The Healing Power of Hip Hop

The Healing Power of Hip Hop

Raphael Travis Jr.

Intersections of Race, Ethnicity, and Culture
Gary Y. Okihiro, Series Editor

 PRAEGER™

An Imprint of ABC-CLIO, LLC
Santa Barbara, California • Denver, Colorado

Library of Congress Cataloging-in-Publication Data

Travis, Raphael, author.
  The healing power of hip hop / Raphael Travis Jr.
    pages cm.—(Intersections of race, ethnicity, and culture)
  Includes bibliographical references and index.
  ISBN 978-1-4408-3130-0 (alk. paper)—ISBN 978-1-4408-3131-7 (ebook)
1. Rap (Music)—Social aspects.   2. Hip hop—Social aspects.   I. Title.
  ML3918.R37T73 2016
    782.421649—dc23   2015029366

ISBN: 978-1-4408-3130-0
EISBN: 978-1-4408-3131-7

20 19 18 17 16   1 2 3 4 5

This book is also available on the World Wide Web as an eBook.
Visit www.abc-clio.com for details.

Praeger
An Imprint of ABC-CLIO, LLC

ABC-CLIO, LLC
130 Cremona Drive, P.O. Box 1911
Santa Barbara, California 93116-1911

This book is printed on acid-free paper ∞

Manufactured in the United States of America

**For my children Morgan and Niko, my brother Najee,
and my goddaughters Abijah and Sanai**

May you one day fully understand
the *strength* from which you come,
the *love* that surrounds you,
and the *power* you have
to make our world a better place.

Contents

Series Foreword

Intersectionality, named by critical race scholar Kimberlé Crenshaw in 1989, references the multiple and conjoining forces that constrain and oppress all peoples. Two decades before Crenshaw's articulation, activist Frances Beale organized the Black Women's Alliance and then the Third World Women's Alliance to mobilize against the racism, sexism, heterosexism, and classism faced by women of color in the United States. Critically important was Beale's recognition that African Americans, American Indians, Asian Americans, and Latinas comprised a collective group, across racialized divides, as women of color or, in the parlance of the 1960s and 1970s, Third World women. The wider term linked the condition of women of color in the United States with women in Africa, Asia, and the Caribbean and Latin America.

African American women of the Combahee River Collective, a Black feminist group formed in Boston in 1974, best described what Crenshaw later called intersectionality. We are committed, the Combahee River Statement declared in April 1977, "to struggling against racial, sexual, heterosexual, and class oppression, and see as our particular task the development of integrated analysis and practice based upon the fact that the major systems of oppression are interlocking. The synthesis of those oppressions creates the conditions of our lives." Significantly, the theorists of the Collective observed from their everyday life experiences that the forces that oppressed them were systematic and intersecting. They were not random but organized, and not additive as in racism plus sexism plus heterosexism but relational and overlapping as in gendered races, sexualized genders, and so forth.

The power of those analyses and practices must not escape us in the twenty-first century. They are as fresh and vital as when they were first experienced and theorized. This series, "Intersections of Race, Ethnicity, and Culture," aspires to continue and extend the struggles against all forms of oppression. Our authors understand the past as prologue, and they offer fresh perspectives to contemporary social issues in highly accessible language. Moreover, our authors present engagements beyond the white/nonwhite binary to relations among peoples of color and enlarge upon the U.S. social formation as race but also and simultaneously gender, sexuality, class, and nation. Finally, their studies show how peoples of color cast a different light on the United States, revealing the nation in its fullness and verity.

Peoples of color have reshaped America fundamentally, and we establish that claim in this series.

Gary Y. Okihiro

Acknowledgments

Thank you. Seriously, I want to acknowledge you. If you are a part of my life, I have been inspired in some way by you. I have learned from you. I have been supported by you. I have shared good times and not so good times. I have laughed with you. We have jokes that only we understand and memories that make each day just a little bit brighter. Thank you for being you.

Dnika, as the person who knows me better than any other person on the planet, you know how much I appreciate the people in my life, so you can tell everyone that I'm not lying to make them feel important. Of course, thank you Dnika. Thank you for your support in everything that I set out to do. I know, it's always something I'm working on. And this book was another one of those "things." This was a labor of love and you were along for the ride from the beginning. Without you, there is no way this book would have been completed. The starts, the stops, the enthusiasm, the frustrations, the highs, the lows, and then finally the euphoria of completion. You were that quiet and steady rock all the way down to those final three days in Knoxville. Thank you.

Thank you mom and dad for showing me what hard work looks like—every day. Mom, all of this is from and for you. Thank you. Dad, I will always remember. Grandpops, thank you for always being the solid foundation I needed. To grandma—from your grandbaby—thank you for being a walking angel and cutting through distance, time, and circumstances to be a constant presence of love, strength, and pride for all of us. Thank you also for showing me it is okay to laugh, at everything. This spirit of being able to pull out the best amid the biggest challenges is an underlying premise to all of my work, including this book. To my incredibly supportive in-laws, aunts, uncles, cousins, and other family and loved ones—each of you are shining lights that inspire me to do and be better.

Thank you to Laurel Street. While I may be far away, you are always close to my heart and the source for all of my hopes, dreams, aspirations, and wishes for better in the world. To Tyrus, D.R., Blake, Allen, Rahmel, Sean, Chuckie, and Jeff. My love of Hip Hop started right there on Laurel Street from trying to rhyme, to write graffiti on pants, to mix and play music out of my window, to b-boying at Pathmark and Roosevelt Field. To Janice Miles, Concerned Citizens for Roslyn Youth, and Patricia James for a steady hand of encouragement and support to all of our youth in and around Laurel Street. Thank you to Hempstead, my weekend home away from home. To Lincoln Park, to Campbell Park, that might as well have been Madison Square Garden to me as a kid. To the many friends of Raphael Sr., in Hempstead, who offered unconditional love and support, and just the right mix of guidance and honest fun to help keep me on track.

To WBAU, Red Alert and Mr. Magic—the original 98.7 and 107.5 FM in New York—and the late night mix shows. To Jamaica Avenue and buying cassettes and mixtapes on the street. To the Rock N Fresh Crew. To EPMD, who solidified my love for true flow in lyricism. To my favorite emcees and groups that embody that flow (say whatever you want—these are *my* favorites) EPMD, Jadakiss, AZ, Fabolous, Public Enemy, De La Soul, Blue Scholars, Lupe Fiasco, Rapsody, Talib Kweli, Kendrick Lamar, and Biggie and Pac. And, to Statik Selektah for figuring out the magic of that boom bap sound and keeping it alive for newer generations.

Thank you to my academic mentors Neal Halfon, Mark Schuster, and Richard Lerner for bringing me from the practice world to the world of research and the active empirical search for the best ways of investing in the long-term health and well-being of our youth. To the Robert Wood Johnson Foundation and Debra Joy Perez, for investing in my early research career years and role modeling how to focus one's career on the study of youth of color while also moving beyond the study of problems to the study of successes. These principles guide the work in this book. Thank you to my supportive collegues and inspiring students at Texas State University.

Thank you to the many ambassadors of Hip Hop culture who go unrecognized, unrewarded, and unknown but work tirelessly to bring this amazing culture to our youth free of all the biases, stereotypes, and prejudices foisted on Hip Hop. To the more well-known ambassadors inspiring me and many others: Chris Emdin and the #HipHopEd movement, Timothy

Jones, Asheru, Mazi Mutafa, Ian Levy, Cendrine Robinson, Tomas Alvarez III, Natalie Schere, Elliot Gann, Amil Cook, Mark Anthony Neal, James Peterson, Sam Seidel, Marc Lamont Hill, Emery Petchauer, Edgar Tyson, Edward Vogel with Rhymes and Reasons, MK Asante Jr., Brad Porfilio, Debangshu Roychoudhury, Lauren Gardner, and LeConte Dill.

Thank you to Janice Johnson and the GrassROOTS Community Foundation for representing a tireless commitment to improving health and well-being at the community level and seeing (not just hoping for) the results in the lives of girls and women of color. Thank you also for your encouragement of my work and many of the ideas expressed in this book. A similar thank you to the Community Coalition, CADRE, the Youth Justice Coalition, the Advancement Project–Los Angeles, and JUICE for your commitment to youth and justice.

Thank you to the Austin area team of Hip Hop ambassadors continuously representing for the culture: Scott Bowman, SaulPaul, Tim Eubanks, Joshua Childs, Minkah Makalani, Bavu Blakes, Ray Cordero, Sherri Benn, Darrion ChiClopz Borders, and Mindz of a Different Kind. Thank you to TXPOST, and the Austin area supporters of youth who refuse to buy into stereotypes about youth and youth of color. Instead, you help to ensure youth reach their potential and let everyone know how great our young people are along the way: Steve Medel, Sarah Stone, Shannon Sandrea, Sonia Gaillard, Stephen Kinney, Clifford Gillard, Laura Garcia LaFuente, Suzanne Hershey, Sabine "BiNi" Foster, Ricardo Zavala, Jesse Silva, Shirlene Justice, Katy Aus, and the entirety of United Way for Greater Austin.

Thank you to my SB and GriotStarters family for your commitment to the idea of family, and continuous exchange of music and mixes over the years: Jack, Bob, Chuck Dobard, Kobina, Cory, and Maurice. Thank you to my UVA brethren, for working and playing hard, always to a soundtrack: Sam, Byron, and Richard. Thank you Mary Jo Garcia Biggs for seeing potential in my work and forwarding the idea of this book on to ABC-CLIO. Thank you to Kim Kennedy-White and ABC-CLIO for your support throughout the development of this book, and to Tim Misir for your editorial support and appreciation of the culture. A special thank you to Alexis Maston for capturing the essence of this book and its stories within the beautiful poem "For Every Rose."

For Every Rose

There was a mothering bush
Giving it a powerful push
. . . To grow
Beyond its circumstances
Beyond concrete walls and enclosed spaces
To rise out of darkest and harshest of places
To make it in the depth of the bleak
By climbing the limbs of the symbolic rose tree
It overcame the statistical probability
Of defeat
But it did not endure alone
The rose was pushed by the rosebush
That it called home
A community of rough patches and thorns
Aided in the esteem that the rose adorned
That provided shelter during the storm
It now stands in bloomed form

This is the classic
Story of Hip Hop's ambassadors
Using their communities as motivations
To become ambassadors of states
Using the shoulders of generations past
To unlatch the gates
They are the sons and daughters
Roses pushing through streams without waters
Dreams without borders
Who will not falter nor fail
With one another they will prevail

The sisters and brothers of this generation
Their branches stretch farther than
Situations that they are facing
Than limits of skies and zones of dreams
These roses that grew from blocks of concrete
Using their creativity as leaps
Of endurance
These who live amongst the ruins . . . and survive
These rose scented Black lives
That matter

For every rose
There was a mothering bush
Giving it a powerful push
. . . To grow
      Dr. Alexis Maston (God's Def Poet)

Introduction

The rise of rap music and related genres appears to be the single most important event that has shaped the musical structure of the American charts between 1960 and 2010.[1]

Do you listen to music or do you just skim through it?
                                        Jay Z, on "Renegade"

Hip Hop changes lives. It brings into expression the soul's yearning for meaning and connection. At its core, a raw power pervades the culture of Hip Hop—celebrated through its beats, art, movement, analysis, lyrical dialogue, rhythm, overall musicality, and style. With this power and sense of urgency, Hip Hop has had a forty-year history of giving voice to the voiceless, allowing people a renewed freedom of cultural expression, and giving people tools to liberate themselves from a belief that their external conditions define them. In this vein, Hip Hop fuels life.

Hip Hop music is a multibillion dollar industry, but Hip Hop is also an economic and cultural powerhouse. Recent research suggests that Hip Hop music has been the single biggest influence on the song structure of music on U.S. charts between 1960 and 2010. This has economic implications because of the relationships between chart popularity, audience exposure, and purchases.

A global appetite for Hip Hop has also exploded, with tentacles reaching beyond its origins in the United States to every other continent, and particularly vibrant regional scenes in places like France, China, South Africa, the United Kingdom, and the Caribbean. In the United States, Hip Hop's influence has elevated a powerful echelon of artists to become game-changing CEOs, like Sean Combs (aka Puff Daddy/P. Diddy/Diddy), Dr. Dre, Sean Carter (aka Jay Z), and 50 Cent, each in a race to be the first with a net value of $1 billion; philanthropists, chronicled well by the website and organization *Hip Hop Gives Back*; and community activists and artists consistently at the forefront of social and political issues influencing communities in need, such as Talib Kweli, Jasiri X, and more recently, Jidenna.

Hip Hop culture's longstanding goal has always been to become better one way or another. Afrika Bambaataa and the United Zulu Nation describe this as peace, love, unity, and having fun. Others talk about the goals of authenticity, individuality, autonomy, creativity, survival, utilitarianism, being active, participation, mobilization, resistance, protest, and action. Ultimately, these goals are highly prized values that coalesce into Hip Hop's tendency toward creative self and community improvement. This propensity shows up as empowering opportunities within the most marginalized communities. Yet Hip Hop is often misunderstood. Common assumptions and rhetoric about Hip Hop culture distill its complexity into a monolithic or singular expression of rap music. Additionally, these common assumptions are often negative and rooted in controversy.

While immersed in writing a good portion of this book, I had Rapsody's album *Beauty and the Beast* on heavy rotation. In many ways, the album's title compellingly speaks realism about the complexity of Hip Hop culture. On one hand, Rapsody represents the "beauty" of Hip Hop literally and figuratively: that is, the artistry, intellectual depth, technological expertise, pride and resilience, discoveries and innovation, entrepreneurial spirit, personal and communal improvement, and fun that launched a worldwide movement of empowerment.

On the other hand, we cannot ignore the elements of Hip Hop culture that mirror systemic and institutionalized oppression, exploitation, and profit from the suffering of others. This is the "beast" that gives many of us pause. These risky elements have given Hip Hop culture the reputation of being a source of negative influence among youth and communities of color. Many Hip Hop artists are scapegoats for this negativity. It is from this vantage point we must profess, "It is okay until it is not okay anymore." (One of my favorite sayings, and I wish I knew who to give credit to for it.)

Let us consider why it is not okay anymore. From a big picture perspective, it is no longer right to have limited discourse and narratives about what constitutes contemporary Hip Hop culture, how it is used, the implications of this use, or its potential to influence learning and growth. In mainstream popular culture, Hip Hop—particularly rap music—is treated like fast food and so both the "good" and "bad" art is easily consumed and disposed of, quickly buried beneath the next wave of new "art" created.

Yet, Hip Hop culture is incredibly dynamic and nuanced. At its simplest and most generic, Hip Hop culture is the ongoing use of beat and groove-driven music, beat-inspired movement, street art, and lyrical manipulation to creatively better oneself. Note that this improvement can be achieved either in a superficial, short-sighted manner, or a more growth-oriented, long-term manner. At its most complex and culturally rich, Hip Hop culture is . . . well, that is the rest of this book.

Participants in Hip Hop culture use and repurpose specific tools like turntables, Digital Audio Workstations (DAWs), paint, break beats, and samples to innovate within the culture. Hip Hop also has a unique set of aesthetics and styles that influence how tools and environments are used and manipulated for maximum expression and creativity. Finally, the relative consistency of Hip Hop's context-specific values such as *persistence* and, at times, *resistance* (also under the umbrella of self and community improvement) in the face of adverse social conditions distinguishes it from other forms of art and culture.

This book explores Hip Hop's healing powers by elaborating upon the tools, direction, narratives, and voices of the culture, demonstrating how it has been used, past and present, to help people improve their lives. It pays close attention to Hip Hop's applicability to the unique lived experience of the Black community in the United States while recognizing the critical role of intersectionality.

Chapter 1 reintroduces Hip Hop as a culture in the hope of erasing potential misconceptions that may affect how readers interpret this global phenomenon and the rest of the book. It helps to explain the culture in all its richness and splendor, including the legacy of art, social identity, and social movements from which it emerges. The main cultural artifacts used in its appropriation are reviewed along with the values guiding their use. All of the culture's elements, including deejaying, emceeing, b-boying and b-girling, graffiti and street art, and knowledge of self, are reviewed as the vehicles by which artifacts are used, shared, and interacted with.

Chapter 2 builds upon this exploration of Hip Hop's origins with a discussion of the complexity of Black racial identity in the United States and how Hip Hop became part of mainstream pop culture. Black racial identity is considered alongside the recognition that there is not a singular African American culture, that multiracial identities are more commonplace, and that the largest portions of the contemporary Black immigrant community come from African countries and the Caribbean. The influence of the entertainment industry on Hip Hop culture and how this has evolved over time is also reviewed. The prominent role of this industry provides context for changes in trends in the culture's riskiest content.

Chapter 3 provides early examples of Hip Hop's healing power at the individual and community levels. The ability of individuals to embrace the culture as a source of motivation and inspiration for self and community improvement has been embedded in its values and social narratives from the start. Hip Hop is introduced as a natural resource, a fuel with the material essence of its power described as *tools, direction*, and *narratives*. Tools are the skills embedded in participating in the culture (e.g., critical analysis and communication in emceeing, researching, archiving, and remixing by deejays and producers). Direction is the consolidation of Hip Hop's values into a superordinate value of "better" or self and community improvement. Narratives are the five specific dimensions of improvement or "better" most often found in Hip Hop. At the same time, the chapter concludes with a recognition that risky attitudes and behaviors can be present amid empowering narratives. The five dimensions of esteem, resilience, growth, community, and change are examined closely and identified as the pillars of the Individual and Community Empowerment (ICE) framework in the subsequent chapters.

Chapters 4 through 7 link specific Hip Hop narratives to self and community improvement while introducing the concept of Hip Hop's musical canon, or Hip Hop's essential tracks that should be, and often are, embedded in the culture's collective conscience as part of its institutional memory. By integrating specific tracks into the discussions, and having gained a contextual understanding of Hip Hop's legacy from earlier chapters, we can better appreciate the steady and continuously expanding empowering potential of Hip Hop culture, along with the powerful relevance of archiving and reuse of its material.

Chapter 4 focuses on narratives that reflect issues of esteem, identity, and feeling better. Chapter 5 focuses on narratives that reflect resilience, context and doing better. Chapter 6 focuses on growth, skill-building, and being better as a person, as well as having a sense of community, solidarity, and a better sense of belonging. Chapter 7 focuses on change, pressure against injustice, and better community conditions. Each chapter concludes with a look into Hip Hop's musical canon and the lineage of tracks the capture the essence of these narratives. A number of its more popular exemplars are provided.

Chapter 8 provides a conceptual foundation for planning and measurement based on existing research on music, health, and well-being. Chapter 8 begins with Stefan Koelsch's model of how interacting with music helps generate emotions that begin a sequence of events with the potential to influence health and well-being. The three main ways of interacting with music are discussed: health-musicking (i.e., the deliberate functional use of music by oneself), everyday listening, and professionally mediated interactions such as with a social worker or teacher. The chapter also discusses a new way of looking at well-being, particularly for Black youth, through the lens of Raphael Travis and Tamara Leech's Empowerment-based Positive Youth Development (EMPYD) model. It is a newer model of healthy development that is culture-bound, empowerment-based, and action-oriented. It offers many new opportunities to understand growth and development and ways to intervene for Black youth. Key aspects of this model are how features of positive development are interrelated so that they reinforce and build upon one another. It also features how a sense of community and engaged citizenship are at the core of positive development for youth of color as opposed to outcomes. Much of the content is applicable to all youth; however, this model emphasizes research that explicitly used Black youth as samples for their data analyses.

Chapter 8 helps outline how the learning and growth principles of EMPYD can be applied to a specific framework for understanding how Hip Hop's value driven narratives of self and community improvement are empowering. In other words, all of the various ways that people appropriate Hip Hop culture to improve themselves, to get better, or to feel empowered can be captured within the five narrative dimensions mentioned earlier. In summary, the Individual and Community Empowerment (ICE) framework includes the dimensions of esteem, resilience, and growth (i.e., individual empowerment), and community and change (i.e., community empowerment).

These theoretical and conceptual chapters create a foundation for understanding Chapters 9 through 12, which showcase how Hip Hop is integrated across four professional domains, with perspectives from some of Hip Hop's leading cultural ambassadors. Chapter 9 pertains to physical health, Chapter 10 focuses on education, Chapter 11 examines out-of-school time (OST) and communities of change, and Chapter 12 discusses mental health. Contemporary voices in the field—Hip Hop's new types of cultural ambassadors—help punctuate information about work being done and unique opportunities offered by Hip Hop culture. They include:

- Dr. Chris Emdin, emcee and co-founder of #HipHopEd—a unique cultural platform embracing the intersection of Hip Hop and education—and associate professor in the Department of Mathematics, Science and Technology at Teachers College, Columbia University.

- Mazi Mutafa, executive director of Words, Beats, and Life, Inc., a Washington, DC, arts-based educational program focused on using the transformative power of Hip Hop culture to help youth and communities.
- Gabriel "Asheru" Benn, Peabody Award winning emcee, international Hip Hop educator, and founder of the Washington, DC-area community service organization Guerilla Arts Ink, which specializes in education through arts, cultural programming, and professional development.
- Timothy D. Jones, emcee, chief visionary officer of #HipHopEd, and director of healthy connections for Martha's Table, a Washington, DC-area program working with children and families in the fields of education, nutrition, and poverty.
- Dr. Elliot Gann, producer and executive director of Today's Future Sound, an Oakland-area program that brings mobile music production and deejaying to K–12 schools, community centers, and a range of youth-centered events.
- Ian Levy, emcee, high school counselor, and doctoral student at Teachers College, Columbia University.
- Dr. Cendrine Robinson, a psychologist with experience integrating Hip Hop culture into mental health strategies with people involved in the criminal justice system.
- Natalie Davis, executive director of an out-of-school time program in southeastern United States. The program centers on using all elements of Hip Hop culture to promote education, health, and positive development for youth.
- Timothy Eubanks, supervisor for the Austin Healthy Adolescent (AHA) program in Austin, Texas. The program engages, empowers, and collaborates with communities across Travis County to support youth ages 10 to 18 in taking ownership of their own health and working to advance the health of their communities.
- Darrion "Chi" Borders, emcee and community peer health educator who works with the Austin Healthy Adolescent program. He helps promote adolescent engagement in youth programming and community efforts.

Chapter 9 looks at physical health by focusing on understanding the landscape of health development for the Black community, where Hip Hop–integrated strategies have concentrated, and future opportunities. Similarly, Chapters 10 through 12 offer information about the general trends as they relate to the Black community, Hip Hop–oriented strategies working toward improving outcomes, and where opportunities seem to exist for future work.

Chapter 10 highlights the importance of student engagement and trends in suspension and expulsion within education. It also includes specific examples of the use of Hip Hop in education to better engage youth and support their efforts to address disparities. Critical pedagogical strategies are discussed for their deliberate emphasis on equity and justice—key aspects of the Black educational experience.

Chapter 11 describes traditional and less traditional OST activities. For example, traditional initiatives are more often community based and geographical in scope, while more innovative settings can include virtual communities like #HipHopEd. Attention is paid to the difference between strategies focused on youth well-being only and those also having a community equity and justice interest.

Chapter 12 discusses the unique social and environmental realities that contribute to mental health. This is followed by a brief overview of the origins of Hip Hop–based therapy and counseling. The chapter continues with discussion of the relationship between mind and body and its connection to health. This chapter also offers distinctions among deficit-oriented strategies and the promise of growth and empowerment-based strategies

Whether you are an educator, caregiver, youth worker, health professional, or simply a curious reader, as you get started with this book, please take some time to reflect on your own assumptions, viewpoints, and perspectives about Hip Hop culture and the Black community. To help you in this effort, consider the following thirteen questions at the onset and throughout:

1. What might you have misunderstood about Hip Hop culture?
2. How might changes in the entertainment industry influence how Hip Hop culture is understood?
3. How might the risky elements of Hip Hop culture uniquely threaten the Black community?
4. What emotions and feelings do music and art evoke for you when you consider your own musical and artistic preferences?
5. In what ways do you use music in your own life?
6. In what ways does music help you feel better?
7. In what ways does music help you cope with life's challenges?
8. In what ways does music motivate you to become a better person?
9. What role does music play in helping you connect with important people in your life?
10. What have you learned about yourself or the world around you through your varied musical experiences?

11. What connections do you see between how others appreciate Hip Hop culture and how you interact with and appreciate any form of music and art?
12. How can you capitalize on the healing power of Hip Hop to better help the young people in your life learn and grow?
13. How will you begin?

CHAPTER 1

Unpacking the Culture of Hip Hop

Beats boom from a portable black speaker system as the audience slowly enters the room. This melodic sound, filled with enough bass to properly go along with the lyrics, immediately piques their curiosity. Members of the audience quickly grab the resource-filled handouts available at the room's entrance while trickling in to their seats. My enthusiasm and my nerves peak as I turn down the music and draw the audience's attention to the first slide. A graphic of me in my b-boy stance with big glasses and a Chicago Bulls hat is projected brightly in the front of the room.

"Welcome, everyone!" I begin. "Today our dialogue will begin with a focus on Hip Hop culture as a strategy of working with youth." I continue to tell them a little about my own story and how Hip Hop culture has been a continuous source of inspiration in my life, from my days as a youth with the b-boy name "Treacherous T," to my love of graffiti, to saving my money to buy my own turntables, all the way up to later life and the empowering process of making mixtapes. I continue on to a slide that is divided in half with two simple questions: "How is your use of Hip Hop helpful?" and "How is your use of Hip Hop hurtful?" I briefly scan the room looking for points of confusion or interest. Happy to see heads nodding affirmatively in the crowd, I am relieved to see that these nods of agreement are not limited to millennials and the younger generation or those with varied hues of brown skin. Others seemed engaged, though a little confused.

One person toward the back of the room raises her hand. "Raphael, I have a question," she asks, standing. "What's the difference between rap and Hip Hop?" I hear the resounding grumbling in the room, "Yes." "Good question!" "Hmmm . . ." Several others in different parts of the room chime in. I am not surprised. The question about the difference between rap and Hip Hop is without fail the most common question I face in public discussions and workshops about Hip Hop culture. Amid this discussion, another audience member follows this question with the next most common one: "What about all that foul language?" This time the audience is silent.

This chapter addresses the first question of rap vs. Hip Hop, then further explains the evolution and elements of Hip Hop culture from which rap (or rap music) is derived. This discussion of Hip Hop culture speaks to the broader content of the book, contested meanings and actual *use* of all elements as a powerful force in the ongoing health and well-being of the Black community and society at large. The question of "foul language" is also important and an example of the risks embedded within the empowering aspects of Hip Hop, which we will continue to revisit throughout this book.

RAP VS. HIP HOP

"Rap is something you do, but hip-hop is something you live."

—KRS-One

Rap and Hip Hop are often viewed as one and the same. It is commonplace to use the terms interchangeably. Yet to call Hip Hop rap is a misnomer. The decontextualized skill of emceeing, or rhyming over beats is "rap" and "rap music." This is what "you do," as noted by KRS-One, as a verbal art form and what we hear when listening to the lyrics within rap music. As a broader construct, Hip Hop encompasses a culture of which rapping or rap music *can be* a part. Simply put, rapping and rap music does not equate with the much larger sociohistorical culture of Hip Hop. Hip Hop is a fun and communally experienced cultural phenomenon embodying core elements of emceeing (rap music), deejaying, graffiti (and street art), b-boying (and b-girling), entrepreneurship, and knowledge of self, with values of self and community improvement—all of which continue to evolve as lived experiences across generations, racial and ethnic groups, socioeconomic statuses, genders, and regional boundaries.

Importantly, rap music is where many of the questions around foul language reside. This is the music people hear on the radio, the lyrics they see paired with explicit imagery in videos, and the explicit words being sung casually by youth in hallways, classrooms, streets, cars, and homes. Embedded in this question of lyrics and content is a powerful and important dialogue about the commercial viability, consumerism, and commoditization of the rap music component of Hip Hop culture. The nature of how entertainment and Hip Hop culture developed into a market that reinforces and glorifies risky messages is discussed at greater length later in the book (see Chapter 2). However, the riskier themes and messages dominant in more commercial rap music, in particular, often make risky behaviors seem normative or necessary to feel better or to become a better person. These riskier messages disproportionately glorify and thus elevate drug and alcohol use and violence; unhealthy—even misogynistic—attitudes toward women, girls, and relationships; family or community conflict; and a devaluation of school and traditional employment. Each of these risky areas is well-debated among scholars, community leaders, youth workers, parents, and even Hip Hop artists. From the lens of this book, staying entrenched in critical dialogue about risky messages, attitudes, and behaviors reflects a personal and professional struggle among many listeners and fans of rap music—particularly for those who have a steadfast commitment to harnessing Hip Hop's healing power.

How do we handle the risky messages that blast through our speakers when listening to popular music? At the same time, and in contrast, how do we use Hip Hop culture and its elements, as fuel to channel its power for learning, growth, and positive change? To start, let's build a foundation of understanding and unpack the elements of Hip Hop culture as detailed in this chapter. We can use this to build on Hip Hop's values of self and community improvement. We can recognize risk, but build upon the empowering elements to promote esteem, resilience, growth, community, and change. We can capitalize on the wisdom and commitment of today's Hip Hop ambassadors. These change agents are leading the way with innovative and meaningful uses of Hip Hop across the range of settings within which we find our youth, schools, out-of-school time (OST), and health and mental health settings. We can prioritize the roles of identity, contextual realities, healthy relationships, and community belonging in the lives of youth—all anchored in and by music. We can provide artists a viable alternative for using their expert knowledge and skills toward promoting health and well-being. We can pair their excellence and mastery with learning and growth of youth, and we can boldly move forward in a way that integrates identity, culture, strengths, and action toward positive change. Instead of rap music being quickly consumed and discarded as fleeting entertainment, it will instead be recognized as the renewable growth resource *and* self-sustaining economy that it is. This opens opportunities for artists, for

youth, for communities, and for a wide range of professions. This book offers a language and structure for understanding how to anchor Hip Hop
culture in these empowering aspects while recognizing but inhibiting risk.

DEEPENING AN UNDERSTANDING OF HIP HOP AS CULTURE

Defining Culture

Hip Hop scholars and practitioners force us to recognize that although
we focus on the South Bronx as the birthplace of Hip Hop, all culture exists
along a timeline with commonalities from the past and new elements that
distinguish it from the past.[1] The focus of this book is on Hip Hop culture in
its broadest sense. From this we can parcel out new distinct and interrelated
terrains, or "artifacts," and the residual characteristics of Hip Hop's cultural
roots. As we continue to deepen our understanding of Hip Hop culture and
this book's emphasis on specific terrains within Hip Hop culture, let us first
look at the concept of culture in general with a little more depth.

The most observable aspects of culture can be found in its artifacts, that
is, what you can see, touch, and feel. Less observable, but the glue that binds
culture together, are its shared values. The least visible, but where divergence
sometimes surfaces for members of a given culture, are the underlying assumptions associated with each shared value.[2] This is a useful way to consider Hip Hop culture, especially as we seek to better understand how it has
evolved over time to occupy shared spaces in mainstream popular culture.

Culture is also not uniformly experienced, both unique environments
and unique individual personalities contribute to how culture is taken in
and interpreted. Taking this a step further, this then relates to how others
experience them as a representative of the culture. As seen below, culture is
learned and culture can be a motivator for action.

> Cultural representations . . . are internalized by individuals, though
> not equally. Some are internalized very superficially and are the
> equivalent of cultural clichés. Others are deeply internalized and in-
> vested with emotion of affect. These can instigate behavior by being
> connected to desirable goals or end states.[3]

Similar ideas about culture can be found looking through Etic and Emic
lenses. While artifacts and shared values exist in Hip Hop (Etic), we simultaneously have unique generational and personality driven ways of interpreting and expressing it (Emic).[4]

Hip Hop Culture

It is at this juncture of interrelatedness that this book engages Hip Hop culture. What are often described as the elements of Hip Hop are discussed in this book within the context of three levels of cultural artifacts: primary, secondary, and tertiary. This book emphasizes the microphone, turntable, Digital Audio Workstation (DAW), break, sample, paint, stencil, and other singular items (primary artifacts) creatively manipulated within *emceeing, deejaying*, graffiti, b-boying/b-girling (or breakdancing), and *knowledge of self* as major contributors to the use and production of *beats, hooks, lyrics*, and *mixtapes* (tertiary artifacts) as tools of engagement in Hip Hop. However, there is no denying the understanding that the full repertoire of Hip Hop's cultural artifacts—to be discussed shortly—allow one to truly appreciate Hip Hop's healing power. It is also the *secondary* artifacts, often discussed as "the aesthetics" of Hip Hop which continually bring innovation to the culture.[5]

Again, these interrelated artifacts are embedded within unique cultural *values* and *assumptions* that help bring forth Hip Hop's power. These values, such as individuality, authenticity, survival, creativity, unity, and protest, when looked at collectively, can be understood as a superordinate value of *betterment*, or active participation in positive growth and well-being. By recognizing how vastly different assumptions can exist about how to achieve the same value of improvement, or working toward "better," helps to explain how Hip Hop culture's more high-risk characteristics can exist *alongside* its most empowering elements. This particular constellation of artifacts, values, and assumptions, as a new community-level set of relationships and experiences, was born in the Bronx. Each individual's capacity to engage this culture for his or her own improvement—whether at the individual or community level—has been the powerful gift of the culture taken forth in the decades since.

HIP HOP ARTIFACTS AND VALUES

The constantly evolving culture we know as Hip Hop includes its main elements of *emceeing, deejaying, b-boying*, and *graffiti* at its core, along with a *"knowledge of self,"* which Afrika Bambaataa declared just as important as the other elements. Contemporary definitions of Hip Hop also include added elements, such as the style of *clothing and dress* and *entrepreneurship*.[6] These elements make use of Hip Hop's primary artifacts, the materials used in creative ways to give Hip Hop life, such as the microphone, turntable, DAW, break, and sample. Their use within Hip Hop's elements by individuals that identify with Hip Hop culture is distinct from their use in other arenas by individuals not identifying with the culture.

Secondary artifacts, often discussed as the aesthetics or style of Hip Hop, include the skills, abilities, and ways of doing things that have uniquely Hip Hop manifestations such as the *cypher* (also spelled cipher or cipha), *battling, sampling and looping, remixing, digging, call and response*, and *communication and language*.[7] Still further are a tertiary group of artifacts that can be classified as both derivatives of and raw materials for primary and secondary artifacts. These materials of [cultural] engagement are *beats, hooks, lyrics*, and *mixtapes*. When considering the full array of primary artifacts, tertiary artifacts also include graffiti's *tags, throw-ups*, and *pieces*, and b-boy and b-girl *dance moves*. Even still, among cultural adherents, all of these are continually unpacked, uniquely interpreted and reinterpreted.

Hip Hop Culture's Primary Artifacts and Unique Subcultures

On his track "Rap vs. Hip Hop," KRS-One says, "Rap is something you do, Hip Hop is something you live." At the same time, each element of Hip Hop (e.g., emceeing) is a (sub)culture in and of itself too. These are active communities and movements in which individuals aspire to be a member of and represent. When they obtain membership, they value this membership and accompanying sense of belonging. Furthermore, these Hip Hop communities, although overlapping in many ways, have their own boundaries and values. Thus, the attraction to one element of the culture may not mean sustained energy into all or even any other aspect of the culture. For example, many b-boys exist in a world largely devoid of what one would consider rap music but are hardcore b-boys steeped in the culture.[8] Being a b-boy is a look, an attitude, an approach to mastering the range of b-boy skills, and a synergy of teaching and learning amid well-respected history and traditions.[9] Further, classic b-boy anthems are mostly funk records, with *no emceeing at all*.

Similarly, graffiti artists are often mostly concerned with their art and may not listen to rap music at all. Historically, "graffiti writers listened to rock and punk, but their tastes in music played no role in whether or not they were viewed as real writers, nor should we interpret this to mean that 'punk' or 'rock' are code for white and 'funk' is code for black."[10] When you look at the classic graffiti movie *Style Wars* you see many of the writers are non-Black, many do not reference any other Hip Hop elements, and one of the central protagonists sports a Van Halen T-shirt. Similarly, reflecting on his early days deejaying, DJ Q-Bert, a pioneer of deejaying and member of turntablism trio the Invisibl Skratch Piklz, said,

[In the early nineties] we were totally like on another branch of Hip Hop. . . . We love rap and stuff, but what they were doing with DJs in the background, just fill in stuff, we just totally blocked it out, we were in our own world.[11]

Hip Hop Culture's Founding Values

Hip Hop as a culture is infinitely more expansive than learning the skills of each element. Each element of the culture is its own universe, with its own history, symbols, norms, subcultures, and internal debates. However, amid this complexity is some degree of commonality and shared social, political, and economic history that birthed Hip Hop's core, the unique manifestation of artifacts, values, and assumptions that we know as Hip Hop culture. It is cognitive, and of the physical body as much as it is an outpouring of skill. It is personal and social. It is practiced, but it is also improvisational at its core.[12] These are the spaces where Hip Hop's values can be understood.

At the onset of what became labeled as Hip Hop culture, Afrika Bambaataa's United Zulu Nation (UZN) sought to offer a different path forward for his neighborhood community *and* surrounding communities. Amid a tumultuous social environment, Bambaataa championed a new set of community values, bringing people together with the motto, "Peace, Love, Unity and Having Fun." The environment of the time was plagued by longstanding gang violence, a lifestyle Bambaataa grew to move away from. Not only was he moving away from it, but he was doing so with a renewed sense of urgency around his Black identity and his sense of community solidarity.[13] Graffiti artist Ray Abrahante (BOM5) said in Jeff Chang's *Can't Stop Won't Stop*, that Bambaataa was inspiring with his efforts to establish solidarity. "[Bambaataa was saying] This gang thing, the cops put us up to this stuff. Society put us all here to fight against each other and kill us off, and we're not getting nowhere."[14] This led to the transformation of his crew into The Organization to the Zulu Nation, and eventually the United Zulu Nation. Bambaataa was clear. "My vision was to try to organize as many as I could to stop the violence," he said.[15]

Inherent in this quest forward were two more of Hip Hop's values, what Chang identified in his synopsis of what UZN celebrated as it embraced this new community vision: survival and creation or creativity.[16] Implicit in this creativity is participation and improvisation, or freestyling. In addition to artists, Hip Hop audiences are expected to be active in the engagement and perpetuation of the culture. From the expected call-and-response tradition of any live show today, to the fact that active engagement of youth in an alternative lifestyle and activities was Bambaataa's founding principle for UZN, participation is a prized cultural value.

Hip Hop culture is also grounded in the values of *individualism, autonomy,* and *freedom.* There is a fierce identity streak that undergirds all of Hip Hop's artifacts, and it is this individualized expression that helps drive innovation. Linked closely to this is the highly contentious but essential value of *authenticity,* which manifests through the "narratives, storytelling, testifying, and witnessing" that help bring Hip Hop culture's social environment and contextual backdrops to life.[17]

In all of the varied manifestations of engaging Hip Hop's artifacts, the goal is consistently to become better. Through Hip Hop, identities are affirmed, strengths are realized, and joys are shared. People cope, survive, and thrive in the most challenging of situations with Hip Hop. Skills are mastered, roles are modeled, and traditions are honored as essential to the culture. Communities unify as collections of individuals, and both individuals and communities show resilience and *get better* while embracing the best of Hip Hop culture.

EMCEES AND DEEJAYS: BEATS, HOOKS, LYRICS, AND MIXTAPES AS TOOLS OF ENGAGEMENT

After Marley Marl changed the game with his new mode of sampling on Eric B. & Rakim's "I Know You Got Soul," Public Enemy's Bomb Squad got busy in the studio. In the summer of 1987, the incomparable screeching-siren driven "Rebel Without a Pause" was the result. Public Enemy producer Hank Shocklee reflected, "That record ripped through the Bronx, ripped through Brooklyn, ripped through upper Manhattan, ripped through Queens" and everybody was checking for that loud noise.[18] This is a testament to the power of beats relative to lyrics. *Beats* invite you in. *Hooks* give you an easy way to participate. *Lyrics* tell you a story for you to interpret and act upon, or not.

"Rapping skills involve verbal mastery, mastery of delivery, creativity, personal style and virtuosity."[19] An emcee integrates verbal mastery and the skills of rhyming with attention to the immediate environment, with the intent of "rocking" the crowd.[20] An emcee embraces the fine line between battling and collective energy of the cypher. It is using the mastery of communication, observation, analysis, a strong emotional IQ, social skill, and personal flow to transform the listener's experience.

"There are quiet brooding MC's, loud abrasive ones, and technically accurate ones. They share one thing. They connect to the listener," Dr. Chris Emdin said about emceeing.[21] This is discussed in the context of *style,* or that "unique, individualistic ambience with which a person invests his or her presence and being . . . the aesthetic finesse with which any kind of statement, attitude or value is delivered."[22] He notes that this ability to generate a consistent and distinct style is a precursor for establishing a positive reputation. A quality emcee allows people to step into a story and take a journey. The power of the emcee to transport the listener is based on a premise of authenticity, but via the power of storytelling and its embedded persuasiveness.

People have written extensively on the fluid boundary between life and art within Hip Hop culture.[23] Many interpretations of "keeping it real" exist. Each emcee is unique but the veil of authenticity within the culture is real. "We have to be about what we're saying. . . . People are going to expect you to live what you say and will test us on it. If the streets don't test us on it, God will," legendary Hip Hop deejay DJ Premier said, echoing this premise.[24] Keeping it real can also mean refusing conscious efforts to "cross over" to appeal to primarily white audiences and losing culturally-based styles of composition. It can mean keeping the artistry alongside a strong sense of community and avoiding "pop music" stylings, and for others it means not just telling how life is in the hood but also overemphasizing the highest risk elements of the hood. Because the reality is that there are many, many untold stories about Black community life.[25]

Therefore, when we think of emceeing and Hip Hop culture's associated value of authenticity or "keeping it real," we recognize that emcees may choose to use a microphone with or without beats to embrace the highest risk elements of establishing a "hard" or "street/hood" persona.[26] Alternatively, they may create narratives with less risky aspects of authenticity geared toward individual and community improvement, such as being true to yourself and representing where you are from, your culture, and the more empowering elements of Hip Hop.[27] Rap music is a particular use of Hip Hop culture's artifacts, but the associated lyrics, narratives, emceeing and deejaying, and increasingly production and beatmaking, can vary wildly with respect to the visible or auditory threads to the history and values of the culture.

EMCEEING: MULTIPLE OVERLAPPING HISTORIES

The more distal history of the emcee enjoys contributions from a range of cultural forefathers. Within the broader Black diaspora is the West African griot. Within the more recent history of Black music in the United States are the introspective and emotional slave hollers and the blues, along with the scatting of Cab Calloway and Louis Armstrong. There are the sociopolitical narratives of soul music and funk during the Civil Rights, Black Power, and Black Arts movements. And there are the street conscious and poetic stylings of the Last Poets and the Watts Prophets, street/jive-talking or *rapping*, and "toasting" about Black folk heroes in stories and film.[28] All helped to shape the distinctive, urgent, context-driven, and creative storytelling style of the modern emcee.

Similarly important to note is that the immediate history of the emcee in Hip Hop was rooted in deejaying, as the two were integrally related. Early emcees sought to engage the crowd but also to enhance the visibility and profile of, and essentially a "connection with" the deejay.[29] DJ Hollywood is credited as the king of popularizing the creative, often rhyming, style *while* deejaying and commanding the energy of the crowd.[30] Famous call-and-response phrases like "Throw your hands in the air" and "Somebody say 'Hoooo!'" are credited to DJ Hollywood.

DJ Kool Herc also began speaking over his extended breaks, but he handed over the reins to other emcees. Jeffrey Ogbar calls the origin of emceeing the result of deejays' request for lyrical assistance and labels them "lyrical DJs."[31] To differentiate by name, the emcee (M.C.) is considered the "master of ceremony."[32] The same occurred for West Coast deejays who were the feature because they brought the music. Emcees accompanied the deejay. As deejaying grew in complexity with DJ Grandmaster Flash and DJ Grand Wizard Theodore, so did the complexity of emceeing and the number of participants in the performance. It is as much an elaborate physical and social orchestration as it is auditory and verbal.[33]

Deejaying: . . . And Turntablism, Beat-Making, and Production

The deejay—not to be confused with the Jamaican deejay (the emcee)—was the highest-profile of Hip Hop's elements because the deejay had the music. The deejay was responsible for keeping the crowd engaged. "The deejay was the source of the energy. Because it was his responsibility to find the music, the selection of music, what types of rhythms the people would feel in the audience," DJ Grand Mixer DXT, one of the founding deejays in the culture, said. Important to note is that deejays in general, and Hip Hop deejays specifically, played *any* musical sounds, and *any* genre that got the crowd moving. The deejay allowed/blessed the emcee to pick up the microphone. The deejay "was the backbone" and the emcees were the arms and legs and everything else to make him colorful."[34]

Early deejays that preceded the "Hip Hop culture" era but likely nonetheless contributed to its earliest roots also existed in all the Bronx's surrounding boroughs. Several important elements were their appeal to youth culture, their public and community-specific orientation, and their dedication to massive sound, sound quality, and technology.[35] These "outdoor discotheques" provided the blueprints for the first "Hip Hop" park jams.[36] Evidence of these park jams existed across the boroughs, as was the steady advance in technical skill in mixing songs and eventually emceeing over tracks. DJ Grandmaster Flowers, The Mixologist—the area's first "Grandmaster" preceding Flash—and other well-known deejays of the time are credited with contributing to the craft: DJ Donny Lawrence (The Dance Master), DJ King Charles, Pete DJ Jones, and Master D/DJ Lance.[37]

Worth noting is that within Jamaican and Caribbean culture, deejays "toast" over live and prerecorded music. This tradition and the heavy trend of immigration from the Caribbean to New York between 1965 and 1970 is likely a contributor to the fact that three prominent architects of Hip Hop culture's deejays were of Caribbean descent: DJ Kool Herc, Afrika Bambaataa, and DJ Grandmaster Flash.[38] DJ Babu, of the Hip Hop trio Dilated Peoples, introduced the concept of the deejay as a "turntablist" by naming himself one.[39]

Digging: Deejays as Researchers and Archivists

Historians are excellent researchers, well-versed in the historical record, preservationists of temporally significant information and artifacts, and above all appreciative of time, place, and how it is recorded. Aside from using turntables as actual instruments, deejays similarly function as excellent researchers and archivists, but with regard to sound bites.

First, deejays must have a deep appreciation of melody, harmony, and rhythm. Deejays must be excellent researchers to assemble the requisite palate of songs from records, eight-track tapes, CDs, MP3s, and other sound files to rock a party. To gather the appropriate tracks, they must know the history and range of music options and be open to further exploration of music beyond stereotypical boundaries. In their search past and present, they must have an instinct for preserving the highest quality sounds (and words and moods as conveyed on record) and the instruments to help convey and augment these sounds. To have a depth of understanding about quality, deejays must also pay close attention to the culture(s) within which the sounds, words, and moods were created.

Culturally specific art likely resonates the most within that culture, however, if you are not necessarily a card-carrying member of that culture yet are able to cognitively, emotionally, or spiritually "access" that space, you can capture its power. Of course, some art is universally powerful and able to tap into the psyche of humanity, but deejays are often able to find even the most obscure pieces of work and use them to powerful ends within Hip Hop culture.

Deejays and producers who research sounds, words, and moods (i.e., "samples") for later use in a new piece of their own work call this process "digging." It is akin to a researcher finding words, quotes, and topical evidence to help support their thesis in a paper or book they are developing. As Joseph Schloss points out, "The aesthetic delight that producers take in finding a good sample is comparable to that of a wine connoisseur savoring a fine vintage."[40] In order to create and put forward their own highest quality art, deejays must be familiar with trends in sound, instrumentation, and lyrical expression in the same manner that researchers must be aware of research trajectories, methods, and research results.

Digging is a skill often born of convenience (e.g., parent's/home record collections), but it is a skill that can be developed, refined, and continually expanded—akin to the difference between an emerging scholar and a seasoned research scholar. Schloss highlights the importance of corollary functions of digging on top of acquiring sound material as "displaying a commitment to Hip Hop culture, paying dues, educating oneself for knowledge, using material as a source of creativity, and socialization."[41]

For producers who are seasoned diggers, the evidence is on full display through the music they create. "Rap made up for its [perceived] lack of melody, with its sense of reminder" Chuck D. said while discussing the depth of research and digging of his production team, The Bomb Squad. "To make a PE record you had to comb through thousands of records. There was so much research that had to be in each record . . . so incredibly difficult," The Bomb Squad's Hank Shocklee said.[42] This trend was quickly muted with the controversial advent of sampling requirements and fees shortly thereafter.[43]

When talking about his own digging habits, in a scene from the movie *Scratch*, DJ Shadow resembles the graduate student of generations past emerging from depths of library stacks with a pile of books to check out. "This is research." The record store owner where he is located adds, "He comes in regularly and spends the day and always comes up with a [large] stack."

DJ Shadow shares, "This is my little nirvana. I take the art of digging seriously. It's an incredible archive of music culture." He echoes Chuck D.'s essentialism of sampling as reminder but also humanizes the experience, "It's also a humbling experience. It's like a big pile of broken dreams. . . . Almost none of these artists still have a career. If you're making records, mixtapes, or whatever . . . you're sort of adding to this pile. In ten years down the line, you're going to be in here," DJ Shadow says in the film.

A person's record collection or crates are their material archives, but so is their mind. For example, DJ Jazzy Jay leads viewers through his collection with, "Come down into the dungeon. This is . . . the bulk of my collection. I've got records dating back to the early thirties. I've got three or four hundred thousand altogether. . . . I know so many breaks. I'm a walking encyclopedia."[44]

Renegades of Funk: True Hip Hop Historians

The Renegades of Funk tour, with DJ Shadow and Cut Chemist, highlighted the etic and emic aspects of the overall culture and the deejaying and digging subcultures. The two deejays used only vinyl pulled from Afrika Bambaataa's actual collection of over forty thousand records, now archived at Cornell University. DJ Shadow highlighted how the collection includes a wide range of genres, indicative of the foundation of the culture and its classic breaks across a wide range of musical genres beyond rap. The program portrayed "Bambaataa as an artist, exploring the influence of his classics like 'Planet Rock'; Bambaataa as a collector, and the genre-defining breaks he discovered; and Bambaataa as a peacemaker and force for social change."[45]

The Austin leg of the tour in 2014, which I enthusiastically attended, was a reminder of Hip Hop culture's ability to innovate while reminding the audience of the culture's rich legacy and UZN's core values of peace, love, unity, and having fun.

Deejaying: Science, Technology, Engineering, Math. (S.T.E.M.)

Within Hip Hop culture, music engineering and production have always been about technology, innovation, and sonic power.[46] Deejays are excellent at timing and have the mathematical skills necessary to maintain the pace, tempo, and track of shifting moods.[47] But they have also always been immersed in technology, using turntables, faders, drum machines, and now DAW software and computers, among other things, to create music. Today, deejays and beatmakers continue to reinterpret uses of technology for the precise sounds they desire.[48]

The mastery of these S.T.E.M. skills continues as deejaying culture morphed into production culture and a new range of associated skills. Hip Hop is a "sound" culture as much as anything else.[49] The enormous variability and innovation available to lyrical delivery, sampling, beat development, and remixing makes this understandable.

When we revisit sampling, it is about creating new sounds from older sounds in the same way scholars develop and publish new theories informed by prior published theories and ideas. For deejays and producers, the first step is digging to find the best older sounds. Sampling is taking the old sound and bringing it to life in a new way. Producers choose how much old vs. new material is included in the new sound and how it is arranged. Thus, Hip Hop can be incredibly rich, layered, and complex sonically with no words at all. When you add in locale, different regions often have their own unique sound palate, all with the right to claim a legitimate place at the table of Hip Hop culture.[50]

BEYOND RAP MUSIC: THE BROADER HIP HOP CULTURE AESTHETIC

B-Boying and B-Girling

Legendary b-boy Jorge "Popmaster Fabel" Pabon of the Rock Steady Crew and United Zulu Nation called b-boying and b-girling "physical graffiti" in his article seeking to help unravel the story of Hip Hop's various dance forms.[51] Deejaying and b-boying/b-girling, or breakdancing, was not limited to the East Coast, as the West Coast developed a vibrant mobile deejay and locking culture of their own in the mid-1960s. This transformation of the Black social scene with greater mobility of parties and flexibility in music selection was the genesis of the modern West Coast Hip Hop culture that emerged in the late 1970s. The multicultural nature of California only enhanced the growth and innovation in the emerging culture, across all Hip Hop's elements: b-boying, emceeing, deejaying, and graffiti.[52]

The dancing associated with Hip Hop culture and its evolution over time has blended dance forms from both the East and West coasts of the United States. The West Coast cultural movement included funk dancing and popping and locking. New York City's contribution to Hip Hop dance was b-boying/b-girling and uprocking.[53] Adding to the complexity of the dance repertoire was taking the dancing to the floor through footwork and ground moves.[54] The b-boy dancing on the extended "breaks" popularized by DJ Kool Herc gradually became more and more complex as dancers practiced what they saw and made up new moves to outdo one another.[55]

The continued progression of ground moves brought about the advent of "power moves," which gained widespread notoriety and media attention.[56] The battle element, although present in all aspects of b-boying, was closely linked to "rocking" or "uprocking" where dancing mimicked fighting and warring between dancers. The style and structure of battling among uprockers and b-boys differed a bit and are discussed in more detail by Pabon and others.[57] The New York b-boying was aggressive, "militaristic," and "on a mission to terrorize the dance floor."[58]

Locking drew from a wide range of influences, expanding the original basic locking of joints and arms to a range of steps and moves called "Boogaloo."[59] The more advanced repertoire of moves includes "isolated sharp angles, hip rotations, and the use of every part of the body . . . moving the body continuously in different directions."[60] However, different cities and regions in California had a range of unique funk-driven moves that were popularized according to their own timelines and with their own histories.[61]

The result, however, is a cornucopia of dance moves that lend themselves to Hip Hop culture. Contemporary interpretations of the range of dances cause several challenges to strict adherents to the integrity of b-boy form and culture, including a hybridization of forms disconnected from its sociohistorical roots, their respective musical influences notwithstanding.[62] Contemporary expressions of b-boying and b-girling often overemphasize power moves, while contemporary expressions of uprocking often overemphasize jerking. These tendencies of overemphasis, or disproportionate emphasis, touch upon other elements of the culture that we will highlight later.

Graffiti and Street Art

Graffiti art is considered the spoken, written, and physical language of Hip Hop culture.[63] Examples of graffiti art date back to the earliest walls of cave-dwellers, and the West Coast Latino community had a *cholo* style of graffiti and tagging in the late 1960s. However, graffiti most closely associated with Hip Hop culture is thought to have begun in the late 1960s with "Cornbread" of Philadelphia and "TAKI 183" of Washington Heights in New York.[64] It began with simple tags and progressed to the manipulation of letters and characters, and eventually full pieces that incorporated letters, characters, and background imagery.[65]

New York's elaborate subway system contributed greatly to the culture by incentivizing quantity and location of graffiti.[66] The most cars covered and the most visible (and difficult to access) locales provided instant recognition for the writer and were what separated legends (King or Queen) from the average writer (Toy). Early writers were distinguished from bombers in that bombers focused on tags in quantity and not the development of throw-ups or pieces. Some writers created pieces solely for aesthetic reasons, while other writers created pieces with messages about social, political, and economic issues.

The early 1980s saw a progression of Hip Hop culture-influenced graffiti in the western United States and in Europe. Asia and South America followed soon after.[67] Newer renditions of graffiti have shed the constraints of spray paint to include stenciling, chalk, oil paints, stickers, and a variety of tools to create an array of desired 2D and 3D words, figures, thematic pieces, and backgrounds.[68] In an attempt to disassociate themselves from the stigma of graffiti as vandalism and criminal activity, many refer to graffiti art as street art, aerosol art, post-graffiti, or neo-graffiti.[69]

THE SKILL AND CRAFT OF HIP HOP

For the remainder of this book, when we talk about Hip Hop culture we assume primary artifacts as materials used among the elements of emceeing, deejaying, b-boying/b-girling, graffiti/street art, and knowledge of self (e.g., the microphone, turntable, DAW, break, and sample). We assume secondary artifacts as the aesthetics of Hip Hop, to help bring primary and tertiary artifacts to life—such as through sampling and looping, the battle, the cypher, digging/archiving, and remixing. We also consider the tertiary artifacts as products within the culture that can also be reorganized through the aesthetics of the culture—to create newer, more complex and creative artistic pieces. These include beats, hooks, lyrics, mixes/mixtapes, throw ups, pieces, and [dance] moves.

We also assume the coalescence of all these artifacts into the very fabric of the people in society who identify with Hip Hop culture. These primary, secondary, and tertiary artifacts also include the embedded values of the culture and accompanying assumptions to varying degrees depending on each person's uniqueness. Contemporary society benefits from Hip Hop's cultural ambassadors who embody the full repertoire of artifacts, values, and assumptions that make Hip Hop unique.

When we talk about advancements in the culture, we are concerned about the mastery of the skills and teaching the skills associated with the various artifacts of the culture. But we are also concerned about the scaffolding of skills and innovation. For example, in deejaying, the temporal progression of improvisation brought about mixing/blending, scratching, transforming, beat juggling, flaring, and body tricks.[70] In graffiti, the scaffolding is in the creative skills associated with the increasing complexity of pieces. For example, in early New York subway graffiti, the progression went as follows: tags, throw-ups, pieces, top-to-bottoms, end-to-ends, whole cars, and whole trains.[71]

Finally, this book is concerned with the realities of everyday life that fuel priorities, creativity, and innovations in the culture, or as Tia DeNora says, "how art articulates social life, inasmuch as social life articulates art."[72]

THE FIERCE URGENCY OF NOW

This book emphasizes Hip Hop culture's beats, hooks, and lyrics as the drivers of narratives that reflect Hip Hop's range of core values. At their simplest, these values help people get better in their own unique ways. With the help of Hip Hop's unique blend of artifacts, self-improvement efforts started together in the community, they progressed with individual use for both personal and social goals, and sit today as a part of everyday life and as part of a wide range of professional uses.

The entirety of Hip Hop culture is embedded within the psyche and physiology of today's Hip Hop cultural ambassadors. This is what they carry forward. They recognize the brilliance and interdisciplinary mastery of all of Hip Hop's commonly mentioned five elements. They understand the urgency of battling or working hard to "show and prove" improving upon and teaching your craft(s) while at the same time affirming your or your community's authentic identity. They appreciate that sampling/ collage, remixing, language appropriation, blurring boundaries, in depth research and critical analysis, and a utilitarian approach amid a simultaneous concern for presentation is a given during the creative process. Finally, they are committed to the principles of peace, love, unity, and fun as a part of this tapestry. This is the Hip Hop culture and foundation upon which many of today's cultural ambassadors and leaders of contemporary youth settings are bred. It is this totality from which their approach to health and well-being stems.

These sensibilities are coupled with a commitment to help youth achieve their best, and for their communities to be resilient sources of strength and sustenance. It is here where the synergy between these cultural ambassadors and the younger generation's own distinct personal relationship to Hip Hop culture exists, and where it has the most potential to contribute to the health and well-being of the Black population in the United States.

CHAPTER 2

Racial Identity, Hip Hop Culture, and the Shift to Mainstream Pop Culture

The battle over the right to "claim" Hip Hop culture has been waged in the public eye and within the culture since its inception. Jeffrey Ogbar suggests that authenticity plays a gatekeeping role for legitimate participation in Hip Hop culture. He argues that its multicultural origins cannot be ignored and the complexity by which cultural insiders, including artists themselves, negotiate race and ethnicity often makes authenticity a moving target.[1] Imani Perry, however, while agreeing that Hip Hop has multicultural roots and contributors, considers it to be a form of Black music.[2] She anchors her argument on four points: (1) its language is primarily African American vernacular English; (2) it has a political location in society distinctly ascribed to Black people, music, and cultural forms; (3) it is derived from Black American oral culture; and (4) it is derived from Black American music traditions.[3] Mark Fenster departs from essentialist notions and helps to bring attention to the heterogeneity of all cultures. At the same time, he recognizes the powerful role of Hip Hop culture in articulating identities within specific environments, like the social and political realities of the Black community.[4]

Hip Hop culture's focus on the histories, experiences, and perspectives of communities of color is critical to unpacking its relevance as a tool of empowerment and change from the individual to macro levels. These distinctions span and intersect cultural contexts, which include but are not limited to racial and ethnic backgrounds (within and across communities of color), region, age, gender, and economic status. This chapter offers a lens to understand Hip Hop's cultural roots in the Black community, how it morphed from a subculture into the mainstream media and popular culture, and what this means for Hip Hop's underlying values of self and community improvement.

HIP HOP CULTURE THROUGH A MULTICULTURAL LENS

Hip Hop culture's roots in the Bronx borough of New York are undeniably multicultural with Black and Puerto Rican youth providing the lion's share of creative energy and occupying the social, political, and economic space from which these energies emerged.[5] In the Bronx, DJ Kool Herc brought cultural influences from his Jamaican roots, including the use of massive sound systems; dub (instrumental) versions of music to talk, scat, and improvise over; microphones in an echo chamber; and more. However, all races and all boroughs, not just the Bronx, claim contributions to the overall cultural stew that bubbled up as Hip Hop. South Bronx and Uptown both had a rich Puerto Rican culture that brought salsa, high energy, and an acrobatic and communal dance spirit to the area.[6] Latino music also had a rich, funky, percussive, and traditionally live performance element that contributed to the culture.

We know of the extensive Caribbean contributions to the culture's origins, including DJ Kool Herc, Afrika Bambaataa, and DJ Grandmaster Flash at the onset.[7] The corporatization of the culture has contributed to diluting society's recognition of Puerto Rican influences in early Hip Hop culture because b-boying and graffiti are less marketable to the mainstream.[8] Without exposure, their contributions have been inaccessible and effectively erased to newcomers to the culture.[9] On the equally multicultural West Coast, the street, mobile deejay partying, and dancing that became associated with Hip Hop culture had contributions from Latino, Black, and Asian communities.[10] There is also the more distal, yet integral history of activism and the Black Power and Black Arts movements that helped shape the culture.[11]

The culture thrives across all continents today. In the United States, residents whose cultural backgrounds span the regions of South Asia, East Asia, West Africa, and Southern Africa embrace Hip Hop culture through each of its elements.[12] Multicultural engagement of Hip Hop continues to have implications for individuals as much as it does for communities. Today, Hip

Hop has a worldwide presence, and people participate in the culture in a variety of ways, from the most simple beat-driven body movement (e.g., head nodding when you hear a song you like from a passing car), to embracing it as a lifestyle and appreciating the culture's social, political, and artistic roots. For the purposes of this book, we celebrate Hip Hop's multicultural history and also focus on elements specific to the Black community, including issues in education, health, well-being, and the social environment.

UNPACKING DISTINCT BLACK IDENTITIES IN HIP HOP CULTURE

Critical to the discussion of the healing power of Hip Hop is a need to shift from several outdated assumptions that Hip Hop is only for those who identify with Black culture, that Hip Hop cannot play a unique and culturally specific role in the lives of Black people, or even that Black people identify as one homogeneous group. Issues of class, nationality, faith, complexion, and gender intersect prominently with race in the Black community. Perry helps us move past this false pretense of an essential Black monolith in the United States, or "romantic AfroAtlanticism." Instead, she proposes the utility of an underlying question, "What kind of Black American are you?" focusing instead on prioritized communities of identity.[13] A few of these identity-related tensions are discussed below.

Eugene Robinson's account of more pronounced class and social divisions within the Black community and Christina Greer's notions of "elevated minority status" among United States' and foreign-born Blacks suggest that differing experiences of identity may exist.[14] Craig Watkins similarly recognized tensions and conflicts that occur among people of African descent in the United States.[15]

Identity takes on specific significance in developing individual life goals, navigating life challenges, and in how one chooses to interact with Hip Hop culture—whether creating as an artist, or listening or experiencing the works of another.[16] Although the Black community in the United States is often heuristically lumped together socially, politically, and economically as a non-dominant group, there are substantive divisions that play out within and between subgroups. This is to-date an underexplored area in Hip Hop research. Variability in within-group identity and identity development may relate to variability in the appropriation of Hip Hop culture as a resource. Even if we were able to disentangle the "splintered" mainstream from what Robinson labels "the transcendent," "abandoned," and "emergent" groups, we would still have to respect the within-group differences in each group.[17]

MK Asante notes these tensions, in which a focus on individual successes can seemingly overlook the hard reality of economic disparities and inequities within the U.S. Black community. He suggests that for the Black middle class, status and material goods are traps and disincentives to advocating for anything beyond incremental social changes and suggests this is the reason structural and institutional oppression persists, and why the momentum for broader solidarity is waning.[18]

This splintering of identities becomes more apparent if we continue the exploration of this dichotomy: mainstream vs. abandoned (in the words of Robinson). Further division continues to mount when, in some instances, individuals who identify as mainstream see the circumstances that the abandoned face as "ghetto" or "beneath" them.[19] Arguments suggest that this is due partly to assimilation by the mainstream. Newer generations of the mainstream are not as firmly entrenched within majority-Black social networks and contexts. Neighborhoods, schools, and even music and media are less socially homogeneous.[20] Assimilation has the potential to influence individual and social identities. Robinson offers his sense of caution as it relates to identity, "[We] marched, studied, and worked our way to the point where we are assimilating, but we have reservations about assimilation if it means giving up our separate identity."[21]

Greer also examines shared and divergent identities among Black U.S. residents. However, she looks closely at ethnic differences in identity and how this relates to self-interests and individual level concerns. Her ultimate question is more solution-focused and policy-oriented. She asks, "How can Blacks use their shared racial identity and distinct ethnicities to create long-lasting policy that decreases competition for scarce and/or seemingly scarce resources?"[22] As we continue to break down these larger assumptions and categories, it helps elucidate how identity, personal and collective goals, and ultimately Hip Hop culture can be embraced and used in an array of social landscapes.

GRIOTS AND GRIOTTES: KEEPERS OF ORAL CULTURE

The *griot* or *griotte*, a role occupied by both men and women, is a part of the broader African diaspora and extended culture of the Black community. Integral to West African culture, they are "masters of words and music" and were oral keepers of culture through storytelling, poetry, and music.[23] The countries most often associated with the griot tradition include Senegal, Mali, Niger, Gambia, and Burkina Faso. An important feature of their early roles was to be consultants to rulers, leaders, and decision

Hip Hop Culture, the Community, and Black Identities: The Influence of Afrika Bambaataa

A significant section of Hip Hop's cultural roots is grounded in the thoughts and practices of Afrika Bambaataa. He was a walking reminder of the connection between identity and community, as he stayed anchored in his community while also forging a new path forward. Gangs of the time, with which he was affiliated, sought to maintain their turf and protect their community, while their members sought to avoid beatings, robberies, and harassment.[24] Bambaataa drew from his cultural roots within and outside of music and foresaw a new normal. He was educated through materials from the Black Panther Information Center, and his home life was steeped in music and its messages of growth, community, and change. Bambaataa was present at a gang truce brokered by the Ghetto Brothers and a witness to the testimonials about change such as that given by Benjy Melendez. "We're not a gang anymore. We want to help Blacks and Puerto Ricans to live in a better environment," Melendez said at the Peace Treaty.[25] He formed a new family that channeled their energies toward music and dance.

We had a lot of gang violence, also a lot of social awareness. Civil rights movement, human rights movement, love power movement, Vietnam War, Malcolm X, Honorable Elijah Muhammed—Nation of Islam, Beatles, Sly and the Family Stone . . . people were ready for change. UZN was to get everybody away from the negative and move them toward the positive. We had a large following . . . they followed me to the music. It was originally for the Black and Latino community . . . once we started making recordings and took it downtown, that's when it began to reach other cultures. Music itself is colorless. Comes from all races.[26]

His social influence channeled a following of his interests, into the new music being promoted by DJ Kool Herc, which "was more funky" than the most popular deejay in his home community.

makers. Music and words were intertwined with their histories and genealogies.[27]

Griots are the musical storytellers, narrators, and witnesses working on behalf of others within a culture.[28] They tend to occupy the same family and occupy the same social space; a caste. Griots might be political as well, as Adama Drame recounts his father's actions as a griot in 1950s West Africa:

> My father, Saliphu Drame, was a renowned musician. In the 1950s, he was Burkina Faso's first artist ever to record an album. Saliphu Drame was a great tamar, a so-called speaking drum player. He also did wonders with his voice. He was a great speaker. He was one of the first griots when Africa was still colonial to become politically involved. He urged people at the threshold of independence to take their fate in their own hands to break free of backwardness and start cultivating the land of their fathers. He argued that owning your own land was the foundation of a decent living and that no one is going to work that for you, so breed their cattle for them.[29]

Griots are not universally revered. Apprehensions toward them stem from a fear of the power of words, the perception that griots are cultural outsiders, and a discomfort with the freedoms associated with their unconventional behavior (e.g., shouting, singing and dancing, demanding gifts).[30] The expectation by some griots of gifts in return has led to a devaluing of their work, as people believe it lacks substance and is merely for reward.[31]

While there is great diversity among griots, there is also great commonality. At their core are their mastery of communication, their alignment with music, their use of men and women in these roles, and their potential contributions to communities. These characteristics are noteworthy as we investigate the evolution of the emcee as contemporary regional extensions of the griot, and ultimately the African diaspora.

PROPHETS: SPEAKING WITH INSIGHT ABOUT THE PRESENT AND THE FUTURE

A prophet is gifted with profound moral insight, able to speak to the future, and an effective spokesperson for a cause or group.[32] While prophets are often associated with biblical roles, they are also often poets. The Black community has been afforded prophets across contexts who have led movements seeking better conditions for their communities. These individuals helped form the infrastructure for advancements in civil rights and the associated gains socially, politically, and economically. These moral leaders were at the vanguard of positive social change and from different vantage points. Some, like the Reverend Dr. Martin Luther King Jr., were more aligned with civil disobedience and nonviolence as the platform for change. Others, like the Black Panther Party for Self-Defense and the Young Lords, were more aligned with self-defense: both are potentially confrontational strategies but nonetheless different ways of seeking to change the status quo. No matter the perspective, they articulated the desire for community improvements, better conditions across a range of settings in which Black people found themselves receiving unfair, disparate, and oppressive treatment.

Sometimes people affirmed and celebrated figures in entertainment. In a genre of film that has come to be known as Blaxploitation, certain characters were celebrated, like Shaft, The Mack, and Foxy Brown, because of pride in being powerful in general, but also in challenging institutionalized oppression on the big screen.[33] Debates persist today as to whether these images were more minstrelsy or part of the movement. Detractors say this was no more than a perpetuation of stereotypes and validation of the Black male as hypersexual, violent, and delinquent. Others do not ignore these stereotypes, yet they argue that these individuals were defiant of oppressive norms, proud, and strong instigators of an alternative reality.[34]

Each Hip Hop pioneer has a personal history that manifested in how the culture was expressed. These leaders drew upon their own cultural ambassadors to create new voices, identities, and community spaces. These leaders also recognized the importance of their environments, including the social, economic, and political realities of the time. "Hip Hop came out of the government's attempt to crush leadership in our communities," Popmaster Fabel of the b-boy and b-girl Rock Steady Crew said.[35] The backdrop of cultural and social devastation for young people at that time is captured well in films like *80 Blocks from Tiffany's*, depicting the attempts of youth to find their voice and identity and a sense of family within the early Bronx street organizations.[36]

MOVEMENTS OF POWER AND ART: BLACK POWER, THE BLACK ARTS MOVEMENT (BAM), AND SOUL

United States Black history has several notable cultural and aesthetic peaks during which intellectuals and artists exist as movements toward galvanizing racial pride, solidarity, and action toward social change. The Harlem Renaissance, an arts movement from the 1920s and 1930s, sought to distance

itself from an "Old Negro" philosophy that catered to systemic White su-
premacy and Black inferiority. Instead, it ushered in what was perceived as
an authentic "New Negro" ideology that was proud and empowered.[37] However, in distancing itself through harsh critiques of prior generations, it also
served as a generational and within-culture wedge that continues to play out
within and between generations of artistic movements.

Between 1965 and 1970, the Black Arts Movement was ideologically
aligned with the Black Power Movement seeking to bridge its efforts with
political and economic progress by focusing on the psychological liberation and reeducation of the Black community. The goal of this literary-
based movement was to change dominant societal values in the United
States to allow greater equity in power sharing across societal systems, and
transformation within Black culture where self-love and racial solidarity
was prioritized.[38]

The "soul" aesthetic is also equated with its coexistence alongside the
Black Arts Movement during this period, including but not limited to music,
dress, language, hairstyles, food, art, and film. These were cultural expressions that evoked pride, solidarity, a counternarrative to dominant or mainstream U.S. culture, and a bridge to authentic African culture.[39] Many cite
Sam Cooke's 1963 single "A Change Is Gonna Come" as the official beginning of the soul music era that lasted until the early 1970s.[40] Some of the
prominent artists of the era were Curtis Mayfield, Aretha Franklin, Nina
Simone, Etta James, James Brown, Otis Redding, and Marvin Gaye.

Art has a social function. Art is power, with the ability to "speak" and
inspire reflection and agency in an ongoing dialogue within the culture
as much as it is outside the culture.[41] Rabaka reiterated Franz Fanon's
view that these artistic movements were "the art of social transformation
and human liberation . . . creating pathways of hope toward a brighter
future."[42]

YOUNG, GIFTED, AND BLACK

Nina Simone's "Young, Gifted, and Black" was named the official Black
national anthem by a remodeled and more nationalistic Congress of Racial
Equality (C.O.R.E.)—a thumb of the nose, or at least a deliberate contrast
to the Civil Rights Movement's Negro national anthem "Lift Every Voice."[43]
Spike Lee made a similar statement of contrast when he used a soft jazz
version of "Lift" in the movie opening of his 1989 film *Do the Right Thing*
but then made a sharp contrast by switching to Public Enemy's protest anthem "Fight the Power" and an infectious sampling of sound and imagery
with Rosie Perez dancing.[44]

Beyond the specific content of Simone's "Young, Gifted, and Black," the heuristic power has lived on within Hip Hop culture's collective imagination. It has been reinterpreted in a variety of uniquely specific ways by legendary Hip Hop emcees Big Daddy Kane and Jay Z, "underground" artist Gist, and most recently by emcee and community activist Jasiri X with youth members of his *1Hood* media academy. Spike Lee, Big Daddy Kane, Jay Z, and Jasiri X are all reminders of different approaches to achieve the same goal, and reminders of art and social politics as "two sides of a bridgeless gap in political consciousness and mobilizations of the Black United States."[45]

"I CAN'T LIVE WITHOUT MY RADIO": THE EVOLUTION OF RAP MUSIC IN THE MAINSTREAM MEDIA

> "When it's real, you doing this without a record contract."
> —Nas, "The Genesis"

Timothy Jones, of #HipHopEd and Martha's Table, believes that Hip Hop culture's history is essentially a tale of two eras, "Before Industry" and "After Industry."

Before Industry

Ironically, one of the first voices in the corporate discourse around Hip Hop music to help shape a shift in attitudes from rap as a fad to rap as a cultural product was Hip Hop pioneer and business mogul Russell Simmons. He had a terrible showing in his initial business pitch (to Warner Brothers) within the world of major record labels. In 1985 he got a second chance, this time to pitch to Columbia Records. Simmons laid out in exhaustive detail his Def Jam vision and its sphere of influence. But what set this empire and commercialization explosion in motion was his insistence that rap music was "more than Black music, it was teen music."[46]

Def Jam was multiracial in its leadership, in its musical acts, and in the business dealings that led to its commercial success. Dan Charnas pointed out the irony in race, politics, and artistry during these early years of ascension into the mainstream:

> The Beastie Boys were a White group with a Black DJ, managed by a Black man and his White Israeli-American lieutenant. Their Black sounding Hip Hop records were produced by a White man and promoted to White radio programmers by a Black man. They owed their

careers to the endorsement of a Black rap supergroup (Run DMC); and the White MCs now crusaded for a new pro-Black political rap crew (Public Enemy) whose Black friend had just dissed the White rappers in print (Spin magazine). The pro-Black crew, Public Enemy, had been pursued doggedly by a White Jewish record entrepreneur (Rubin) over the mild objections and indifference from his Black partner (Simmons). And Public Enemy was modeled by their Black producer in part after [the revolutionary politics and stance of] a White punk band (The Clash).[47]

Hip Hop and rap music was recognized in the music trade in the early 1980s as little more than a fad, eventually held together by independent labels. Even to those that respected the art within the industry, like Nelson George at *Billboard*, it meant little without press, major label funding, or a more prominent positive narrative.[48] This came in 1985 and 1986.

After Industry

At once Hip Hop went from a culture seeking to be understood to something whose commercial viability could no longer be ignored. Independent labels were absorbed by the majors but kept around because they were cultural insiders.[49] The rap music element of Hip Hop culture was more easily packaged and commoditized as a product than other aspects of the culture like b-boying.[50] In one of the few systematic research efforts to determine music purchasing habits by race, Whites accounted for 60 percent of rap music purchases by 2004.[51] That is down from a number that hovered between 70 and 75 percent between 1995 and 2001. But even in 2009 the top two most preferred music types among millennials (ages 18–34) were rap and Hip Hop (followed by reggae in third place).[52]

In a Pitchfork video looking back at Public Enemy's second album *It Takes a Nation of Millions to Hold Us Back*, frontman Chuck D. made it clear that its goal was to increase social consciousness through sounds and words to "wake motherfuckers up!"[53] Despite only selling 300,000 copies of their first album, their new sound and approach saw them going platinum in a little more than a year after its 1988 release, selling more than one million copies. But these social and political critiques within mainstream rap music, common to artists like Public Enemy, X-Clan, and others, were eventually phased out. Ogbar speculates that for some gatekeepers, that type of music was too much for the new White audience, unlike more "implicitly black" and negative references like "niggas," "bitches," and "hos," which came to dominate mainstream rap music.[54] Fast-forward to the present, two decades later, and this trend has continued unabated.[55] How this is possible is examined in the following sections.

And Then There Were Three . . . Record Labels

Many consider 1988 one of the greatest years in Hip Hop history, with timeless releases across an incredible variety of styles, such as *It Takes a Nation of Millions to Hold Us Back* by Public Enemy, *Strictly Business* by EPMD, *Straight Outta Compton* by N.W.A., *The Great Adventures of Slick Rick* by Slick Rick, *By All Means Necessary* by Boogie Down Productions, *Follow the Leader* by Eric B. and Rakim, *Long Live the Kane* by Big Daddy Kane, *Straight Out the Jungle* by the Jungle Brothers, and *Power* by Ice-T. Back then, there were six major record labels: Warner Music Group, EMI, CBS Records (later Sony), BMG, Universal Music Group, and Polygram. Only three major record labels remain today: Universal Music Group, Sony Music Entertainment, and Warner Music Group, further consolidating distribution outlets. They are now "entertainment" groups controlling recording, publishing, and access to the avenues of distribution. According to global copyright research service Music & Copyright's blog, these labels control 75 percent of the combined physical and digital music market and 80 percent of the digital music market.

When two cultures come together, often one culture's artifacts are reframed and explained within the second, receiving culture in a way that allows an easier integration.[56] For Hip Hop, absorption into mainstream culture, has meant a narrower range of (1) voices represented in the art, (2) social critiques, and (3) overt declarations of cultural pride and nationalism. These results have skewed the types of identities associated with Hip Hop culture and identities associated with being a Black person in the United States.[57]

Historically, Hip Hop culture represented a broad range of "ideas, experiences, and viewpoints" for the Black community, from the most risky to the most empowering and critical voices.[58] This explains how in 1987 it was possible to have LL Cool J, Run DMC, and Public Enemy on the same record label, Def Jam. The same year, a pro-Black, community conscious, cultural shift in production quality and lyricism took place and the voices of Chuck D., Rakim, and KRS-One permanently changed the landscape of rap music.[59]

Two preeminent voices at the onset of this shifting landscape were Rakim and Chuck D. They brought cultural nationalism to the forefront of Hip Hop culture—through mainstream outlets. Rakim's lyrics took you on an infectious journey of individual empowerment, while Chuck's lyricism highlighted the need for community empowerment—what Greg Tate labeled the "innerview" and "overview" respectively.[60] Both "views" are the scaffolding of evolving cultural identities, the critical analyses that undergird Hip Hop's valued "knowledge of self."[61] However, contemporary mainstream Hip Hop music tends to disproportionately present a singularized and decontextualized Black voice and experience.[62] Bettina Love echoes these sentiments when comparing her research of young girls' experiences to her own early life experiences with Hip Hop culture:

> Juxtaposing Slick Rick's and N.W.A.'s lyrics to Lil' Wayne or Kanye West, one sees that there are more similarities than differences. . . . Music that questions society in terms of racism, sexism, classism and xenophobic attitudes are rarely heard on popular radio stations and TV stations. . . . Black youth have limited access to rap music and images that celebrate the multiple and varying identities of Black life, but unlimited access to the trope of Black females as sex objects who are uneducated, promiscuous, and poor decision makers.[63]

Black youth culture has turned into a commodity.[64] First, it has been commercialized as an entertainment product, but also as one within preexisting stereotypic cultural frames about youth of color and society. Next, it is sold by a consolidated few.[65] Hip Hop culture is no longer seen in its entirety.

Who's Your A&R?

Another way to help understand Hip Hop's commoditization is to look closely at the artistry pipeline, overseen by artist and repertoire (A&R) executives that scout, cultivate, and promote talent. We continue to see regular monetization of voices willing to celebrate violence, misogyny, and substance use (and distribution). For example, artist Bobby Shmurda—real name Acquille Pollard—was recently signed to a multiple album, seven-figure deal with Epic Records off of the strength of his song "Hot Boy," buoyed by the viral clip of his "Shmoney Dance" circulated on the Vine social media app. "Hot Boy" peaked at No. 6 and spent fifteen weeks on Billboard's Hot 100 chart. After being arrested for potential conspiracy in gun violence and illegal drug distribution with his Brooklyn neighborhood crew GS9—also the name of the label imprint he was given by Epic upon signing his contract—he spoke of this art, entertainment, and monetization dynamic. From jail he stated how his "lyrics were fabricated because that's what's selling nowadays."[66] Whether he is guilty or not matters less than the recognition of what product is rewarded and monetized, as long as it/he stays out of jail.

Industry Rule No. 4080

In 1991, on "Check the Rhime" from their instant classic *The Low End Theory*, A Tribe Called Quest penned one of the many universally recognized phrases of the culture as they simultaneously gave listeners insight about a major frustration of Hip Hop artists: "Industry rule number 4080, record company people are shady." At the time of the album's recording, the group was working out differences with their record label Jive, a subsidiary of RCA Music Group, about staying true to their artistic vision of the music and culture. They continue on the song with, "Rap is not pop, if you call it that then stop."

Fast forward almost a quarter century, and Lupe Fiasco on "Dots and Lines," off his 2015 release *Tetsuo & Youth*, goes into detail about being beholden to record companies. He does it in a way that only Lupe can, through brilliant wordplay, complex analogies, and the type of figurative expressions that give you a crystal-clear understanding of his perceived challenges. However, equally important, he weaves in food for thought about identity, a sense of self, the implications for society at large, especially youth, and the value of considering alternatives to getting caught up in the industry machine. "Don't sine [sign]."

Kendrick Lamar essentially continues this discussion through the thematic inclusion of "Lucy" on his 2015 album *To Pimp a Butterfly*, released about twenty years to the date after Tupac Shakur's third album *Me Against the World*, and at 78 minutes long, double the length of Nas's 39-minute magnum opus *Illmatic* released a little more than twenty years prior. "Lucy," short for Lucifer, is a personification of the most exploitative, parasitic, and profit-driven elements of the entertainment industry—and its residual trappings and risks for artists. On "For Sale?" Lamar states, "Lucy got paper work on top of paper work. I want you to know that Lucy got you. All your life I watched you. And now you all grown up then sign this contract if that's possible."

However, in the same way that Tupac straddled the lines between mainstream trappings of a singular stereotypic story of Black life and narratives that move back and forth between Rakim's innerview and Chuck D's overview, several artists are showing glimpses of this today. Kendrick Lamar is one of a few emcees enjoying mainstream success while maintaining a wide range of critical content. For example, he released "i" with "The Blacker the Berry" and "u" on the same album. He deftly articulates introspection, accountability, protest, and hope within these three tracks.

Art is shaped by a commercially driven industry, even among the most visible and successful artists. Lupe Fiasco, in an interview with Sway Calloway on *Sway in the Morning*, said that he seeks to release material that aligns with his creative vision as much as commercial interests. Lupe has notoriously battled Atlantic Records over the content of his records. The push for commercial viability can inhibit the expression of complexities about the lived experiences of the Black community, but more importantly, it limits the range of empowering opportunities available for those that engage with the culture.

HIP HOP EXPOSURE AND RISK: UNDERSTANDING

The mainstream success of Hip Hop culture has allowed tremendous exposure, popularity, and wealth generation. Several Hip Hop elements and their associated artifacts are well known, widely available, and universally practiced. However, a closer look at the culture begs the question: which elements, which artifacts, and which values are most readily transmitted within contemporary society? Next, which are internalized with depth, and which are engaged only at a superficial level?

For example, if we are looking at the values of peace, love, unity, and having fun, which ones are prominently featured in the most commercialized representation of Hip Hop culture? It is fair to say some semblance of "having fun and unity" exists, but with tremendous variability in the proportions of high- and low-risk versions of self-improvement?

When we examine Hip Hop's elements—b-boying, deejaying, graffiti, emceeing, and knowledge of self—what is featured most prominently within the entertainment industry? Is it fair to say that emceeing and deejaying are prominent, b-boying has been commodified into "street dance," graffiti has been largely criminalized with limited opportunities for public art spaces, and knowledge of self is limited to the most high risk aspects of self-improvement? The type of knowledge of self in commercialized Hip Hop culture privileges fun, skews the representation of some of the culture's assumptions about battling and authenticity (e.g., mastery, competition, and one-upmanship), and essentializes high-risk unity, thus limiting the culture's most empowering values. Upon reflecting on the state of the most commercial aspects of the culture, Asheru, emcee and founder of Guerilla Arts Ink, stated his concern about the net effect of such industry-driven trends on the Black community: "They are using our own art form to build up fear and paranoia about us."

THE ENTERTAINMENT INDUSTRY, HIGH RISK CONTENT, AND PARENTAL ADVISORIES

In 1986 Def Jam released its first platinum-selling album, *Licensed to Ill* by the Beastie Boys, an all-White group, but chose not to include the song "Scenario" because Columbia felt its lyrics were objectionable.[67] One year earlier the first Parental Advisory Labels (PAL) were issued to help alert parents to explicit content on music albums. "Scenario" was an homage to the explicit lyrical style of Philadelphia emcee Schooly D, who Rick Rubin, the album's producer, and the Beasties followed closely. The song's lyrics included the line, "shot homeboy in the motherfucking face."[68] Since then, rap music in popular culture has grown progressively more lenient with lyrics. Think about Columbia's roster (now a part of Sony Music Entertainment) of artists since. With 50 Cent, DMX, Snoop Dogg, and T.I. alone, it is notable how the nature of allowable content has changed.

Concerns about contemporary rap music continue among parents, educators, and youth workers as high-risk messages have grown more prominent in popular culture and the mainstream.[69] A specific causal link between rap music exposure and undesirable outcomes is weak, especially as researchers continue to identify more important mediators between exposure and outcomes. However, the ability to mitigate potential risk in any capacity is a worthy public health goal and should be a priority. Real public health challenges and epidemics exist related to substance abuse, reproductive and sexual health, violence, nutrition and physical activity, access to health services, and social determinants of health. Further, the Black community is uniquely and disparately influenced in many of these categories.[70]

RADIO AND GOING PLATINUM VS. THE INTERNET

With people trying to be fiscally responsible, and through social media and the internet, people often look out for when content from their favorite artist is leaked (i.e., subversively uploaded early to the internet), rather than for the official release date, when they can purchase it from a music outlet. This trend has greatly altered how both artists and record companies make a profit. In 2015 prominent Hip Hop artists Drake and Talib Kweli released full albums unannounced in advance, Drake for purchase, and Kweli *for free* via the internet. In the same way Hip Hop culture crossed over successfully into mainstream music, it also shifted into other forms of entertainment and popular culture in the late 1980s and early 1990s. Television shows with a majority Black cast, such as the *Arsenio Hall Show, The Fresh*

Prince of Bel Air, In Living Color, Martin, Living Single, New York Undercover, and *Def Comedy Jam* became more common. That brief cultural explosion ended as abruptly as Hip Hop's golden era. Fox, which profited greatly from shows like *In Living Color* and *Martin,* signed a lucrative NFL deal in 1994 and slowly shed its majority Black shows from the schedule. By 1999, of the top 26 shows on major network television, none had a leading Black protagonist and 86 percent of the casts were White.[71] Perhaps now is the time for another major network cultural shift.

What Would Cookie Say?

A young boy is walking down the stairs in his home. He is wearing his mother's high-heeled shoes and is walking uneasily. He also has her headscarf wrapped around his head as he continues down to the bottom of the stairs. Suddenly the room quiets as all eyes catch the boy entering the room. As the boy's father turns and notices his son, he becomes visibly enraged and immediately jumps to his feet. He charges toward the boy, grabbing him aggressively while verbally berating him. The father pulls his son out of the house, down the stairs, and into the backyard. He lifts up the lid of the trash can, then lifts up his son and puts him completely inside. He slams the lid shut.

The imagery of this scene between father and son is as heartbreaking as it is a reminder of the toxic depths of homophobia in our communities. That it occurred on prime time television is a surprise. That it occurred on a show whose entire setting and context is based on a fictionalized corporate/mainstream Hip Hop record label is also surprising. That it occurred with a predominantly Black cast, on Fox, is well. . . In the first few episodes of the show, there is drug distribution, parent incarceration, same sex relationships, biracial relationships, homophobia, homicide, mental health issues, and a degenerative disease affliction.

The aforementioned show, *Empire,* enjoyed unprecedented success in its first season. Its 5.1 rating made it the top show among the Big 4 networks in the important 18–49 demographic, averaging 13 million viewers, the best first season on any network since *Grey's Anatomy* in 2005. These numbers do not reflect the fact that viewership for the show rose each week, reaching a 6.9 rating and 17 million viewers for its final episode.[72]

We Want More

Is it time to innovate a new demand, one that cannot be so easily downloaded and dismissed? Can something in the popular culture be more than "artificial, frivolous, and temporary," in the more substantive manner that the Arts and Power movements pushed for decades earlier?[73] According to Questlove of Hip Hop icons The Roots, there is at least one bona fide example in Hip Hop history of a crossover from the mainstream into something more—The Beastie Boys:

> Is this all what it leads up to? Come out the gate rowdy and fightin'... and then gain spiritual enlightenment down the line? The same guy who had "twin sisters in the bed" was now offering women (wives, mothers, & sisters) love and respect to the end. And you know what? They actually made being "square" kinda cool. I know the Boys are going down in history as "first white act this" and "video pioneers that" and blah blah blah ... but I'd like to acknowledge that they are truly rock's most realized group. (Not hip hop but all music really). You really don't see many audiences willing to go where their leaders take them once said audience gets comfortable with a position—I mean even the Beatles imploded 5 years post spiritual enlightenment. I mean did we really expect the most thoughtful mature considerate act in music to be the same brats who gave us *Licensed To Ill*?[74]

Maybe someone was listening and watching. Chicago emcee Chance the Rapper helped bring this dynamic full circle when his freely distributed album enjoyed widespread acclaim:

> The whole point of Acid Rap was just to ask people a question: does the music business side of this dictate what type of project this is? If it's all original music and it's got this much emotion around it and it connects this way with this many people, is it a mixtape? What's an album these days, anyways? Cause I didn't sell it, does that mean it's not an official release? So I might not ever drop a for-sale project. Maybe I'll just make my money touring.[75]

HEALING WITHIN AND BETWEEN

Mazi Mutafa, founder and executive director of Words, Beats, and Life, Inc. in Washington, DC, a Hip Hop–oriented non-profit dedicated to transforming young lives, helped me to understand his vision of Hip Hop's universal appeal. He used an informal acronym for his organization, W.B.A.L.I.: "Whites, Blacks, Asians, Latinos, and Indians—the whole human family." He emphasized Words, Beats, and Life's insistence on using Hip Hop as a vehicle for transforming the human race.

The voices of individuals identifying as Latino, White, Asian, and other cultures have been a steady force within Hip Hop evolution to the mainstream. At the same time, we recognize that within Hip Hop culture exists a distinctly Black thread that has deep social and historical ties to the griots and prophets within and across cultures, but also across prior generations. These profound Black voices simultaneously and giftedly brought forth the art and the politics of the Black experience. Embedded within Hip Hop culture are its artifacts and values, exemplified by artistic mastery—lyrical, visual, physical, and audio. In spite of major changes in distribution, exposure, and how artists are rewarded, Hip Hop's ascension into the mainstream has not deterred its underlying values that speak to the individual as much as the community.

We now have a new generation of adults who work with youth—Hip Hop's cultural ambassadors who promote its artifacts and values. In the following chapters we will hear more from them about their thoughts on Hip Hop's empowering capacity and how they are making a difference in education, out-of-school time, mental health, and physical health. These ambassadors embody society's multiracial realities. They build bridges across cultures while maintaining a distinct core of community pride. Many are artists themselves, blessed with gifts of communication and artistry in their own unique styles. Most importantly, they position themselves personally and professionally within new mainstream and technological realities to push for better—better for themselves, better for other individuals, and better for the communities they value.

CHAPTER 3

Hip Hop's History of Healing and Empowerment in High-Risk Environments

People like Hip Hop. Its popularity spans all facets of the culture—the storytelling, the sounds, the visual artistry, the dancing, and ability for its narratives to help people look inward as well as outward for better. There is power drawn from Hip Hop culture. Everyday individuals, marginalized groups, and communities rely on Hip Hop in all its forms to speak truth to power. For some, it is the draw of having a voice, whether spoken, written, or drawn, expressed sonically or in movement. For others, it is speaking reality into existence or validating their reality. In doing so, Hip Hop becomes inspiration for those who have lost hope, and a cathartic release for those needing to let wilt away hurt, fear, or despair. Hip Hop is also fun, active, exciting, and participatory. For some, the fun is in the adventure, intrigue, and taboo of rebellious, dangerous, or risky attitudes and behaviors. For others, Hip Hop is motivational, helping to spur action, sometimes to just keep on moving during tough times, at other times a chance to do something complex and creative.

There are also those who want the opportunity to connect with and belong to innovative communities of artists, to create art that inspires or instills pride in the communities they value. Finally, there are those who want the chance to use it as a tool to make the groups and places they value better. In this chapter we explain how these differing uses of Hip Hop showcase its healing power and introduce how people have continued to harness its most powerful aspects to improve their lives. A closer look at the culture shows that shared values have persisted over time and have a common theme of wanting "better." It is here that we see that valuing improvement, for individuals and the community, has always existed in the culture and is a major source of its healing power.

A HIP HOP NATION

People liked Hip Hop culture in the 1970s, when the yet-unnamed culture was still being formed. The United Zulu Nation brought rival crews and a mix of races and ethnicities together under one roof for a party of deejaying, emceeing, and dance with b-boys and b-girls to divert energy and attention toward fun and something more positive.[1] People liked Hip Hop culture in the 1980s, when it burst into the mainstream. People liked Hip Hop culture in the 1990s, when many argue it splintered into its biggest variety of styles and forms. People liked Hip Hop in the 2000s when, although more homogenized in the mainstream, the culture firmly entrenched itself into popular culture as the dominant preferred music genre for young adults. And today, when it has transformed into a global multibillion-dollar industry that touches all aspects of social life, people still love Hip Hop culture, warts and all. However, only recently has the question of "why?" been asked—empirically.

In the various ways Hip Hop culture is expressed, the desire for *better* is the common value by which identities are affirmed, strengths are realized, and joys are shared. Again, people cope and thrive in the most challenging situations. Skills are mastered, roles are modeled, and traditions are honored as essential to the culture. Communities bring together individuals and demonstrate resilience. Despite ever-present controversies and debates over negative and positive influences, Hip Hop is a mainstay in popular culture today. At its best, Hip Hop heals, among artists, listeners, observers, and communities of all different racial and ethnic groups, nationalities, geographies, genders, and economic standing. To better understand Hip Hop's positive influence, the following sections will discuss Hip Hop at the community level and then at the individual level.

WE, THE COMMUNITY

Hip Hop Public Health's (HHPH) Hip Hop Healthy Eating And Living in Schools (HEALS) is an initiative that integrates music and dance grounded in Hip Hop culture, with health promotion to emphasize positive choices around nutrition and physical activity. Hip Hop pioneer Doug E. Fresh is the vice president of entertainment—bridging entertainment and education—helping guide this program to over 25,000 students. He doesn't just sing about it, he lives it too, as a vegetarian for over 25 years. HHPH is a formal initiative based in the Bronx, the geographical heart of Hip Hop's roots. However, this community interest and the desire for Hip Hop to play a role in improving circumstances has been around since the birth of Hip Hop culture.

The film *Flyin' Cut Sleeves* also shows how in the backdrop of cultural and social devastation of the early 1970s young people attempted to find their voice, identity, and a sense of family in Bronx street organizations. Many felt this was a government-induced devastation. Again, Popmaster Fabel felt the chaos, instability, and neglect was government-induced, a deliberate attempt to eliminate social change–oriented leadership in communities of color.[2] This community leadership must be understood in the context of the social, economic, and political realities of the time. This was, after all, one of the poorest sections of one of New York's poorest boroughs, and predominantly a community of Black and Latino residents. Prominent in the period immediately preceding the onset of Hip Hop culture, and ultimately feeding the knowledge and attitudes of the culture, were policy-induced economic devastation and the Black Power and Black Arts movements.

The power movements were by nature community based and driven by efforts to make positive change, health notwithstanding. Prominent organizations with histories of engaging in community-based public health campaigns were the Garveyites, the Black Panther Party (BPP, including the local New York and Bronx chapters) and the Young Lords (YLP), which had its focus on Puerto Rican and allied cultural interests. These movements existed among a variety of social movements engaged in sustained efforts toward positive social change for the improvement of Black communities. They included the Revolutionary Action Movement (RAM), the Republic of New Africa, Maulana Karenga's US, Amiri Baraka's Congress of African Peoples, and the Black Panther Party (originally called the Black Panther Party for Self-Defense).[3]

The Black Panther Party developed and maintained public health and education programs such as its free breakfast program and liberation schools. The objective was to meet the needs of individuals and the community. These ideas were reflected in the child's pledge, "I pledge to develop my mind and body to the greatest extent possible. I will learn all that I can in order to give my best to my people in their struggle for liberation."[4] An interesting connection to Hip Hip culture is Lamumba Shakur, father of Hip Hop legend Tupac Amaru Shakur, whose name means "Shining, Serpent, Blessed One," who led the New York chapter of the Panthers.

Like the Black Panther Party, as quickly as the Young Lords Party (YLP) rose in prominence and function, it dissolved. The breakdown came from changes in philosophy among its members; a willingness to allow alternative voices in the decision-making structure; and reported sabotage, pressure, and attacks from the Federal Bureau of Investigation (FBI). Its campaign to "disrupt, misdirect, discredit, or otherwise neutralize" the Panthers and similar organizations like the YLP began in 1967.[5] It worked. However, building upon the community well-being goals of the Black Panthers and the Young Lords were groups like the Ghetto Brothers, the reformed Spades, and the Zulu Nation founded by Afrika Bambaataa. The social movement messages of self and community improvement were not lost.

The Bronx Community

Bronx-area youth faced pressure from wider society and from their immediate social environment. Not only was broader society alienating socially, economically, and through physical neglect because of questionable public policies that directly influenced Black and Puerto Rican residents, there was also teen violence from gangs across races and ethnicities.[6] However, the knowledge and attitudes about community well-being from the prior social movements persisted. New public health campaigns targeted at youth crews in the Bronx and other parts of the city popped up. Distinct health/well-being campaigns included No Angel Dust; No Junkies Allowed After 10 O'Clock; Get Rid of the Pushers; Do Not Drink, Smoke, or Take Drugs; and Stay in School Until You Get a Diploma. There were breakfast programs, advocacy for better healthcare, and "heavy-handed policing."[7]

Reflections on a city-funded effort to promote community well-being through the Youth Services Agency (YSA) helps paint a picture of how tenuous strategies that emphasize investment in strengths and building community assets can be. Black Benjie, a member of the Ghetto Brothers street gang described the YSA initiative and the support of Manny Dominguez (his teacher) and wife Rita Fecher, "You gave us acceptance, love, trust, goals, you as a teacher/your hope . . . ."[8] The couple helped secure an actual storefront clubhouse to use for community-focused programs, with funding from the YSA. Unfortunately, after the gang truce of 1971, the Bronx Youth Gang Task Force began operations and the promise of sustained initiatives for community health and well-being began to deteriorate. The YSA infrastructure began to dissolve with the elimination of

gang conflict mediation efforts and unfunded applications to provide services and programs. The actual storefront was eventually closed because of
budget cuts.[9]

Partying in the Name of Peace

The year 1973 saw a now-legendary party at 1520 Sedgwick Avenue
in the Bronx, New York, with sixteen-year-old Kool Herc as the deejay.
It is cited as one of the flagship moments in deejaying, emceeing, and
b-boying/b-girling. Afrika Bambaataa, another of Hip Hop's founding
fathers, began his transition to deejaying not long after, learning from older
former Spades. By 1975, after returning from a trip to Africa, he was recruiting others to come together, have fun, and create art in the name of peace.

Communal well-being was not necessarily the dominant ethos for youth
at the time, nor was it the oft-romanticized and unified "birth" of all Hip
Hop elements at once as a tool of social justice to combat oppressive conditions. However, when the United Zulu Nation became formalized, it *was* a
deliberate mobilization and organized effort to promote resilience and
solidarity. Again, Bambaataa validated this when he stated, "My vision was
to try to organize as many as I could to stop the violence. So I went around
different areas telling them to join [Zulu Nation] and stop your fighting."[10]
The observable outcomes were people being brought together in peace,
unity, and fun.

WE, THE LISTENERS

Many listeners have had a consistent connection to Hip Hop throughout history with a sense of belonging and the desire for community self-improvement. The concept of *Nommo*, or the potential energy of expression—words,
language, visual, song, dance—is a source of power among members of the
African diaspora.[11] At one end Hip Hop music offers energy for personal
growth. At the other end of the spectrum its power helps inform resistance
and is a tool for positive social change or "social transformation."[12] Within
Hip Hop's canon are many exemplars of records linked to positive community change—whether seeking improvements to the system or improvements
in the community's attitudes or behaviors to achieve a better end state.

"Fight the Power" by Public Enemy is one such song that speaks to this
type of potential transformation and set the tone for many future records
about change in Hip Hop history. The 1990 edition of the *Chronicle of
Higher Education* captures observations about how the track permeated
student culture at the time: "Some Black students are beginning to assert

pride in their cultural heritage by wearing African-style clothing and hair styles . . . new groups as alternatives to traditional fraternities and sororities. The organizations concentrate on improving conditions for Blacks in communities surrounding campuses and on educating college students on the history of Black Americans."[13]

The Push and Pull of Identity for Listeners

Hip Hop can be an influence on identity, pushing and pulling it when working toward positive change for the conditions of the Black community, influencing members of the culture and society at large. When rap or Hip Hop is contextualized as part of a movement toward social change, one assumption is that belonging and community identification has already been established. The goal of Hip Hop in these instances is positive social change, where it inspires individual and collective pressure on the systems within which these valued communities exist to help direct more energy toward improving conditions and the ability to meet these community's needs.[14] An alternative perspective is that Hip Hop helps shift identities in the community that need shifting, akin to the core Hip Hop element of building knowledge of self.

A major shift in the prominence of community solidarity, pro-Black identity, and social and political strength-driven content in Hip Hop occurred in mainstream Hip Hop culture in the late 1980s. Interestingly enough though, in early media and literature narratives about Hip Hop music the division between "conscious, political, or activist" rap and "gangsta rap," was fluid as it was often lumped together as violent and radical.[15] Violent and radical were conflated in rhetoric as the predominant concern about Hip Hop's negative influences.

ME, THE ARTIST

We must remember too that artists are artists, meaning that over time they strengthen their skills, develop mastery, and ultimately *create*. The battle is an important aspect of Hip Hop culture, a place where skills are honed. The urge to be better than and one up others is part and parcel of skill-building, a cultural assumption of mastery and competition. Learning for most writers, b-boys, and emcees is to get better at their craft, but many also want to be recognized and acknowledged as better, and higher in status, than other practitioners.[16]

In graffiti you want to "King" an area and achieve local celebrity status for being consistent in producing many high-quality pieces.[17] As a b-boy, you want to rock the cypher so hard that your opponent dare not re-enter the middle of the cypher.[18] As an emcee, if you are battling, you want to rock the cypher so much that there is no doubt from everyone in the crowd that you are superior.[19] "It's kinda like a training field . . . teaches you delivery. . . . You got to react under pressure. . . . It's gladiators. It's jousting," emcee Ras Kaas said about the cypher in an interview with H. Samy Alim, who called it "a litmus test for modern day griots."[20] For each area there is also the need to be consistent with your quality. These efforts at self-improvement prioritize the idea of being better and an ongoing competitiveness for validation.

Me, the Emcee

"I'm trying not to lose my head. It's like a jungle sometimes, it makes me wonder how I keep from going under." These lyrics from the track "The Message" dealt with the social and emotional influences of trying to survive within an adversity filled social environment. Its urgent yet cathartic tone connected with people immediately. This even surprised Grandmaster Melle Mel, who said in a 1992 interview with NPR that he was surprised at the song's success in the club even when played after an immensely popular song like "Planet Rock." As an all-time Hip Hop classic and story about life for some residents within low-income urban communities, "The Message" continues as representative of part of Hip Hop's musical canon. It anchors identity, helps set the tone for personal improvement by situating one's context, and outlining the potential objectives to work toward.

Artists continue to offer up narratives of their own authentic story and share their unique ways of coping. This thematic journey of survival continues to resonate with listeners. As DJ Premier stated in *Scratch*, "We're speaking for the youth that are being misunderstand by parents and police. So we're speaking for them. Some of those people don't have a voice to let themselves be heard. But Hip Hop has always done that. It's always let the generation that's in trouble show their views of what society is like to them."[21] There are the explicit lyrical testimonials that connect to feeling, doing, and being better, but then there is also the imagery and other content associated with songs and videos.

The Graffiti Writer: In Visibility

The appeal of being a graffiti artist can be from the rush of doing something illegal as much as it can be the sense of voice and agency it offers.[22]

The art form can represent the aesthetic and creative or artistic elements of the tagger's identity. One of the first things to understand about graffiti writers is that they can simultaneously be conspicuously visible and unknown and anonymous. They are public art, but writers do not use their real name and create their pieces and throw-ups out of the public eye.[23]

The primary purpose of writing is to announce to the world, "I am somebody, I have a voice that needs to be noticed." Similarly, graffiti writers work hard to establish their own voice beyond existing parameters and constraints of youth in their social and political spaces. For writers who take it to another level beyond the general mastery of skills (e.g., working from letters in their name, to being able to master any letter in the alphabet), they make social statements where their work talks to other writers and the public as a whole.[24] Having a social and political voice is not as common among graffiti artists, but it is mentioned with regularity and is a feature of contemporary entrepreneurial, professional, and social change efforts.

In the documentary *Getting Up*, graffiti artists speak about the positive emotional and physiological effects of their creative process. They talk about the rush and the high, the cathartic effects in times of pain, the feeling of immense power and invincibility, and the potential for celebrity and fame.[25] However, artists have also been willing to speak to the risky elements of the culture, including interactions with law enforcement, beef or conflict with other writers, and even health concerns. Writers report anxiety, addictive risky behavior, and violence as unhealthy aspects of graffiti culture.[26] One of the most sobering quotes came from legendary graffiti writer Mike "Iz the Wiz" in the movie *Style Wars Revisited* while reflecting on his major kidney problems twenty years after his original film interviews. After talking about all the paint fumes, steel dust, and cement dust he was exposed to as a writer, he continued, "I would trade it all back for perfect health . . . every drop of fame, every drop of glory. I would give it all back in a heartbeat if I had my health."[27] He died in 2009 at fifty years of age.[28]

Me, the Listener

How does Hip Hop culture help the average listener? The average listener, or participant in Hip Hop culture, is not necessarily competing against "battle artists." Instead they are working with material produced by compensated artists, or art as a deliberate product. This presents an interesting question about differences that might exist for interacting with art as a deliberate product and its ability to help (or harm).

Empirical research was late to weigh in on the helpful and harmful aspects of Hip Hop culture. Christine Hansen offered an early critique of the experimental literature that showed both negative and somewhat prosocial effects associated with watching rap videos.[29] Moving forward, contemporary discussions of the value of music (all music) include people's deliberate selection and use of music as a resource for their own well-being. Newer theoretical models incorporate these multidirectional processes so that it is not that listeners are passive recipients influenced by music exposure. Instead, children and adults alike exercise agency in their interaction with music as a creative resource, appropriating music for psychosocial well-being.[30]

Self-health refers to the specific and purposeful use of music as a tool of health promotion. It is a strategic appropriation of music by the everyday music listener in the moment without the assistance of a professional.[31] Emotional regulation, motivation and focus, and belonging and social bonding have been identified as consistent and common reasons for appropriating music.[32] One comprehensive literature review by Thomas Schäfer and colleagues identified 129 distinct uses for music. The study had a large sample to rate these uses and found the most common reasons overlapped substantially with previous findings: regulation of arousal and mood, achievement of greater self-awareness, and expression of social relatedness.[33]

FROM EMOTIONAL REGULATION TO OVERALL IMPROVEMENTS

Researchers who looked specifically at the appropriation of music by younger people found that they believe it helps them to feel better, because it is often a badge of identity and because it can be used as a bridge within relationships and social networks.[34]

How and why people interact with music, especially rap, were extended by Raphael Travis and Anne Deepak with five dimensions of empowerment (Figure 3.1).[35] These dimensions were elaborated upon as people's ongoing efforts at improvement (i.e., to feel better [esteem], to do better [resilience], to be better [growth], to better belong [community], and to achieve better community conditions [change]).[36] These attitudes correspond to Hip Hop's core values of self-improvement at both the individual and community levels, and encompass the broad range of music themes and use-of-music functions discussed by researchers before. Again, these uses range from emotional regulation, to identity development and self-awareness, to catharsis, to psychosocial development and belonging, to being actors in solidarity toward positive social change.[37]

Figure 3.1. Empowerment Narratives as Esteem, Resilience, Growth, Community, and Change

From this perspective, individuals are engaged in a deliberate process of self-improvement, self-health, getting better, or empowerment, where Hip Hop culture is used as "a vitalizing, life spark, an energy that burns . . . where the capacity to articulate and experience feeling is achieved and located on a social plane; it is made real in relation to self and other(s)."[38] The individual and community empowerment framework's connection to health and well-being, including both empowerment and risk, can best be understood alongside the underlying psychosocial processes of empowerment-based positive youth development (EMPYD) and life-course health development.[39]

These processes are consistent with research evidence showing the relevance of appropriating music for functional strategies across the lifespan into later life.[40] Further distinguishing this approach from much of the literature on positive or prosocial effects of media engagement is the assumption that the nature of the media and its utility for empowering use is completely unique and subjective, influenced by one's circumstances, personality, and characteristics.[41] The important distinction is that we must think about emphasizing "prosocial appraisal of media" alongside "prosocial content."[42]

MUSIC AND THE BRAIN: REWARD AND REASONS

The anticipation of and enthusiasm about the functional uses of music is also rewarding, via the release of dopamine by the brain into the bloodstream.[43] Subsequent functional uses, whether it is to improve mood, inspire activity, to reinforce healthy decision-making, or to enhance a sense of connectedness among friends, compound these psychological and physiological rewards. Pairings occur and associations are established between the music and a wide range of attitudes, behaviors, and experiences. The extent to which these are empowering experiences helps shed light on one dimension of music's healing power.

UNDERLYING COMMONALITIES AND HIP HOP CULTURE'S NEW CULTURAL AMBASSADORS

Hip Hop's ascension into the mainstream coexists with struggles by Black youth and communities to live long, healthy, and productive lives. A new generation of individuals, Hip Hop's new cultural ambassadors, have been strengthened by their own immersion and development in the culture. These new ambassadors have used Hip Hop's unique cultural artifacts and values to create synergy within their social networks and with their own professional development to create a new empowerment-based reality for what it means to be a helping professional.

These ambassadors use beats, hooks, lyrics, breaks, the assumption of knowledge of self, individual and collective self-improvement, resilence, mentorship, the cypher, and a host of other cultural tools and values as building blocks for learning and healthy development. These cultural insiders share collective memories grounded in these evolving narratives, yet they recognize how much room still exists for unique new understandings and pathways to self-improvement.

HIP HOP CULTURE: INTERGENERATIONAL DÉJÀ VU

It is empowerment-based for Hip Hop's cultural ambassadors (how it began for them), and empowerment-driven (the process by which it manifests) when helping young people and their communities grow and develop over time. These ambassadors are able to simultaneously embody and operationalize empowerment through themes of esteem, resilience, growth, and community to change lives. We have seen these building block narratives repeated in Hip Hop's musical canon throughout the forty-year history of Hip Hop culture. These narratives of self-improvement articulate social contexts, and their empowering and risky realities, which brings us to the multigenerational nature of Hip Hop culture.

Although Hip Hop is thought of as a "youth culture" we must not insist Hip Hop should only be geared toward youth or that its helpful elements are for the concerns of youth only. Adults are still maturing and growing in their own right. More importantly, adults play crucial roles in the developmental infrastructure of youth and the overall ecosystem of society. The next few chapters describe these narratives: culture-based resources that help explain Hip Hop's healing power or pathways to positive health and well-being, with exciting evidence of success.

HIP HOP CULTURE AS A NATURAL RESOURCE: TOOLS, DIRECTION, AND DEVELOPMENTAL NARRATIVES

If we extend our understanding of music as a cultural artifact or "semiotic force" to the unique history and context of Hip Hop culture, it allows us to understand both opportunities and challenges of contemporary Hip Hop with greater flexibility.[44] Hip Hop's new cultural ambassadors recognize that on the one hand, as discussed above, we can unshackle our thinking about Hip Hop culture with false divisions across generations. On the other hand, we can also explore the unique characteristics of the culture as a natural resource, a fuel and energy that is renewable and available for ongoing appropriation for learning, growth, and the well-being of individuals and communities.

Hip Hop's history has deep roots in Black social movements, both conservative and radical.[45] Four decades of evidence to support this exist, along with today's cultural artifacts and values that can be cultivated, strengthened, and refined. The results leave today's youth and young adults with the tools, direction, and developmental narratives to meet the needs of individuals and communities.

Tools

Tools refer to the innovative skills and competencies, or traditions of mastery, uniquely developed within the culture across all of its primary, secondary, and tertiary artifacts, whether technological, physical or technical, cognitive or psychological, social/interpersonal or entrepreneurial. These tools are often anchored in the utilitarian values of creatively using whatever is in one's immediate environment to expand a basic level of skill, and then adding personal "style or soul" to it.[46]

To be able to participate in the oft-cited aesthetics of Hip Hop, one must be armed with the tools of the trade, a range of cognitive, social, and physical competencies.[47] For example, the act of deejaying includes knowledge of how to use and integrate an ever-expanding universe of technology, both hardware and software. Digging requires research, archiving, and memory; sampling, looping, layering, and remixing requires basic mathematical knowledge, but also impeccable precision, improvisation, and creativity. High-quality emceeing requires astute observation, critical analysis, and masterful communication and linguistic skills. These are but a miniscule few of the skills that manifest as human and social capital uniquely among adherents of Hip Hop culture. This does not mean that similar skills cannot exist among others, however, there are unique skill-building opportunities among the culture's artifacts that are not reliant on the dominant structural systems of learning or socialization (e.g., school).

Direction

Direction refers to deliberate artistic mediated movement toward Hip Hop's superordinate value of improvement and empowerment, but in an individually unique and desired way. It is a personal choice. This alone allows us to understand that, along with promoted ideals like love, peace, unity, and having fun, is a spirit of individualism and freedom that has always been present and has always offered a creative tension within the culture. It starts with an artist's name, as a reflection of their identity and the communities within which they associate, and moves on from there.[48] It helps explain the prominence of the battle and cypher within the culture, and the ongoing discourse between individual needs and community needs within any culture.

The individuality, freedom, and autonomy that people have on their path of growth and development also allows room for the wide variety of voices in Hip Hop. For example, there are a multitude of ideas and narratives about what social change should look like in Hip Hop culture. Although always subject to interpretation in social- and political-themed narratives there are "radical" voices, "moderate" voices, and "conservative" voices. Further, some voices start out conservative and become more radical. We can also have radical nonviolence and civil disobedience, or less confrontational methods. At the same time there are radical voices that become more conservative. Within the Black community, there are voices that align directly with the urban and rural poor, while others align more closely with the broader African diaspora. There are also voices that are more global and multicultural alongside voices that are less diverse and more homogeneous. All of the above voices can find a home in Hip Hop. Each voice can be just as committed to the culture and be just as determined in their work within a progressive movement toward better conditions for all in the United States.

Narratives

Narratives are specific dimensions of empowerment and improvement that help describe how people appropriate various aspects of Hip Hop culture. In this book we concentrate on how these narratives surface among the beats, hooks, and lyrics (and mixtapes) in Hip Hop culture. These narratives are about getting better as individuals and as members of groups and communities. They capture the specific details about what is most empowering and what is risky. Hip Hop's narratives aid our understanding of music's relationship to personal growth and well-being.

The quality of how narratives are articulated has crystallized over decades and now exists at an incredibly proficient level of conceptualization, innovation, and delivery. Simply put, contemporary emcees, deejays, and producers are excellent and widespread. However, only a fraction of their potential has been tapped, either as text for functional use, or as raw material for developing new yet-undetermined cultural artifacts. Some scholars and practitioners lament that Hip Hop culture's artifacts and raw materials have been exploited and commoditized to the point that they only benefit those in positions of ownership. However, if one takes a step back and analyzes Hip Hop culture's resources from the tools, direction, and narratives perspective, the picture is substantially brighter.

The empowering aspects of the culture are universally embraced across generations, transcend (artificial) temporal and generational boundaries, and continue to reinforce what has been a historic relationship between arts and politics.[49] Further, the multiple iterations of Hip Hop culture in the past forty years have as much commonality as they do differences. The result, recognized by Hip Hop's new cultural ambassadors, is the opportunity to use the tools of the culture to revisit common, meaningful narratives of improvement and create opportunities to promote community well-being in limitless new and creative ways.

THE RAWEST MATERIALS: BEATS, HOOKS, AND LYRICS (AND MIXTAPES)

A common refrain heard among casual fans of rap music is "I just like the beats." Sometimes, the focus is on beats because of poor lyrical interpretation by the listener.[50] However, when we closely analyze Hip Hop's developmental narratives, beats are as important as hooks and lyrics. This is often the first thing that captures one's attention and thus can be a gateway to musical experiences or help to reinforce them.

There is also a musical canon specific to beats and instrumentals as much as there is an overall Hip Hop musical canon of tracks that include beats, hooks, and lyrics. For example, b-boys and b-girls are accustomed to interacting with ("rocking") primarily beat-based tracks like "Apache" and "It's Just Begun." According to b-boy Alien Ness, "I think, just for the sake of spirituality, you should get into those beats. Because those are the beats that moved the original b-boys, and it had to be for a reason . . . really see what it is about that beat that moved people and moves you."[51]

The Hook Gestalt (Imagination)

One of the most commonly reported experiences among music listeners is that they enjoy the beat of a song but do not really evaluate the song on a cognitive level with conscious awareness, and this happens in particular with Hip Hop. A close second in common experiences is when the listener really enjoys the beat of a song, *and* the hook, but does not evaluate the lyrics on a conscious level. This is similar to the principle of imagination as discussed by Koelsch: "the emotional effects of imagining that what was perceived in the music would actually be true . . . and imagining oneself in a situation with a particular emotional quality [that] might enhance that particular emotion (e.g., imagining oneself being happy, heroic, or successful)."[52]

Imagining allows the listener to remove or ignore lyrics, especially those that may upon conscious evaluation evoke dissonance or incompatibility with one's personal values. If you hear Drake's "Started from the Bottom, Now We're Here!" or "All I Do is Win!" and then use your "imagination" to fill in your own personal narrative of resilience or achievement that is compatible with your evolving but relatively stable personal story of improvement, then you have an entirely new and likely rewarding and positive emotive relationship with a song. The idea of imagining provides great insight into why people connect so well with Hip Hop's hooks, regardless of whether they know or understand the rest of the lyrics.

Lyrics to Go

We must also look at the lyrics, simultaneously lambasted for being immoral, materialistic, and misogynistic, while praised for being cathartic and socially critical. Do these narratives have a definite meaning that must be identified and translated by a few "experts"? Or, do they have some level of intended meaning that is open ended and left for interpretation? This is no easy feat when we consider artistic fluidity in Hip Hop. In Perry's discussion of Hip Hop's use of multiple and sometimes conflicting registers, in the tradition of "signifyin(g)," she notes how these conflicts make it difficult for listeners to interpret music.[53] Lupe Fiasco, for example, is a master at creating layers of meaning. Should it be interpreted according to the deeper registers or the most superficial, more accessible ones? Or, do we instead privilege the listener and engager of the artifact to develop their own meaning and purpose, regardless of artistic intent?

Emcee, enterprenuer, and actor 50 Cent added to this discussion about perspectives and intent while describing one particular creative process. He talked about the multiple specific perspectives he could have taken when writing about the shooting death of Mike Brown. Brown was an unarmed young Black male killed by a police officer in Ferguson, Missouri. His death was a pivotal spark in the contemporary Black Lives Matter movement seeking to address perceived police harassment and brutality as well as injustices in the overall criminal justice system. As an artist, 50 Cent emphasized his freedom to take on a range of perspectives, including that of the police officer. He highlighted how artists value autonomy, as well as their empathic and critical analytical skills. Implicit in this premise is the importance of paying attention to what the listener engages. Is it a complete suspension of personal values to adopt the most likely attitude of the narrator? Is it the emotion and feeling engendered by the art? It is something else? As important is listener reaction to material. What is the knowledge gained, the attitude shift, and the behavioral response?

Black people today have the opportunity to negotiate these narratives in explicit ways, taking them at face value but then also in implicit, personal, and subjective ways. Tensions exist around interpretations of whether these patterns of engagement contribute to the ongoing subjugation of the Black community. Does it amount to tacit approval of oppression and marginalization of the Black community if one shapes their art in a way they feel benefits them, but it is more broadly interpreted as socially oppressive? Is this a sanctioning of exploitation?

I propose, first, that logistically we can interpret, define, analyze, and react to (i.e., engage) Hip Hop's narratives in many ways. We may also do so in a variety of settings or situations ("arenas"), alone, socially, and in partnership with others that share specialized cultural knowledge, whether a counselor, educator, health promoter, or other professional ("agents") and with different goals ("agendas").[54] Second, we can be simultaneously aware of both its empowering *and* risky elements—that is, not be naïve to its potential toxicity for the self and for others.

Taking this a step further to other elements of Hip Hop culture, b-boying and b-girling have their specific moves and routines; graffiti writers have their tags, throw-ups, and pieces; and deejays have their sets and mixtapes. It is in this domain where we have yet to scratch the surface in terms of using these artifacts collectively in innovative ways to inform a *new* generation of innovative derivative artifacts more aligned with empowering directions of betterment. To do so, we must identify core narratives and artifacts as part of Hip Hop's overall cultural canon, such as emceeing, deejaying, graffiti, and b-boying interrelated with knowledge of self and explicate their value and use for health and well-being. Second, we must invest in researching and developing a wide range of derivative artifacts. This will also help eliminate Hip Hop's artificial generational barriers. We have reduced the use of beats, hooks, and lyrics to the equivalent of a #2 order at your favorite local fast food restaurant. Consume and discard—quickly. It is up to us to create a more wide-ranging and diverse product line to engage.

BUILDING ON HIP HOP'S HISTORY OF HELPING AND HEALING

Again, people like Hip Hop culture. We have four decades of evidence that show people recognize its value in helping them in ways that they value. Hip Hop culture has had a long history of being appropriated for helpful reasons, some of which can be tied back to a community-interest engendered within the broader culture of social movements. Hip Hop's value is evident at the community level and the individual level. Inspiration for better ranges from simply improving mood to the desire for widespread social change. The multiple decades and generations that the culture spans has allowed some level of depth and sophistication in understanding its value as a resource, yet still we are only scratching the surface. A new generation of cultural ambassadors has started using Hip Hop culture as a resource to promote learning and growth among youth and young adults across a wide range of settings.

The following chapters highlight historical consistencies in Hip Hop's narratives and examples of how people use them for improvement (i.e., both empowering and risky elements). Hip Hop's new ambassadors embody and operationalize these empowering narratives of esteem, resilience, growth, and community to positively influence youth lives in areas of education, out-of-school time, mental health, and physical health. We juxtapose these discussions with questions about what this means for the Black community. What is it about Black use of Hip Hop culture that can and does aid self-improvement as part of a universal identity, and as part of distinct social identities within the diaspora? While highlighting these narrative themes and areas in which ambassadors concentrate, this book also provides models to help better understand these pathways to positive health and well-being with exciting evidence of success.

CHAPTER 4

Affirming Identities: Hip Hop Values, Esteem, and Black Experiences

CONCEPTUAL UNDERPINNINGS OF HIP HOP'S HEALING POWER

Hip Hop gives people a unique opportunity to have a voice. It allows maximum creativity and expression of self in writing, speaking, movement, and overall artisanship. Historically, new voices emerged in the crosshairs of profound social, economic, and political alienation. In addition to Hip Hop's artistic elements, the culture has continued to forge a set of values that give new generations direction through narratives that highlight esteem, resilience, growth, community, and positive social change. Hip Hop is empowering. Amid understandably controversial aspects of the culture, Hip Hop continues to have a meaning and a place as a culture and art form in transforming identities for the better. This continues in informal and formal uses of Hip Hop today to heal and increase empowerment of individuals and communities across cultural and regional boundaries. This prompts the central question: How does Hip Hop help to empower, transform, and heal?

This chapter and the three that follow focus on how Hip Hop helps to empower by offering direction for self and community improvement through its five narrative dimensions. At the same time, these chapters look at the specific implications for people who identify with the Black community. Empowerment, transformation, the quest to get better, and self and community improvement similarly encompass values that have evolved from Hip Hop's birth. These values underscore the myriad ways that people appropriate Hip Hop culture in their personal lives. Five narrative dimensions will describe these values and help further clarify how the culture is presented and engaged: *esteem* (Chapter 4), *resilience* (Chapter 5), *growth* (Chapter 6), *community* (also Chapter 6), and *change* (Chapter 7). They are presented alongside their particular significance for the Black community.

For example, Chapter 5 on resilience discusses it as the *context* for *identity*, which is at the heart of esteem narratives discussed in Chapter 4. Further, the discussion of resilience is closely linked to Hip Hop's specific values of survival and authenticity. Within these discussions are voices from Hip Hop's new cultural ambassadors who have been using Hip Hop culture and its narratives to help offer youth context and direction for their own education and well-being. These chapters recognize that among these narratives of empowerment and the quest to get better are also its risky elements. The rest of this chapter focuses on the dimension of esteem and begins with a brief discussion of how to conceptualize the many ways that people appropriate or use Hip Hop culture, whether formally or informally.

HIP HOP'S HEALING THROUGH TRANSFORMATION

Today's leaders recognize Hip Hop's transformative potential for *anyone* who identifies with the culture and appropriates it to get better in life. At the same time, recognition exists for the unique cultural resonance within the Black community. Two voices below capture these layers of universal and distinct relevance of Hip Hop culture.

Mazi Mutafa, executive director of Words, Beats, and Life, Inc., spoke about Hip Hop culture's transformative power for humanity, emphasizing his faith. He emphasizes his faith as a Muslim as an important element of his personal identity and appreciation of the global community:

Humanity trumps racial identity. The young people in my program are all that human family I described. Whites, Blacks, Latinos, and more, they're connected to this culture because this culture is a human expression. The idea of the visual element, the kinesthetic element, the technology and music, and the vocal percussion—you can find that in every ethnic group in the whole human history. The question is less about racial identity and more about a culture of transformation.[1]

Timothy Jones, chief visionary officer of #HipHopEd and director of the Healthy Connections program at Martha's Table, recognizes this universality in power. However, he also spoke to the potential unique benefits to the Black and Latino communities in the United States. It is from this perspective that we begin our discussion of narratives of esteem and their intersection with identity in the Black community.

> Hip Hop's ability to heal is available across the board. But the capacity to fully transform may be higher for Black and Brown because we still identify this as our narrative. [Other racial and ethnic groups] may think it speaks "to" them as opposed to "for" them. So for us in a lot of instances, this came from our belly. It's like how you might be that close friend, but we are just "play" cousins, we're not really "blood" cousins. But I think Hip Hop's power to connect, and help, and shape and heal is across the board. We see that in classrooms.[2]

TO AFFIRM OR NOT TO AFFIRM: HIP HOP CULTURE, BLACK RACIAL IDENTITY, AND ESTEEM

Does Hip Hop have an implicit responsibility to affirm the individual and collective identity of the Black community? That is a question for contemporary artists, fans, and critics of Hip Hop culture. It is not quite as simple as that, however, as tension exists because aspects of the culture can be empowering and risky at the same time. Hip Hop can help both build and destroy. In "Represent," Nas says, "Somehow the rap game reminds me of the crack game."[3] In a bit of foreshadowing, the lyric deftly encapsulates (pun intended) the simultaneous potential to enrich and hollow out identity in the same way that the illegal drug trade can both enrich and hollow out the strength and sustenance of families and communities.

Identity development, a feature of daily life, has a unique relevance in the health development of a Black person because of the strong racialization in U.S. society and the substantial evidence of social determinants of health. A strong identity is helpful for maintaining positive esteem but also for inhibiting depression.[4] Research also shows that Black youth who are socialized with affirming and positive messages about their race and ethnicity are more able to distinguish between positive and negative stereotypes.[5] Identity is consistently explored in contemporary Hip Hop and inevitably bridges person and environment. These context-driven discourses and narratives involving identity are anchored in the lived experiences of any Black person. Often, these social realities offer a glimpse into the roots of self-esteem, resilience, growth and community belonging, and ultimately personal well-being.

As we explore examples of narratives that have the ability to simultaneous affirm and assault Black identity, we also introduce the broader rap music canon as the collective archive for Hip Hop's empowering narratives. The first dimension of esteem is grounded in identity and sets the tone for other areas of improvement. The emcee Common emphasizes the powerful light Hip Hop shines on identity formation, "[You] say what you think, who you are, where you stand, your perspective."[6]

Just as in the larger Black community, in Hip Hop culture there has always been an ongoing intra-group dialogue among members of the Black community that involves looking in the metaphoric mirror and to "the system" to formulate ideas about individual and collective racial or ethnic identity. This has existed since the earliest songs shedding light on social realities, including "The Message" written by Grandmaster Melle Mel of Grandmaster Flash and the Furious Five and "My Philosophy," written by KRS-One of Boogie Down Productions.

The full range of these reflexive discourses, sometimes arguments, is beyond the scope of this book and covered in more depth by others such as Tricia Rose in *Hip Hop Wars*.[7] However, several songs exist as exemplars of the complexity of Black identity in the United States and how identity intersects with esteem and other evaluations of self. From a standpoint of usefulness, these tracks can be cathartic, opportunities to reflect, inspire, and feel better.

These tracks are the first layer of Hip Hop culture's musical canon, an ever-expanding archive of beats, hooks, and lyrics that inspire improvement. In music, there are reasons why certain songs become "hits": They connect. They speak to something inside us. Sometimes it is physiological—an infectious beat that immediately gets in our bones and takes us before we know what has happened. Sometimes it is the hook or chorus that grabs us and we find meaning in it regardless of whether we know the lyrics to the rest of the song or not. Other times, it is the lyrics, and in truly special instances, it is a combination of two or more features.

IDENTITY AND COMMUNITY: CONTEXT MATTERS

We have seen the consistent direction offered by Hip Hop's empowering role throughout history. In the previous chapters we have established the underlying dimensions of self and community improvement, and linked them to the rich history and strong relationship between Black art and sociopolitical movements. We recognize that amid the popularity and wealth that is a result of Hip Hop's by mainstream success has been a consolidation of the entertainment industry, which limits the variety of Black experiences presented in mainstream outlets. Subsequently, this has also increased the opportunity for risky attitudes and behaviors to be portrayed and even glorified in these narratives.

Despite these industry-related challenges, it is still possible to pinpoint Hip Hop's usefulness as a resource.[8] Hip Hop's popularity allows a consistent stream of new material. Therefore, innovative art and culture can be a mainstay for self and community improvement, as opposed to being decontextualized and easily discarded or forgotten.

Each geographical region also has its own unique contextual reality that adds a layer of distinct identity for its inhabitants. If you were raised in New York, Atlanta, Oakland, or the Washington, DC/Maryland/Virginia (DMV) area, you reference different material—words, sounds, and activities specific to that place and time, alongside what is nationally popular.[9] If decontextualized, then esteem-oriented music is easy to dismiss, especially when laced with high-risk messages. However, these tracks can be identity affirming for those who understand and feel a sense of belonging to that context. When contextualized, issues of identity and esteem have powerful connotations, and their usefulness is more easily recognized, as is their potential to be used in a variety of settings and situations. The remainder of this chapter looks at several key issues relating to identity and esteem, including challenges relating to the N-word, status and material items, gender, and societal perceptions. The chapter concludes with specific attention to affirming narratives.

WHO AM I? WHO ARE WE? U.S. NIGGAS: IDENTITY, ESTEEM, AND COMMUNITY

"Young brothers and sisters today have a lack of understanding of what it really means to be Black."

—*Ice Cube, "Us"*

Individuals have their own unique psychosocial footprint that may influence the interpretation and engagement of "cultural artifacts."[10] The same applies for any and all elements of Hip Hop culture. As Black people have a very unique history in the United States and occupy a complex social space in the country, this is no easy feat to disentangle or interpret.

Me, Myself, and I, the Nigga with Attitude

One of the most potent and debated aspects of Black identity is use of the words "nigga" and "nigger." The "N-word," with its ebb and flow of usage, tugs at the heart of identity issues. It also helps us identify the opportunities to be more declarative in determining whether esteem issues are ultimately affirming or assaulting within Hip Hop culture. While an increasing acceptance of vernacular distinctiveness across cultures, like the use of African American Vernacular English, helps the public understand the differences in intentionality between the word "nigger" and "nigga," debates and racial politics around its use still persist.[11]

Hip Hop culture has been one of the main targets and also ammunition for eliminating the use of any word with the root "nigg-." Emcees have not been silent on the issue of the N-word either. Looking back, Tupac Shakur helped appropriate "nigga" by making it an acronym for Never Ignorant about Getting Goals Accomplished and No Ignorance Got Goals Accomplished.[12] Kendrick Lamar's second album, released in 2015, includes a live recording of his song "i," in which he speaks about the word *negus* as an alternative appropriation of the historic N-word in the United States. Negus, an Amharic word, has been used historically in Ethiopia to refer to royalty.[13]

In another Hip Hop moment, Nas's "Project Roach" begins with Eban Thomas of the Last Poets talking about the absurdity of having a funeral for the word "nigger," which was done formally at the 98th Annual NAACP Convention in Detroit on July 9, 2007. "We need to have a movement to resurrect brothers and sisters, not a funeral for niggers." Thomas suggested that we should instead resurrect terms of relationship and identity that are more affirming and reflective of community pride like "brothers" and "sisters." He used the word "movement" as also indicative of a collective effort toward positive social change. He ended with "because Ns don't die!"

What does this mean? What might it mean? For those identifying with the label and name "nigga," as in N.W.A.'s Niggas Wit Attitudes, whose biopic hit theaters nationally in 2015, approximately 28 years after their ascension to fame, it suggests community resilience and a sense of pride for being able to persevere through sustained adversities. Alternatively, if coming from a place of "I'm not them," whether out of self-hate or not, then it could mean that associated negative behaviors are chronic and ingrained and will never stop no matter how hard one tries to eliminate them. Furthermore, it could be interpreted in an endless variety of ways based on the subjective reality of the interpreter.

Nas continues in "Project Roach" with some clues about what he might be alluding to, by describing how desperate times call for desperate measures, wherever and whenever, using the most visually coarse imagery, "Drinking from your spit . . . climbing on top of your plate, bed, wherever I smell food . . . a roach is what I am fool, the ghetto is my land fool, I'ma never be able to fly like a bumblebee." Depending on where the listener chooses to align his identity can have *vastly* different implications for attitudes and behaviors. Adding fuel for one side of the argument, Thomas ends with, "They're never going to go away. Learn from them what we should not become." This suggests an identity distancing and that there is only one, definitively negative, definition of the word.

On Big K.R.I.T.'s "Another Naïve Individual Glorifying Greed & Encouraging Racism" he speaks within and between communities. When talking "within" the community, these do not appear to be stereotypical assumptions but rather an honest reflection and critique. When speaking "between" communities, there is the declaration that he does not want to be limited to stereotypical assumptions of being Black in America.

The above examples suggest that there is a substantially more complex relationship between "nigger" and "nigga" than simply the vernacular-based argument that one term is used endearingly while the other term is used negatively. Although it is easy to say one is used affectionately ("nigga") and the other is a racist epithet ("nigger"), when we dig a little deeper into Hip Hop's narratives we see that there is actually a wide and complex identity-based landscape among Black people of all ages, classes, and gender, within which people exist and operate individually and socially.[14] The word has power and resonates among many facets of identity, as shown by the emcees above and among those who have a clear understanding of and even engage in its appropriate African American Vernacular English usage.

Externalizing Identity and Esteem: Cultivating Narcissism with Status, Wants, and Needs

Mr. Lee is financially secure. He makes his own money and spends it as he pleases. He recognizes that he is not living "right" but feels he is just living life. It sounds like things are going well for Mr. Lee and that he made a decision to favor money over character and living morally. One might assume that this is sufficient to convey his satisfaction with his current life circumstances. However, he also feels the need to compare himself to others. Since he was able to describe his situation, it only seems fair of him to ask others, "What do you have? How much money do you have in your pocket? How much do you spend when you go shopping?" After Swae Lee finishes, his partner Slim Jimmy builds on this, describing his own situation (pretty much the same) but in his own words. For him, every night includes sinning, fancy cars, smoking weed, and being a spendthrift. This is the epitome of living life. This is the gist of Rae Sremmurd's song "No Type."

Mainstream Rap Music and the System of Externalized Identities

On his track "The White Shoes," the artist Wale speaks cautiously about how too often for people "it ain't about what you're doing, it's about how you're looking." At the end of the day he encourages listeners to avoid this trap. Celebrating status and conspicuous consumption is the de facto norm or expectation among many artists enjoying mainstream Hip Hop success. Esteem and positive emotional feelings are fused with items and status.[15] Songs by newer artists and those getting first-time media exposure often have an esteem-oriented element that speaks to improving one's quality of life through wealth, privileges, and hedonistic experiences that are beyond the means of the average individual.

The ability to live well, feel good about oneself, achieve one's goals, and to celebrate these improvements, successes, and strengths are major components of Hip Hop culture. However, as seen in "No Type," there are often substantial risky attitudes and behaviors associated with songs that adopt this basic premise. The appeal of these lifestyles is uniquely problematic for Black youth when (1) financial incentives exist to create art about status and consumption, and (2) identity is connected to social status, income, and class. Evidence suggests that stress and the physiological accompaniments of stress may increase, particularly among lower income youth.

For example, Elizabeth Sweet's research looked at cultural status items and blood pressure among Black youth. Results found that having or using higher group-evaluated status items like specific types of sneakers, iPods, luxury cars, cell phones, and particular clothing brands was associated with higher blood pressure, and that this was significantly higher for youth with the lowest parental resources. These levels of difference in blood pressure are associated with a much greater risk of later life cardiovascular mortality.[16]

Image management happens face-to-face, but youth also use social media and technology to create favorable public images. The risk is that without a strong established identity, these are false images. Since the nature of technology has an immediate reinforcement feedback loop built in, participation requires a continuous level of attentiveness to these projected (false) identities and the desire to enhance their favorability.[17]

Research suggesting newer generations are more narcissistic than prior generations adds to concern. Specifically, research suggests that individuals born after 1980 are more narcissistic than prior generations, and their values have moved away from intrinsic concerns, like community and belonging, toward extrinsic concerns like image, fame, and money.[18] These findings compound interest in how to help youth improve their ability to build their identity through an honest assessment of their internal strengths, abilities, and worth.

IDENTITY IN THE MAINSTREAM: A HISTORY OF CROSSING OVER

Mainstream appeal and profit were not always a goal of Hip Hop artists. In 1992 EPMD released the classic track "Crossover," in which they preached the value of staying "underground" and not succumbing to the enticements of mainstream profits. That they performed the song live on the very mainstream *Yo! MTV Raps* is for another conversation, but in their eyes at the time, "The rap era's outta control, brothers selling their soul . . . To go gold, going, going, gone, another rapper sold."

The group 3rd Bass's "Pop Goes the Weasel" was even more direct in its critique of artists like MC Hammer who went mainstream. Also of interest is that Prime Minister Pete Nice and MC Serch of 3rd Bass were white and well-accepted in the Hip Hop community as authentic contributors to the culture: "Getting paid to peddle sneakers and soda pop (pop pop pop) . . . I guess it's the fact that you can't be artistic, intricate raps, becoming so simplistic."

In 1988 Boogie Down Productions, under the lyrical leadership of KRS-One, released "My Philosophy," a track that has similarly pointed remarks about the mainstream and Hip Hop but also the potential drawbacks for individual and collective Black identity: "Some MC's be talking and talking; trying to show how black people are walking; but I don't walk this way to portray, or reinforce stereotypes of today." Tensions between profit and the affirmation of positive identities also play out by gender.

Gender and Identity in the Mainstream: My Queen to Your Main B

One of the first glimpses of Dana Owens, better known as Queen Latifah, was in her Fab Five Freddy-directed video for "Ladies First," which saw her dressed head to toe in clothing reflecting her connection to an African cultural heritage. She shares her awareness of, her pride in, and the inspiration she feels from this heritage. In words and images, Ms. Owens offered visual solidarity with the historical apartheid struggle of South Africa while expressing the need for greater equality in power and opportunities for women and men.[19] Black women or "ladies" who were strong, successful, and positive change agents, including Madame CJ Walker, Sojourner Truth, Angela Davis, and Winnie Mandela, were also prominent in the video. Ms. Owens's emcee name, Queen, emphasizes power, respect, and leadership alongside gender, while Latifah means "gentle and kind" in Arabic, offering a powerful duality of delicate strength. Identity is a major issue in Hip Hop culture for sure, but the intersectionality of gender makes it of compounded interest.[20]

A more challenging aspect of Hip Hop, gender, and identity is the increased acceptance of the phrase and idea of deliberately "taking" and having sexual intercourse with another person's significant other. Wiz Khalifa, Ace Hood, David Banner with Bun B., and Too Short have song titles devoted to this theme, some variation of "Take Your Bitch." However, it is prominent in the lyrics of many more songs. In this narrative, not only is the woman not held in high social esteem, she is an easily disposable tool used for hurt or revenge. Evidence exists that continued exposure to these and other negative and stereotypic images of Black women can be associated with lower self-esteem.[21]

Connections between esteem and one's social identity are consistent. According to a study into the link between body image (satisfaction) and esteem that introduced the potential influence of racial identity, "body dissatisfaction was linked to lower self-esteem, however it was only for those African Americans for whom race was less central to their identities."[22] When "Anaconda" by Nikki Minaj emerged as wildly popular (currently with 520 million YouTube hits), it fit nicely into a similar niche that can be interpreted on one hand as young women asserting their sexuality, sexual power, and re-appropriating symbols and roles that seem exploitative and objectifying.[23] On the other hand, it can be seen as perpetuating oppressive gender and race dynamics, sexual exploitation, and ultimately be disempowering for women and girls. In fact, a wax figure dedicated to Nikki Minaj borrowed imagery from her video of this song with her posed on all fours. Highlighting the tense dynamic between celebration and exploitation, shortly after the figure was displayed to the public, photos began to emerge in social media with people posing in explicit positions with the figure. This exploitative dynamic is particularly salient when young girls are informed by the media and as a result denigrate Black women's moral identity, lifestyle, and culture while elevating that of White women.[24] Critical media literacy and critical Hip Hop pedagogy constantly focus on understanding and analyzing these aspects of Black health and well-being.[25]

MASCULINITY, PATERNALISM, AND PROTEST IN THE MAINSTREAM: "REALISM AND GANGSTA RAP"

While thinking about representations in Hip Hop that deal with elements of gender and esteem, it is necessary to revisit concerns about misogyny, violence, and substance use—essentially power and exploitation. The presence of high-risk messages and power dynamics within music, specifically Black music, existed well before the earliest documented concerns about Hip Hop's content and influences.[26] Robin D. G. Kelley, like others, positions social realism in Hip Hop music's narratives during the so-called gangsta rap era as critiques of the social, economic, and political disinvestment and alienation of Los Angeles's Black communities.[27] The resultant poverty and saturation of neighborhoods with crack cocaine and weapons made violence and scrutiny by law enforcement part of the social reality for youth. Death and prison became more normal than not for many South Los Angeles communities. Reflecting on what this means within Hip Hop with regard to esteem, Kelley highlights "how 'I' can be representative of personal and collective experiences."[28] In a review of soul music during the Black Arts Movement era, Rabaka also talks about the collective "I," where the musical "I" is actually a political "we," where an individual artist "serves as a symbol for the collective loves, lives, and struggles of African Americans."[29]

The United States and Us: The Collective "I"

> *"Here's what they think about you . . . 'You gold-teeth-gold-chain-wearing, fried-chicken-and-biscuit-eating, monkey, ape, baboon, big thigh, fast-running, high-jumping, spear-chucking, three-hundred-sixty-degree basketball-dunking, titsun, spade, moulignon. Take your fucking pizza and go the fuck back to Africa.' Think about it."*
> *—Ice Cube on "Turn off the Radio," including Pino's rant from the Spike Lee film,* Do The Right Thing

In the opening skit of the song "Us," the voice of a pre-pubescent boy rattles off to an older man his wish list: a car with a stereo system, rims, jewelry, and fine women. In the midst of the boy's excited delivery, the older man tells him to focus on school and getting a good job. Ice Cube then enters the track, delivering a scathing critique of the Black community of which the listener can assume the little boy is a symptom. He continues on to discuss the perils of the Black community and points blame at "us" as opposed to blaming the "system." He lists the common challenges that are recycled through the Black community's collective conscience over time, with a specific focus on identity. The oft-repeated tropes are that the Black community is responsible for their own failings because of: primal instincts, Black-on-Black homicide, envy, backstabbing, having excess children, illegal drug sales, not reinvesting in their community, antisocial behavior, spending beyond one's means, intimate partner violence, substance abuse, unhealthy nutrition, and gambling. The song ends with a definitive closure, "Nobody gives a fuck about [Us]."

Then there is the alternative *overview*. The current Black Lives Matter movement underscores the belief by many in the Black community that Black lives do not matter to broader society. This perspective influences the interpretation of major events involving Black people, especially when they are victims. The net effect is a belief that even when Blacks are victims, they are treated as the perpetrators. For example, when incidents like the law enforcement involved death of Eric Garner in Staten Island, New York, come to light, while there is immediate public outrage within the Black community, there is often the simultaneous "I'm not surprised." It is a concurrent rage and pessimism. It may be simple rage at a despicable event, but also incredulity that the negative outcome couldn't be different when what was wrong about the situation is so obvious, or it may be a type of self-hate rage at feeling duped again into buying into a system that has relentlessly and systematically betrayed one's culture. The pessimism stems from the latter point, a glass half-empty sense that, well, a constant reminder is needed for society to recognize that Black lives matter.

THAT'S WHY WE GET HIGH

On "Life's a Bitch" emcees Nas and AZ go back and forth with their assessment of life in general, their circumstances, and life expectancy for young Black males like themselves. In their final assessments they are grateful for making it as far as they have, and they are painfully aware that they may not have much longer. It offers them perspective and a rationale for their behavior, "That's why we get high because you never know when you're gonna go!" As part of Hip Hop's musical canon, this song helped solidify the foundation for similar narratives in the decades since, where using substances helps people to feel better about current circumstances.

Since then, many of Hip Hop's narratives share this premise of using substances for emotional regulation and mood stability. In some instances, it is tied more directly to mental health issues. For example, Kid Cudi explicitly states on "The Way I Am" and "Marijuana" how medication was not helping him and that smoking marijuana was a much better treatment.

Feature: Unique Contemporary Challenges Like the Death of Eric Garner

"I can't breathe. I can't breathe. I can't breathe. I can't breathe. I can't breathe. I can't breathe. I can't breathe. I can't breathe. . . ."

—*Eric Garner*

What are some of the unique social and environmental challenges for the Black community that may be associated with identity? As we explore this question, it does not mean that such issues do not exist among other groups. Instead, we recognize certain groups face challenges at disparate levels vis-à-vis other groups, or in such a high proportion that they cause undue harm and risk to their short- and long-term well-being. They include community violence, the criminal justice system and incarceration, voting rights and political representation, educational outcomes, employment and poverty, and policing and the use of excessive force.

Eric Garner repeated "I can't breathe" aloud at least eleven times before his heart stopped while placed in a chokehold from law enforcement officers in broad daylight with people standing by watching and capturing the incident on video. The footage was repeatedly broadcast on television. An unarmed person alive and breathing is minutes later lying dead as a result of a law enforcement officer sworn to uphold public safety. Policing and excessive force has grown to manifest as the dominant new generational issue for Black youth. The issue is intertwined with many other issues where implicit bias is implicated, including the school-to-prison pipeline, biases in arrest and sentencing disparities, and the residual disparities in one's involvement with the criminal justice system.[30] Excessive force is only novel in *how* it is being absorbed as a psychosocial toxin within the ecosystem of young people. It is not that prior generations did not have to deal with the issue of excessive force, but with the 24-hour-news media cycle, social media, and technology, this epidemic exists with greater visibility than ever.[31] Inconsistent indictments and charges against officers in the presence of video evidence is also unique and different than the past. It is a sustained system of psychological violence that one can argue differs from prior criminal justice stressors because of media visibility. It complements any of the range of traumas discussed in the context of the Black experience, such as the legacy of slavery, hypersurveillance, and post-traumatic stress disorder.[32] It is visible, it is precedent-setting, it is definite, it puts into flux definitions of "public safety," and it is intimately linked to identity. It is coping with these challenges and maintaining a positive sense of self that is a priority for the Black community today.

AFFIRMING IDENTITIES: INDIVIDUAL GROWTH AND THE INEXTRICABLE LINK TO (A SENSE OF) COMMUNITY

He Had It Made

The one-hundred-and-thirty-pound, fifteen-year-old Ed had it made like a king twice his age and twice his size. He had money, cars, girls, and even an island of his own. He described himself as "your idol, the highest title, numero uno." He led a life of luxury. At least he did on his record *I Got it Made*. In reality, the Flatbush, Brooklyn native, also known as the emcee Special Ed, did not even have a job at the time of the song's creation.

Ed proclaimed in an interview, "I had a vision . . . obviously I was a teenager and didn't even have a job. I thought of what I considered having it made." This approach to rhyming was culled from Hip Hop pioneers before him like Kurtis Blow and Super Rhymer Jimmy Spicer, who rhymed about the lives, status, and power they likely did not have. Ed had a tremendous confidence in his emceeing skills and thus battling for him was a piece of cake, as he would regularly "Walk up on a cypher, destroy the leader and then they had to disperse." His laid-back style made him, in the words of the producer Twilite Tone, "extraordinary."[33]

Rising Above

His vision of an alternative to the lived experience of the time when needs were high resonated with others in his community who felt that they could make it too. He tried to convey the mindset of being able to accomplish more and have a better life. Another emcee of the time, Dres of the group Black Sheep, stated, "[He was saying] I got it made, you can't put something in front of me to make me fall." Ed was strong and powerful. And although the materialistic dimensions of this track are often cited, the track actually begins with Ed talking about *teaching, having knowledge, maturity, creativity,* and *making positive decisions*. This song was about who he was and set the tone for similar narratives of esteem and resilience that would become staples of the culture for years to come.

Like those who blazed the path before him, Ed also inserted himself into a role that he aspired to. The template for presenting oneself to be held in high esteem is a cornerstone of Hip Hop culture and intersects with Black identity in both empowering and risky ways. At its best, as in the case of Ed and youth from his Brooklyn community who looked up to him, it can be a vision, model, and pro-social path forward in life. At its worst, it can result in an overemphasis on externalized identities and high-risk patterns of behavior to enhance one's personal image, status, and esteem.

From "Me" to "We"

In a powerful exchange of ideas between cultural legends Davey D. and KRS-One in 2005, the two focused squarely on the temporal aspect of identity and what it means for the relation between individual identity and an individual's valued communities or community identity. Where does the "I/me" end and the "we/us" begin? In this discussion, KRS-One emphasized the development of his personal identity over time, moving from a focus on racial or ethnic identity to a more humanity-oriented identity, and a spiritual identity that transcends racial and ethnic identity. At the same time he prioritizes Hip Hop as a culture and being a "Hip Hoppa." He did not dismiss his own racial or ethnic identity outright but recognized that it was not sufficient enough to fully capture the magnitude of his being, society's essence, and his vision for maximizing the well-being of humanity. These are core identity issues that have major implications for thinking about the range of ways that the Black community engages these narratives.

Couple these different philosophical orientations to well-being with additional social and class splintering among Black culture and we can more easily see how people engage and digest Hip Hop's narratives in a wide range of potentially different ways. And when it comes to the want or need for a positive change in circumstances to improve esteem and feel better, where should energy be directed? The fundamental question is, "Where is the locus of responsibility for individual and collective challenges?" Is it us or is it someone or something else, such as the system, that needs to be held accountable?

Hip Hop's Cultural Ambassadors Speak on Collective Responsibility

Timothy Jones is dedicated to making a difference in the lives of people using Hip Hop culture, believing it can help shape, influence, and heal. Specifically, he speaks for its uniquely transformative potential for the Black community. He sees the sustained power in Hip Hop's voice to challenge and elevate minds to transcend the maze of challenges facing many of today's youth:

> There is so much against what it is to be a Black man. I feel that is a soldier spot that I've got to fight until the end. I don't know if twenty years from now, I'm going to be as Hip Hop as I am now. I hope to be. But I know I'm going to be Black. And I know I'm going to be a Black man. And wanting to be head of a Black family and what that means. And attaching to the legacy around that. And shaping history, to rewrite some things.[34]

Asheru speaks to his dedication to making a difference in the lives of Black youth. He does this both as an artist and educator, creating material that inspires, educates, and creates the opportunity to explore social justice issues.

> While teaching, everything changed. I realized the [need] is not just here and there, it's everywhere. I've got to do something. It became a calling. I'm doing something for my community that very few people are in a position to do. . . . When I grew up, mainstream Hip Hop lyrics taught me about everything. I would write Chuck D. lyrics, De La lyrics, Slick Rick, Rakim. I would write them down in a notebook and read them and be so proud of these words that I didn't even write. . . . It changed my whole walk, the way I looked at the world, what it meant to be a Black man, everything I got from Hip Hop. I was raised in that so it always stayed with me. Now, they know the power [of Hip Hop] to mobilize and inform, they say "alright, well let's control the message."[35]

THEY (AND I) KNOW WHO I AM: STRENGTH

Recognizing personal strengths that are not wedded to material items and possessions can be very difficult. Further, the perceived value of personal attributes and positive non-material items may not carry as much external cache and weight. For those seeking the approval of others, this can be a difficult proposition to accept. On "Who I Am," Rapsody echoes this sentiment, "They say the music I'm making ain't paying many dollars. My purpose is priceless, lah lah."

Knowledge of Self (Identity and Consciousness)

One prevention-oriented intervention program sought to celebrate the strengths of Black youth to help enhance self-esteem, racial identity, and parental racial socialization among this demographic. Results revealed that the group experiencing the intervention had higher levels of self-esteem.[36] An awareness of the significant relationship between a strong and positive identity and personal well-being, and its unique cultural salience for the Black community, is only half of the story. Identity and esteem also have to be malleable—that is, there must be evidence that identity and esteem can be positively influenced. This offers listeners a license to speculate not only on potential challenges to identity and esteem but also ways in which they can be enhanced.

THE CANON, PAST AND PRESENT

The songs being added to Hip Hop's musical canon seek to capture the depth of people's feelings in the moment, their identities and concepts of self, their joys, their pain, and the wide variety of strategies they use to lift their spirits and feel a sense of power. As with all of these narrative dimensions, empowerment exists alongside risk. Earlier Hip Hop tracks like "Sucker MCs" by Run DMC, "Got It Made" by Special Ed, "Me, Myself and I" by De La Soul, "Ain't No Half Stepping" by Big Daddy Kane, "I Ain't No Joke" by Eric B. and Rakim, and "Strictly Business" by EPMD paved the way for later tracks.

Songs followed like "What's My Name?" by Snoop Dogg, "For the Love of Money" by Bone Thugs-N-Harmony, "Life's a Bitch" by Nas, "Big Poppa" and "Hypnotize" by Notorious B.I.G., "Diamonds and Wood" by UGK, "My Name Is . . ." by Eminem, and "Big Pimpin" (featuring UGK) and "Nigga What, Nigga Who" by Jay Z. While the Billboard charts are filled with esteem-oriented Hip Hop, several contemporary tracks that follow in the line of these predecessors include, "Man of the Year" by Schoolboy Q, "Over," "All Me," and "The Motto" by Drake, "King Kunta" and "The Blacker the Berry" by Kendrick Lamar, "Black Beetles" by Joey Bada$$, "The Pessimist" by Wale and J. Cole, and "January 28th" by J. Cole.

THE HEALING POWER OF ESTEEM

The desire for a positive sense of self, respect in the eyes of others, and to have status and recognizable talents is not inherently negative or problematic. However, focusing on external validation and risky ways of achieving this status can be problematic. Seeking experiences that reinforce fun, joy, and happiness while minimizing pain is also empowering. The same concerns over risky strategies apply. Youth are constantly creating "esteem narratives." Sometimes they look to broader societal narratives in the media. In other instances they embrace commercially successful music artists as models of a prosperous and hopeful outlook for adulthood. Youth identities are malleable and they may use these narratives in any way to compare and contrast with their own abilities, talents, skills, and strengths, regardless of risk or legality.

Hip Hop's musical canon continues to revisit identity and esteem in conjunction with the collective history of the Black community in the United States. Hip Hop's new cultural ambassadors embrace this as well as a more deliberate cultural landscape for identifying a positive sense of self. Their goal is to help youth be confident independent of materialism or external validation, to strengthen their identity, and to be intrinsically happy. Materialism and validating social support are not inherently negative, however significant risk exists when identity and self-efficacy is contingent upon them.[37] Ambassadors seek for youth to be able to cultivate their healthiest strengths in the face of harsh contextual realities common for many present day Black youth. Hip Hop's esteem narratives offer pathways for expression, reflection, and attitudes that inspire action for self-improvement. The following chapter will focus on resilience and the context and stories that help shape identity and esteem.

CHAPTER 5

Context, Surviving, and Thriving: Resilience and Black Experiences

"Walk a mile in my shoes, then you'd be crazy too" are Tupac Shakur's words on "Nothing to Lose," after laying bare the difficulty of being thirteen, in poverty, fatherless, street-oriented, and witnessing his mother go it alone—in despair. If you really want to know a person, the saying goes that you must walk a mile in their shoes. Everyone has a story that offers a glimpse into the context from which they came. It is this context that helps shape identities while also helping to forge new identities. These contexts are the social environments in which we live, work, and play, where choices dictate how we cope with adversity and shape pathways to well-being.

Hip Hop culture has always offered a window into these contexts with authenticity and realism. This facilitates "transportation" or "presence" for listeners, enhancing believability.[1] How "real" though, has always been a matter of debate. Emcees craft Horatio Alger-type rags-to-riches autobiographical narratives that offer insight into their struggles but also give listeners a template upon which they can project their own stories about surviving and also thriving.[2]

INDIVIDUALIZED COPING

The list of challenges people can experience is long, but even the same type of challenge is unique for every individual. Among these resilience narratives, stories are personal ("me") and distinguished from community-level ("we") narratives that can speak to collective resilience. For example, the Austin-based SaulPaul rhymes in an infectiously powerful way about his ability to rise above profound early life adversity to excel and live his dream. This chapter and discussion relates to these types of individualized experiences of coping with adversity.

Adversity can also be issue specific. For example, the issue of police harassment has been similar across generations, but the setting, context, age, severity, reactions of bystanders, and its lasting impact are different for every individual. These stories are real, vivid, emotional, and in-formative, but are different for each person. Further, artists have their own unique style and flow, and differing abilities when moving between different styles. The result is that any topic can be developed, expressed, and engaged with in myriad ways. This is part of the power of Hip Hop.

Another aspect of the power of Hip Hop culture is its utilitarian spirit. Natalie Davis, executive director of a Hip Hop–integrated youth program in southeastern United State said, "Survival with anything available is a part of our culture. [You] do the most with what you have." Along with her team, she works on connecting youth to solutions to problems. They model for youth as they "critique and evaluate in ways that are not judgmental but still very helpful/critical."[3]

We must also recognize within-culture tensions about the best coping strategies and whether surviving or thriving is the most desired outcome. Do we yield to the pressures of our social landscapes to prioritize survival by any means necessary, or do we aspire to a longer-term vision of growth where attention is paid to delayed gratification and the broader welfare of one's community too? While not a simple dichotomy of choice, the pro-portional emphasis on surviving versus thriving is often ideological and malleable.

OUR STORIES: HIS AND HER STORY

Intensely emotional music can also facilitate the aforementioned "trans-portation" or the experience of "getting lost" in the story.[4] The combination of emotional music and transportation-facilitating narratives has been as-sociated with reduced critical processing, changes in beliefs, and behavioral motivation. In a research study conducted in 2013, 41 percent of youth said "it is easier to listen to rap music that talks about issues in my life than for me to talk to other people about issues in my life."[5] Clinical social worker Ian Levy spoke about his experiences of Hip Hop's power to guide introspection, coping, and growth from adversity. This is what helped directly inform his incorporation of Hip Hop into his professional practice. He talked about how it went beyond theory, or a good idea; he knows firsthand the power of the culture. Despite being a skilled musician—a trumpeter—Hip Hop was able to take him to a place of growth and well-being that he was not able to access through trumpeting.[6]

People connect to narratives in general, but absorption into stories (i.e., transportation) has been shown to influence beliefs.[7] People connect more with stories, a focused integration of attention, imagery, and feelings, within which they can locate themselves.[8] We have an expansive library of stories in Hip Hop that capture aspects of the Black experience, favorable and less favorable. When pressed about perceptions of negativity in these stories, Rakim said, "Negativity [in Hip Hop] is gonna be there. It's gonna be there yesterday, it's gonna be there tomorrow. Can't hide the fact that this crazy shit is going on, but rap is an expression of life. What we gotta do, man, is do a couple of joints explaining what's going."[9] Rakim captures the subtle tension between symptom and cause. Both are realities. When we zoom in on symptoms though, it offers a very different perception of reality compared to when we zoom out to capture its causes as well. At its most empowering, Hip Hop illuminates context.

We continue to recognize that context-driven narratives are also heavily mediated by a larger commercial system of Hip Hop production and distribution. It is also not possible to fully project how individuals uniquely engage with material presented to them. Thus, we examine contemporary Hip Hop products with themes of resilience to offer perspectives about both the challenges and opportunities that exist for Black youth. These youth are undoubtedly still negotiating their identities as Black among the African diaspora, as residents of the United States, as adolescents and young adults, and even as consumers of Hip Hop culture.[10]

This is the context within which identity emerges. These are the stories that are told and retold about one's life, past and present. These are stories of challenges and successes, akin to the old *Wild World of Sports* tagline, "the thrill of victory and the agony of defeat." The narratives here are of adversity but also of bouncing back and coping, or what James Peterson calls the "come up."[11] The challenge as we explore these narratives is that sometimes they offer a narrow and truncated view of the adversities in the Black experience. So while we will often hear about the travails of neighborhood stressors, we rarely hear about mental health, anxiety issues, pressures to balance academic demands, family concerns, peer pressure, and coping with friends facing adversity. Yet these are among the most reported stressors for Black teens.[12]

TRADING WAR STORIES: CATHARSIS
(ABOUT ME OR WHAT I SEE)

From the songs of slave hollers to the blues to Hip Hop, the Black community has a long legacy of music with stories of challenging social realities, offering potential catharsis and relief to artists and listeners alike. Few Hip Hop tracks are more universally known to follow in this tradition than "The Message" and its classic lines, "Don't push me 'cause I'm close to the edge. . . . It's like a jungle sometimes, it makes me wonder how I keep from going under." It is a visceral reminder, as much today as at its original release in 1982, of how desperately real the situation is for many. The idea of drowning in despair is impossible to ignore.

Another track, "6 in the Morning" by Ice-T, brought the nation's attention to a uniquely West Coast phenomenon involving the Los Angeles Police Department. Officers were widely reported to show excessive force, using a battering ram to destroy homes and property during police raids.[13] When Dead Prez took on the educational system from the perspective of a young Black boy in "They Schools," low expectations and an absence of cultural competence by teachers took a front seat. KRS-One's "Sound of the Police" critiqued policing policies long before Rodney King. Tupac's "So Many Tears" helped audiences look at the emotional coping of hood living and the loss of close friends. These songs contributed to Hip Hop's musical canon, a template upon which the unique challenges of present generations could authentically, unapologetically, and creatively express their contextual realities.

A distinction must be made between narratives that describe neighborhood stressors. First, when we look at the landscapes of excessive violence described, substance use, and exploitive misogyny, while being identity- and esteem-based narratives, there are subtle yet fundamental differences among them. While some narratives are described more for affirming and assaultive reasons that are oriented to perceived self-competence and self-worth (the prioritized outcome), others offer an account of challenges, adversities, and the complexities of living that are the context for that self-worth but also leave room for tangible attitudes and means to cope and transcend those adversities and do better (the prioritized outcome). Second, they emphasize individual worth and coping ("me") narratives in contrast to collective worth and coping ("we") narratives that will be discussed in the context of "community" later.

Similar to our discussions of identity, the unique position of being Black in the United States has created a daunting number of social and environmental stressors and disparities, including the police harassment and use of excessive force perceived in the aforementioned deaths of Mike Brown, Eric Garner, and even twelve-year-old Tamir Rice. The following are but a few of the unique contexts from which these identity narratives often emerge: (1) community violence; (2) the criminal justice system, including incarceration and bias; (3) voting rights and political representation; (4) educational quality, zero tolerance/suspension/expulsion policies and outcomes; (5) employment and poverty rates; (6) female-headed households and fatherhood; and (7) police surveillance and use of excessive force. Each of these contextual realities has its own set of smaller issues and within-race/ethnicity dynamics such as gender, class, and skin tone. Further, each of these topics includes the crosscutting stressors of interpersonal and structural or systemic bias. However, the remainder of this book focuses on exploration of the aggregate issue level.

CONTINUOUS TRAUMATIC STRESS

In general, short-term stress and adversity can be a helpful way to recognize one's strengths and resources. However, stress can be toxic when there is insufficient support.[14] Extreme stress in the form of trauma can shatter one's sense of security and cause substantial physiological, psychological, and social problems. The Centers for Disease Control and Prevention define Post-Traumatic Stress Disorder (PTSD) as "an intense physical and emotional response to thoughts and reminders of the event that last long after the traumatic event." It has three broad and often overlapping symptoms: intrusive reliving (flashbacks and intense emotions), numbing and avoidance (of any reminder of trauma), and hyperarousal (on edge, easily provoked), and often occurs with depression, arising from distress and inability to cope. On "Losing My Mind," Pharoahe Monch talks about his post-trauma struggles: "If I could only put the past on a flash drive I'd, for peace of mind, install an external drive so I'd be more driven internally to survive."

PTSD should be considered alongside Continuous Traumatic Stress (CTS) as a phenomenon in many of our communities where the persistent, unpredictable, and faceless nature of threats is often coupled with an absence of sufficient support.[15] Thoughts, anxieties, and behaviors center not on the past but on how to stay safe now and in the future. Again, the existing canon of Hip Hop music creates spaces for all of these areas to rest and be built upon. Cendrine Robinson speaks to her first-hand use of artists like Meek Mill because of his ability to speak to the traumatic realities of youth she works with professionally. She finds that many youth identify with him and the stories he presents about street life, dealing with law enforcement, and other youth stressors.[16]

The pervasiveness of these stressful experiences must be understood as just that—pervasive. Chris Emdin speaks to his own stressful experiences with law enforcement and Hip Hop's role in coping,

> Hip Hop is everything to me. . . . It's a release, comfort, it takes the edge off of the tensions that come with being in this space. Literally, I'm driving up 125th [Street] today and got pulled over. In the last two years I have gotten pulled over at least six or seven times for no reason, once cuffed and taken to Central Booking for no reason. The only thing I know to give me some sanity, to give me a release, to come in afterwards and do my job and not be mad at the world is my music. I use it as therapy.[17]

FEATURE: BLACK LIVES MATTER

In a March 2012 class in the undergraduate Hip Hop Culture and Positive Youth Development course I teach, I allocated extra time during a discussion on resilience to focus on the death of Trayvon Martin. I connected the incident to the history of the use of excessive force by law enforcement officials in the Black community and used the Rodney King and Amadou Diallo cases as examples. I brought in written materials to help my students understand different perspectives about "the talk" that many Black parents feel obligated to have with their young boys.[18] I told them explicitly that I believe the death of Martin will be a story they will hear about long into their adulthood, in the same way people talk about the Rodney King incident. As a class, we discussed what it means to have this Black male vs. police dynamic culturally embedded at such a deep level, and ultimately what coping means—emotionally, socially, physically—for small children, older youth, fathers, mothers, and communities as a whole.

Only two years later, Michael Brown was killed in Ferguson, Missouri. Next, another police shooting death occurred not far away in St. Louis. Twelve-year-old Tamir Rice was also killed in a Cleveland park two seconds after police arrived on the scene. Next was the decision not to indict officers involved in the choking death of Eric Garner in Staten Island, New York. Next was the killing of unarmed Walter Scott, who was shot in the back by a South Carolina police officer, an incident caught on video by a bystander. Next, there was Freddie Gray's spinal damage and death in Baltimore, Maryland. Most recently was the questionable arrest and suspicious death of Sandra Bland in Hempstead, Texas. In between these cases, there were a host of other assaults and deaths of unarmed Black citizens at the hands of law enforcement officers.

When 50 Cent spoke on the freedom of artists to narrate from a range of perspectives, he was speaking about his actual G-Unit rap group writing sessions while watching coverage of the Michael Brown incident. He spoke to the range of potential voices involved in the incident, and ability of artists to easily write about any of the perspectives involved. Several Hip Hop artists released songs addressing this spate of officer-involved killings, following in the footsteps of Jasiri X's "Trayvon." For example, J. Cole's "Be Free" was a highly emotional appeal that was as much a collective appeal as a personal story of coping with lyrics like, "Can you tell me why, every time I step outside I see my niggas die?" In general, the reality of the use of excessive force by the police and injustice in the criminal justice system is a mainstay of Hip Hop culture. From N.W.A.'s anthem "Fuck tha Police," to Blue Scholars' "Oscar Grant," to KRS-One's "Who Protects Us From You?" to Jasiri X's "10 Frisk Commandments," to Dead Prez's "Police State." Most recently, we also have Wu-Tang Clan's "A Better Tomorrow." Lil Boosie's "Hands Up," J-Live's "I Am a Man," and Rapper Big Pooh's "Eyes Wide Open." Although not a Hip Hop artist, Prince wrote the song "Baltimore" in response to the death of Freddie Gray. Similarly, Janelle Monae and her Wondaland crew created the instant-classic anthem "Hell You Talmbout?!" that offers an explicit roll call of the many Black lives lost at the hands of law enforcement.

FEATURE: COPING WITH LOSS

Dealing with the loss of a loved one is a universal pain. Sometimes Hip Hop culture is perceived to be too cavalier about death and dying, but there are numerous tracks that help provide a foundation for such topics in future tracks. The canon on loss and coping would include the precedent-setting songs "They Reminisce Over You (T.R.O.Y.)" by Pete Rock and C. L. Smooth, "Renee" by the Lost Boyz, "Tha Crossroads" by Bone Thugs-N-Harmony, "Life Goes On" and "So Many Tears" by Tupac Shakur, "Miss U" by Notorious B.I.G., "I Seen a Man Die" by Scarface, and "I'll Be Missing You" by Puff Daddy & Faith Evans.

Artists coping with real-world losses in a transparent and creative way drive these songs. The kinds of loss they experience vary, and their songs offer a range of ways to approach coping. They can also be about another's loss, like Wiz Khalifa's "See You Again," a song about the death of Paul Walker, in which Khalifa takes on the perspective of Walker's friends and coworkers. One of the most famous tracks speaking to resilience and overcoming loss is Pete Rock and C. L. Smooth's "They Reminisce Over You (T.R.O.Y.)," nostalgic and celebratory as much as it is a story of loss. The track is dedicated to their friend Troy Dixon, also known as Trouble T. Roy, who died from an accidental fall, hence the title of the track. C. L. Smooth starts at his birth and early life with his single mother. He speaks to her strength and resilience despite challenging times ("positive over negative") and continues to talk about a father figure that provided all the guidance and mentorship he needed. He talks about his faith in him and his grandmother, uncle, and aunt with joy, appreciation, and pride. Along with the incredible sonic backdrop of Pete Rock, it is a timeless classic that helps anchor Hip Hop's musical canon.

Bone Thugs-N-Harmony's "Tha Crossroads" has a notable spirituality in its coverage of losing important people in life. The group's members do not mask their vulnerability in this track, talking openly about sadness, pain, tears, and the need for mutual support. Tupac takes on community violence and the criminal justice system in "Life Goes On," his testament to losing friends to death and incarceration. He talks directly to them as opposed to the narrative form of the other tracks. Like Bone Thugs-N-Harmony, Tupac speaks to his own mortality as well. Again, in "So Many Tears," Tupac talks not only about the emotional difficulty of both his losses but also how his current levels of stress and suffering can be debilitating and prompt suicidal ideation.

Notorious B.I.G. speaks to the death of young men in general but focuses on his two friends, O and Drew, in "Miss U." B.I.G.'s incredible gift of descriptiveness helps bring in different layers to help understand the multiple contexts of these losses—the history of the relationships, the acute moment of death, and the implications of the loss for him and for family members. He talks openly about love and emotional closeness for both friends.

In graffiti culture, writers are often involved in the process of coping when they are recruited to develop pieces for murals in remembrance of people that have passed away. These memorial walls are not only for the specific individual who prompts its commission but they are often also a public and community-wide event. These memorial walls allow grieving, but also celebration and the opportunity for a long-term emotional connection and support for people connected to that person.[19]

FEATURE: FATHERHOOD

"No stability, every year got a new address; never change the view from this window, he seeing mad arrests" are the narrator's words on Rapsody's song "The Man." Instability, both residential and economic, is combined with the traumatic ubiquity of law enforcement presence and criminal activity. This is the stressful life of a young man who assumed a mountain of responsibilities for his home and siblings in the absence of his father. When his father stops by later in life he cannot contain his anger and resentment when finally meeting face-to-face after years of absence. His ongoing high level of stress is palpable in the song.

Fatherhood is another important topic that is often discussed in this dimension of resilience. According to the most recent United States Census, published in 2014, 67 percent of Black children reside in single-parent homes, many of which are headed by single women. The encouraging news is that most recent data, for example, from the National Health Statistics Reports (2013) and the Congressional Research Service, highlight that among non-custodial fathers, Black are consistently the most regularly and actively involved of all racial groups with their children.

Hip Hop culture explores many more narratives and dynamics that intersect with the theme of fatherhood. Beanie Siegel and Jay Z touched on fatherhood on "I Still Got Love For You" almost fifteen years before Rapsody. Jay said, "And the pain I felt all my life you feel in the song; your lack of warmth left a chill in the morn.'" Although the song is filled with raw anger and disappointment, both artists also cite maturity as a reason they can forgive and reconnect. Two tracks, same pain, different outcomes.

FlowStory, an Austin, Texas, organization promoting health and well-being in youth and young adults, uses Hip Hop tracks with fatherhood themes in its Finding Fatherhood Toolkit. As part of Flow Story's "Muzuze" system, toolkits use print and digital media to encourage youth to use music educationally and therapeutically, to learn and to grow. The 2014 edition included more than seventy fatherhood-oriented tracks from Hip Hop's most respected and well-known artists, twenty standalone educational topics to explore, and a wide range of therapeutic prompts to guide their strategic use for learning, health, and well-being.

One of the most gripping combinations of fatherhood-oriented tracks, and a testament to how innovative Hip Hop can be, is "Letter to My Son" by Don Trip, followed by the response to it, "Letter to My Father" by Driicky Graham. Trip's lyrics, "I'm sorry Jaylin, I don't get to see you like I want to. But I just wanna let you know I want to" are followed by Graham's lines, "I just wanna see my father. It's hard to turn the pages when you hardly see the author." The prominence of fatherhood as an issue in the Black community is also evidenced by the prominence of it as a theme in tracks. As Fashawn says on "Man of the House" on his newest album *The Ecology*, "The world on my shoulders, the only thing [my father] ever left."

HIP HOP SAVED MY LIFE

Hip Hop culture can also help people cope with adversity through attempts to master one or more of its cultural elements. The skills needed and process of creating art to express oneself helps, regardless of whether its empowering functions are high- or low-risk. Thus, it is where opportunities arise, whether they are purely economic or mission-driven by the opportunity pathways. Lupe Fiasco, in his second album *Lupe Fiasco's The Cool*, talks about this duality and the opportunity for individuals to turn their lives around. This sentiment rings true for many apologists for artists with high-risk messages containing violence, misogyny, and glorification of substance use. The idea is that it is better to sing about it as a form of entertainment than to do it in reality.

A young man named Christopher felt he was being treated unfairly when he was only trying to earn enough money to feed his daughter. His frustration led him to write a manifesto dedicated to his persecutors. Christopher also revealed his childhood dreams of limousine rides and riches, dreams at a time when things were so desperate he sometimes had no heat, ate sardines for dinner, and went without on birthdays and Christmas. But most important to young Christopher was the positive role that rap and Hip Hop played in turning his life around. As much as he wanted it to, he was unsure whether rapping would work out for him. Despite being a high school dropout, Hip Hop helped him move away from the drug game and crime to a life of wealth and luxury for himself, his mother, and daughter. Christopher Wallace, a.k.a. Notorious B.I.G., embraced this resiliency saying, "Damn right I like the life I live; 'Cause I went from negative to positive."

DON'T ASK ME WHY . . . ASK ME HOW

In the song inspired by his classic poem, "The Rose That Grew from Concrete," Tupac Shakur talks about the amazing feat and spectacle that would be if a rose grew from concrete. He compares this incredible example of resilience to young people and how they make good in the most difficult and challenging environments. He concludes that most people would choose not to ask why the rose had some damaged petals, as they would understand and recognize its "tenacity." He identifies with the rose and ends with, "These are my damaged petals. Don't ask me why . . . ask me how!"

It is easy to wax poetic about choice sometimes, to romanticize the ease of coping with neighborhood stressors and the ease of peaceful conflict resolution when one is removed from the up-close and personal challenges of face-to-face pressure. Some of the most challenging neighborhood environments pressure youth into situations where they feel desperate and focus disproportionately on survival.[20] Decisions made in such situations have very high stakes and can literally be a matter of life and death. When youth are embedded in generational street-life circumstances, where parents, older relatives, and entire social networks have high-risk lifestyles, it only compounds the stress and pressure. Coping involves making difficult choices.

THE JEALOUSY, THE ENVY, THE PHONY, THE FRIENDLY . . . THE SNAKES IN THE GRASS

Questions of authenticity aside, in an interview with Rob Markman on Shade 45's G-Unit Reunion Special, 50 Cent shared his thoughts about people taking shots (i.e., verbal or written attacks) at him in the media. He said he would rather keep himself safe than be victimized after making the assumption that artists are "just rapping." In other words, he prefers to take them at face value as real and authentic and not just "let it go." These are the same choices that most listeners have to make about the art they listen to and engage with, and the lives they live. Is this real? What does it mean for me? How do I want to respond to this? The choice is to survive (at all costs) or choose thriving and pro-social responses (with some risk and some faith).

These reactionary tendencies can be especially challenging in communities if there is an overrepresentation of violent encounters. One can choose how to respond to adversity. However, there is also not necessarily a consistent "right" and "wrong" when mortal survival is at play. Most people align with the perspective that greater value exists in surviving than not. Early Hip Hop tracks like "Just to Get By" by Talib Kweli and "Survival of the Fittest" by Mobb Deep helped accentuate these cultural norms of survival. However, prioritizing survival in the short term, with little attention to longer-term goals and the big picture, presents its own individual and collective high-risk challenges.

STRAIGHT OUTTA SOMEWHERE

In 1991 Hip Hop drew from two poles of influence: Compton and Tennessee. Both came on the heels of Hip Hop's golden age of consciousness.

On the surface they were very different. Compton symbolized the new angst of N.W.A. and similar artists with stories about hood challenges as understood by residents in and around South Central Los Angeles. "Straight Outta Compton" and "Fuck tha Police" opened the media floodgates, and the rest is history. A deeper listen to Ice Cube of N.W.A. finds that amid anger, projection, misogyny, and racial epithets directed outward is also a strong sense of connection and responsibility for the fate of the communities he values by race and geography. Most direct was the desire to reduce Black-on-Black crime at a time that capped one of the most violent periods in the history of Black communities, aided by an influx of crack cocaine and firearms.[21]

Tennessee symbolized Arrested Development's efforts to use contemporary challenges as a way to connect with a vision for the positive potential of Black culture (on *3 Years, 5 Months & 2 Days in the Life Of . . .*). It was also a within-culture plea for the Black community to step into the best version of themselves. So while different, Compton and Tennessee were similar in their value of improvement within the Black community.

CAN'T KNOCK THE HUSTLE: THE BIG BUSINESS OF ILLEGAL DRUGS

East Coast, West Coast, "Dirty South," it's all the same. Many youth in lower-income communities perceive that the illegal sale of drugs are a legitimate opportunity to try and overcome financial adversity.[22] The two biggest-selling illegal drugs in the United States are cocaine and marijuana, accounting for about $69 billion per year in sales.[23] Drug and alcohol sales have been part of the United States' informal economy for a long time, but reports suggest a greater prevalence in Black communities, which saw a significant heroin influx in the 1970s and a particularly devastating influx of crack cocaine in the 1980s.[24] The source of these influxes has been a longstanding point of contention. The sale of illegal drugs is believed to be a multimillion-dollar economy in many impoverished communities, and an industry that is always hiring. However, it also brings increased family instability, gun violence, and mass incarceration to these communities.[25]

Crack cocaine, a cheap alternative to cocaine, hit the streets of urban America in large volumes in the early 1980s, after the War on Drugs had already been announced and at the same time President Ronald Reagan's administration oversaw a substantial reduction in social service programming. Crack was attractive. For the user, it was a more economical way of associating with the glamour of cocaine and had intense addictive qualities. For the seller, it was an immediate, income-generating tool to combat poverty, a recession, and government cutbacks of federal programs and funding.

Two decades later, competing narratives about how to cope with poverty, employment instability, and service constraints remain in Hip Hop's narratives. Is success best obtained through *survival by any means necessary*, or *thriving via healthy long-term decision-making*? The volume of narratives aligned with each side of this tension—to survive or thrive—has expanded considerably. The duality is more pronounced among "underground" artists, as it seems a bit more one sided in the mainstream (by any means necessary), but the same premise exists. How much energy is placed on telling the story of adversity? How much energy should be devoted to overcoming adversity? And ultimately, where is the emphasis in chosen strategies for overcoming? Is it primarily survival by any means necessary? Or is the emphasis on growth? Is there a longer-term plan in place that offers a growth-oriented trajectory; a bridge to the most positive aspects of one's community?

Consider artists like Jay Z and T.I., who are financially successful but pepper their tracks with narratives of their hustling days in the illegal economy. They frame these behaviors with not only how it was necessary for survival but also as a favorable option. On the track "Seen it All," Young Jeezy and Jay Z both share stories about the ups and downs of making it in the drug trade to an infectious beat that perfectly connects with their lyrical wordplay. While we do hear about jail, we hear much more about pride and nostalgia in the activity of the drug trade, which can be interpreted by some as glorification of the activity. This contrasts with Inspectah Deck at the end of "C.R.E.A.M.," where he tries to "kick the truth to the young Black youth" about considering a different path.

Kendrick Lamar speaks to this forced game of survival through a story about a caterpillar and butterfly on "Mortal Man" from his 2015 album *To Pimp a Butterfly*. He is sharing the story with the deceased Tupac Shakur, "The caterpillar is a prisoner to the streets that conceived it, its only job is to eat or consume everything around it." The caterpillar is in survival mode, a form of self-protection from the "mad city" around it. He raps about how this caterpillar is trapped, stagnant, and has a biased view of growth and thriving, until it is finally able to embrace new ideas about reality. Once free of these old constraints the caterpillar is able to grow, spread its own wings, and embrace a new life of potential.

THE TRAP

Some of Hip Hop culture's most famous names have reappropriated systemic community oppression to romanticize it as "The Trap." Although other artists like Ice Cube and Andre 3000 fully identify this system of pathways to death and prison as "A Trap," the industry appears to see it as a source of credibility and legitimacy. Consider T.I.'s album *Trap Muzick*. Consider Gucci Mane's line of mixtapes, *Trap God*, *Trap Back*, and *Trap House*. Each of his mixes has successive volumes, such as *Trap House* 1 through 4. More trap mixtape titles include Young Jeezy's *Trap or Die* series, *Trap to the Future* by Frenchie, *Trap-a-Velli* by Tity Boi or 2 Chainz, and even Iggy Azalea's *Trap Gold*.

Fetty Wap's "Trap Queen" dominated the charts in spring 2015, with a classic ride or die, Bonnie & Clyde, partner-in-crime tale. On this track, Fetty beams at how helpful his girlfriend is with his hustling, and right by his side, "I get high with my baby . . . I be in the kitchen cooking pies with my baby." Still, among these trap narratives remain stories of pressure, stress, adversity, and tension about how best to cope. These narratives are still ultimately about coping and the relationship between environmental stressors and personal responsibility. De La Soul made an early reference to this idea of being a part of some bigger nefarious plan on "Stakes is High" with, "Neighborhoods are now 'hoods 'cause nobody's neighbors . . . experiments when needles and skin connect no wonder where we live is called the projects." On Outkast's "SpottieOttieDopaliscious," Andre 3000 offers a final cautionary line about making the wrong decisions as it relates to Trap life, "So now you back in the trap, just that 'trapped.' Go on and marinate on that."

IT'S US THAT'S KILLING US

The continued challenge is that the same message about free will and personal responsibility can be highly subjective.[26] What is the best path forward for handling stress and adversity, systematic injustice or "the trap," or traumatic experiences? MK Asante discussed how when speaking about personal contributions to community violence and risky behaviors, the newly maligned Bill Cosby and Tupac Shakur say essentially the same thing. Tupac spends a little more time paying attention to the social realities that contribute to, or are root causes of, these circumstances, but the message is essentially the same. Look toward personal responsibility before looking to blame others.

On "White Manz World," Tupac says, "Use your brain. It ain't *them* that's killing us, it's *us* that's killing us." This intra-racial dialogue, similarly punctuated in Kendrick Lamar's emphatic "Hypocrite!" at the conclusion of his track "Blacker the Berry," brings to a head the ever-present reality of coping in a social landscape that is at once filled with race-specific challenges and opportunities.

THRIVING

The idea of thriving moves beyond survival to a longer-term path toward healing. For example, occupying a space between resiliency's survival element and the mentorship aspect of growth is Immortal Technique's "Dance with the Devil." It follows in the pattern of Gang Starr's "Just to Get a Rep." It is a cautionary tale about a young man named Billy seeking to be "the illest hustler the world had ever seen." With an absent father and a mother that was in recovery, he was on endless quest for street credibility and peer validation. He succumbed to the basest peer pressure to prove himself through rape and murder of a stranger only to find out it was his mother. These extreme cautionary tales help bring to light some of the more sensitive topics that are sometimes considered taboo to the point that they are not discussed, such as rape and abuse.

It is at this point of choice where the so-called "conscious" segment of Hip Hop takes center stage. It is the up-front declaration of intentionality and a proclamation of healthy decision-making that takes prominence. In the same way previously discussed narratives are bold assertions of esteem, worth, and context, these thriving-oriented narratives do the same for pro-social decision-making—taking responsibility for doing the right thing, making positive choices. These are the precursors to growth narratives and being at one's best.

The emcee Guru of Gang Starr helped set the tone for conflict resolution as opposed to reactionary retaliation on "Moment of Truth," another track from Hip Hop's musical canon, "The same shiesty cats that you hang with, and do your thang with, could set you up and wet you up." He talks about his own recognition to not judge or overreact to minor situations, preferring to step back and think. He also talks about his need to avoid using substances that will only increase his anxieties. Ultimately he is face-to-face with the most desperate of situations and feels backed into a corner. However, by reflecting on past resiliency, thinking clearly, and through prayer he emerges renewed, strong, and ready to take on the situation, ready to meet his moment of truth.

Similarly, songs like "Can't Stop the Prophet" by Jeru the Damajaly set the table for later songs like "Take a Walk" by Masta Ace, "Kick Push II" by Lupe Fiasco, "Show Me the Good Life" by Blu and Exile, "My Story" by Jean Grae, "Still Standing" by Pharoahe Monch, and other newer, more conscientious takes on resilience. For example, on "Dehydration" from his album *Water*, Mick Jenkins helps listeners consider how to stop being reactionary to help curb the cycle of violence in our communities, just like the aforementioned Guru. The difficulty in making the correct decision is also a feature of these tracks.

USING CONTEXT TO THRIVE

The ability of people to overcome pain and adversity is a powerful step forward in life. Rakim has said the adversity he recognizes and the coping he sees by people in life inspired his art: "When I'm driving through New York, I don't just see a hundred-and-such-and-such street or blasé-blah, I see the pain. I see life itself. I see culture."[27] He also explained how his life-style paralleled his career as an emcee, allowing a knowledge of self to manifest through his craft. He was able to see himself in a new light, and he shares his path from life on the street to life as an emcee speaking about being the best version of himself as a Black man on Earth: "I was rhyming for a while, then I got knowledge of himself like a year before I started making records. I got into that reading so much, and you know, all that was in me. I had the street life in me, but the knowledge was in me, too. So I was speaking on what I knew. Just so happened that it came out the way it did."[28] These narratives of actual growth, of turning over a new leaf, and of making a deliberate step toward being the best version of oneself are what take root with an intention to thrive.

THE CANON, PAST AND PRESENT

The tracks about resilience steadily being added to Hip Hop's musical canon seek to capture the diverse and dynamic stories of people coping with life's challenges and overcoming adversities. Classics like "The Message" by Grandmaster Flash and the Furious Five, "The Breaks" by Kurtis Blow, "Dear Mama" and "So Many Tears" by Tupac, "Code of the Streets" by Gang Starr, "It Was a Good Day" by Ice Cube, "Juicy" by Notorious B.I.G., and "They Reminisce Over You (T.R.O.Y.)" by Pete Rock and C. L. Smooth have provided the foundation for later tracks.

Later songs like "Survival of the Fittest" by Mobb Deep, "Slipping" by DMX, "Hard Knock Life," "Moment of Clarity," and "Can I Live" by Jay Z, "Renegade" by Jay Z and Eminem, "Lost Ones" by Lauryn Hill, and "One Time" by The Roots paved the way for newer tracks like "The Prayer" by Kid Cudi, "Started from the Bottom," the similar "Worst Behavior," and "0 to 100/Catch Up" by Drake, and "Try Me" by Dej Loaf. More empowering and lower-risk tracks with themes of resiliency include "In the Wind" by Joey Bada$$, Big K.R.I.T., and Chauncy Sherod, "Deliver" and "The Coolest" by Lupe Fiasco, "Hard to Choose" and "The Man" by Rapsody, and "So Low" by Talib Kweli.

THE HEALING POWER OF RESILIENCE

Telling your story or hearing someone else's story that resonates with you can be useful. It is an expression of your individual reality, including all of the challenges, stressors, triumphs, and growth. Across Hip Hop's narratives of resilience, we can embrace the many adverse and empowering contexts that shape identities. Hip Hop allows authentic and complex stories to be told in accessible and innovative ways. By either creating or identifying with these narratives, individuals have shown that Hip Hop provides ways to cope with adversity. Alternatively, unhealthy coping strategies include a reliance on high-risk, survival-mode strategies. Differences in perspective on how to move past challenges and stress highlight the difference between an orientation toward survival and an orientation toward thriving. Moving past resentment, anger, and continuous reactionary strategies to cope are critical for positive growth.

Successful coping strategies are a chance for one to think about lessons learned, new opportunities, and realized strengths after overcoming challenges. Experiences of resilience offer people a chance to reflect on their pillars of support—whether family, friends, or faith. Growth emerges from empowering, lower-risk narratives that reinforce the use of one's skills, strengths, and interests to bounce back from challenges. Such narratives found throughout Hip Hop's musical canon can be the foundation of lifelong resilience so that stressors do not keep individuals down but instead propel them forward and help them excel.

CHAPTER 6

My Life, My Community: Growth and Black Experiences

The Universal Zulu Nation's creed of Hip Hop being about "peace, love, unity, and having fun" is a value that champions collective solidarity. However, in order for peace, love, unity, or fun to take place at a collective level, individuals must take a stand for them. One must stand for peace in the face of violence, conflict, or the burning desire for revenge. One must stand for love in the presence of hate or fear. One must stand for unity in the face of divisiveness, conflict, or exploitation. One must stand for fun in the face of sadness, callousness, or nihilism. This is quite an investment in growth and maturity. It contrasts markedly from having only personal concerns, being in survival mode, or wedded to hedonistic immediate gratification. In the middle of major stress, adversity, and challenges, it can be tempting to be reactionary and self-preservationist at the expense of peace, love, and unity.

A BETTER PERSON

Hip Hop's narratives about growth involve building knowledge, improving attitudes, and refining skills to help individuals grow into better people. This type of self-improvement helps people to get better at the things that matter to them. It is discovering, cultivating, strengthening, and sharing that spark, talent, or interest that captures our attention. In the context of Hip Hop, this is using the culture as a platform for building skills—life skills as much as artistic skills. These are cognitive, physical, and social skills. It is about fulfilling one's potential, thriving, and positively contributing to the communities one belongs to. As KRS-One said in his song "My Philosophy," it is about "being a teacher, not a king."

Implicit in this growth is also greater maturity, inclusivity, and empathic connectedness with others. Attention and concern is expressed in all age and circumstantial directions, toward older generations, peers of similar age and circumstances, and younger generations. An ability to cultivate and refine healthy relationships and to be of service to others is a bridge between person and environment. It is the link to valued communities and reinforces mentorship and modeling roles. It is the pathway by which a personal story becomes a community story.

YOUNG, GIFTED, AND BLACK

To be young and Black can mean a wide range of things. A major problem with stereotyping and bias against the Black community is the abbreviated view of success for Black youth offered to the general public. The limited examples of individuals reaching their potential and thriving in arenas outside of predictable stereotypes leads to limited thinking about the Black experience. Talib Kweli's song, "Drugs, Basketball, and Rap," speaks to this monolithic view of Black youth culture that is overemphasized. Hip Hop's healing power exists by expanding narrow societal narratives, and these expansive growth narratives are a consistent reminder of possibility and potential. Young, gifted, and Black can be the norm instead of the exception.

QUESTING BEYOND THE BLOCK: NAS ON LEAVING AND LEARNING

Nas spoke of this dynamic from the perspectives of being both an artist and a Hip Hop fan [of A Tribe Called Quest]. He was growing and developing as a young, Black man and also as an artist, offering growth narratives in solidarity with the Black community. In a 2014 interview with NPR's Ali Shaheed Muhammad and Frannie Kelley on the occasion of the 20th anniversary of his debut album *Illmatic*, Nas said:

> Man, like the album cover, the album title, the whole thing about being on a journey into the world where—you just asked about leaving

the block. A lot of people don't want to leave the block; we all know people who don't want to leave the block. So the Tribe [Called Quest] movement, to me, was encouragement to get out there to the world, to get out and go out . . . to get around the city and learn. And, you know, when you're young, learn what's going on in other neighborhoods.

HEALTHY IS THE NEW GANGSTA

Khnum "Stic" Ibomu of Dead Prez turned over a new leaf, or new "leaves" over the past few years as an influential spokesman for healthy living, including both nutrition—he is now a vegetarian—and physical activity. His RBG Fit Club is a healthy lifestyle movement, and his recent album is titled *The Workout*. The tracks on the album are motivating, inspiring, and filled with tips and information about leading a healthy lifestyle. They speak to both mind and body. They touch on all of the aforementioned value dimensions including esteem, resilience, growth, community, and change, but the overwhelming emphasis is on helping listeners achieve their potential. One of the album's most poignant tracks, "Yoga Mat," is a journey in mindfulness, resilience, discipline, and healthy lifestyles. It is a pathway to self-improvement geared around the metaphor of the yoga mat.

The tag line for Stic's movement is "Well Rounded Well Being" and the front of its latest T-shirt is emblazoned with the slogan "Healthy is the New Gangsta." Stic said that the movement "recognizes the urgency in our communities in general to revolutionize our priorities as it relates to health." The movement's website and materials champion Hip Hop values, as Stic embodies everything he promotes. He is as much "about that life" and an authentic participant in what is promoted as he expects his audience to be. His latest book, *Eat Plants Lift Iron*, is all about reaching fitness and nutrition goals and with a strict vegetarian diet and long-distance running.

SPIRITUALITY

One strand of growth involves spirituality. This does not refer to a dogmatic religious affiliation, although it can. In fact, Alexis Maston has developed a powerful and exciting line of research building on the idea that all the discussed dimensions of empowerment (esteem, resilience, growth, community, and change) are spiritualized within and throughout Hip Hop culture.[1] In her research she also found that individuals use faith and Hip

Hop culture as vehicles for both personal growth and for solidifying their roles as educators and leaders in their communities. In other words, research suggests that there is faith and spirituality that intersects with Hip Hop culture, but there is also a spirituality embedded in each empowering dimension of the culture.

When looking specifically at this growth dimension, one of the more prominent emcees who leads with spirituality and faith is Dee-1. "One Man Army," one of Dee-1's most well-known tracks, is a prime example of Hip Hop's growth narratives in a spiritual realm. On this track, he describes a conversation with God where he at first struggles with his task, then he finds courage and renews his commitment to bring his best foot forward in service to God.

Another Dee-1 track, "Shut Up And Grind," speaks to his ambitions to achieve and grow despite the people and obstacles standing in his way. He also recognizes that he is blessed and must allow these blessings to shine. Most of his songs capture both his personal journey to be at his best and his attempts to mentor others with affirming messages. "Against Us" is about advice he has received: "Don't dim your light. Don't try to be so worried about fitting in with people."

EACH ONE TEACH ONE: MENTORSHIP, MODELING, AND SERVICE

The ultimate manifestation of growth is moving from "me" to "we," from strictly personal concerns to a place of service and giving, as outlined in the above example of Dee-1. This shift does not sacrifice individual growth on the behalf of others because it necessitates a continual refinement and strengthening of skills, gifts, and talents for individuals to be at their best and of greatest service to others. In Hip Hop culture across each of its artifacts, this growth involves teaching, sharing, and reinforcing cultural values and general mentorship.

Most often this orientation toward "we" is directed at younger generations with the goal of helping them to improve their awareness, attitudes, or specific behaviors. KRS-One named his 1990 album *Edutainment* based on this premise. With tracks like "Love's Gonna Get'cha," "Beef," and "30 Cops or More," he embraced the role of *teacher* and took accountability for mentorship and mobilizing for change. It included skits with speaking from Kwame Toure (formerly Stokely Carmichael) of the Black Panther Party speaking about the Black community. This fits well with the historical Black community value of "lifting as we climb."[2]

HEY YOUNG WORLD, ARE YOU BEAMING? BECAUSE THE SHOW GOES ON

Slick Rick's "Hey Young World" provided a blueprint for subsequent tracks seeking to offer guidance and perspective to the younger generation. He talks about life issues from the perspective of a wise elder. He talks about avoiding negative peer pressure—"don't follow these dopes"—and specific negative behaviors to be cautious about engaging in. However, most important in growth narratives are aspirational goals, and on this track, Slick Rick talks about positive growth areas such as school and mastery and skills to reach for.

Lupe Fiasco takes a cue from Slick Rick with the same level of deliberateness on "I'm Beaming." His first verse is a personal affirmation of being at his best. In many ways these statements can be considered his way of establishing his credentials, validating his ability to offer guidance. He punctuates this with, "Do you remember me, the guy from verse one? Failure is my last name, never my first one." On the second verse, he asks youth to aspire, learn, and explore the world. Lupe has an impressive catalog of tracks featuring growth and community narratives, and tracks with strong change narratives.

On "The Show Goes On," Lupe Fiasco makes one of the most powerful and straightforward declarations for growth to youth on record. He first insists that "The world is yours" and acknowledges that he sees his former self in these youth and follows with his commitment to "ghetto" girls and boys around the world, "Africa, to New York, Haiti, then I detour, Oakland out to Auckland, Gaza Strip to Detroit." He reinforces his view of Blackness with the global diaspora and concludes with an affirmation of youth resilience regardless of the specific obstacles they face. On "Ital (Roses)" Lupe first asks his rap peers for a break from the references cocaine, drug sale, and strippers in their music. He then proceeds to offer some perspective for youth, "Ain't no manhood in no bang bang . . . I know some rappers put that in your mainframe."

Mentorship can be in the music or outside the music. Nas spoke about the value of mentorship for him as a person and artist: "I always looked up to dudes that got that wisdom, too. I always know who to hit up for a story. I'll call Eric B. up and Eric B. will fill in the blanks for me about things I didn't know. I talked to—there's a few dudes, man, I'll call and talk to. So I'm there—whoever want to hear me, what I gotta say, I'm here to talk. It's all good; we can talk."[3] A few of the more prominent protégémentor combinations in Hip Hop over the course of history include: Large Professor—Nas, Dr. Dre—Eminem/Snoop Dogg, Jay Z—Kanye West/J.

Cole, Lil' Wayne—Drake/Nikki Minaj, Notorious B.I.G.—Jadakiss/Lil' Kim, Digital Underground—Tupac Shakur, and 9th Wonder—Rapsody.

WE "ARE" ROLE MODELS

When looking at artist intent, we see that many artists seek to inspire others to reach their potential. For example, the Indigo Child (Raury) focuses his art specifically on this idea of developing fan potential. He wants young people to use their access to knowledge and modes of production to their advantage, saying they should "take charge of their lives," adding, "Kids like us grew up with the world at our [fingertips] . . . I want to make this world better." Rapsody echoes these sentiments when reflecting on her own work, saying: "I want to inspire little girls, especially little Black girls." She is a female artist and prioritizes gender, addressing it in a manner that allows mentorship and modeling in a transparent manner. She speaks to her deliberate effort to "bring humility and honesty" to her craft in Hip Hop. She also underscores the importance of a strong identity as a precursor to being of service, while taking accountability for mentorship and modeling. "It's confidence and a lot of patience. You have to be secure with yourself and you have to be confident in what you do and never second guess it, because there's always someone out there that can relate to you and somebody that you're speaking for," Rapsody says about being a woman in Hip Hop.[4]

Rapsody embodies the spirit of a woman from an earlier generation who in so many words shared these aspirations for her own community. A young Nina Simone said to her audience, "These songs are for all you Black folks out there . . . I'm singing only to you."[5] She made a deliberate switch early in her career to use her music for community advancement, at the expense of individual popularity and fame with songs like "Four Women," "Mississippi Goddam," and "Backlash Blues."[6]

THE CANON, PAST AND PRESENT

Tracks in Hip Hop's musical canon seek to showcase narratives that capture the spirit of growth, learning, and building skills. They also reflect being concerned about, in relationship with, and of service to others. Further, these tracks emphasize deliberately choosing to be the best version of oneself. Early tracks that laid the foundation include "Hey Young World" by Slick Rick, "Be" and "The Light" by Common, "Thieves in the Night" and "Joy" by Black Star, "Hip Hop" by Mos Def/Yasiin Bey, "SpottieOttie-Dopaliscious" by Outkast, "I Can" by Nas, and "Love Is Blind" by Eve.

These tracks paved the way for "Jesus Walks" and "Kiss the Sky" by Kanye West, "I'm Beaming" and "The Show Goes On" by Lupe Fiasco, "Not Afraid" and "Lose Yourself" by Eminem, and "Moment for Life" by Nikki Minaj. Newer tracks include "Don't Wanna Be" by Jon Connor, "Hard to Choose" and "I Don't Need It" by Rapsody, "Life" by Big K.R.I.T., and "i" by Kendrick Lamar—a track that highlights the tethered links between identity, esteem, social identity, and community. A strong lineage of anti-drug songs exists too, from "White Lines" by Grandmaster Flash and the Furious Five, to "Pause" by Run DMC, to "Slow Down" by Brand Nubian setting the tone for future tracks.

THE HEALING POWER OF GROWTH

In Hip Hop's growth narratives, the move is from immediate gratification to longer-term goals and what can be. Life is viewed from a place of possibility and potential. At the same time, an increase in personal responsibility is taken for one's thoughts and behaviors. Attention exists to developing confidence through internal strengths and skills linked to futures oriented well-being. These growth narratives talk about maturing, being healthy and whole, and striving to reach one's potential. Although not universally the case, growth is often associated with less risky attitudes and behaviors. These growth narratives are a bridge to community narratives, including mentoring, being a role model for other, and being an upstanding member of prioritized communities.

MY LIFE, MY COMMUNITY

"You know I'm proud to be Black y'all and that's a fact y'all," Run DMC shouted on "Proud to Be Black." Along with "It's Like That," the song was one of the group's few overtly social or political statements on record. The track name-checked Harriet Tubman, Martin Luther King Jr., Malcolm X, George Washington Carver, Jesse Owens, and Muhammad Ali. It also spoke directly about hate in the context of slavery and discrimination.

When Hip Hop's narratives shift from being about "me and my story" to narratives about "we," "us," and "our story," things take a dramatic turn. As mentioned earlier, rap music has included a consistent discourse within *and* between race, gender, and class-based communities. Hip Hop's identity and esteem-oriented narratives are often drawn from solidarity with, or a lack of solidarity between given communities or social identities. These communities have cultural norms, histories, resiliency, and pride. Amid this is an awareness of and attentiveness to their community's conditions, circumstances, and well-being.

A community or social identity can relate to a range of group affiliations, from race, gender, and class, to family, team, neighborhood, spiritual affiliation, club, or gang/crew affiliation. It is any group that a person prioritizes, feels a sense of belonging to, draws strength from, has pride in, and feels he or she has a role in maintaining. To this end, in Hip Hop's musical canon, Kool G. Rap's "Streets of New York," Tupac and Dr. Dre's "California Love," and N.W.A.'s "Straight Outta Compton" fall in the same conversation as Common's "The People," Public Enemy's "Rebel Without a Pause," and other tracks like DMX's "Ruff Ryder's Anthem" and Wiz Khalifa's "We Dem Boyz." Locality has always been centralized in Hip Hop and it allows similarities to exist alongside uniqueness such as with tracks like "Empire State of Mind" by Jay Z and "Compton State of Mind" by Kendrick Lamar.

Nas spoke about what he viewed as his prioritized communities and his artistic obligation to these communities. He spoke of these communities as inspiration in the same way that Rakim did, but he also wanted to create art that spoke back to these communities. For Nas, it is a two-way relationship, especially with his immediate Queensbridge community:

My surroundings. The hip-hop community, also, and to be No. 1—the No. 1 emcee, the No. 1 rapper. Most of us are out to be the best. So that meant I made it for other rappers, I made it for other emcees, I made it for other hip-hop groups. I made it for artists, singers, people in the arts—that's who I made it for. But it comes from the street, so my surroundings wrote that album. I made it for them. It's the theme—it's the theme songs for my surroundings when I made that album, right. These albums was all written and produced by the streets, in a large sense.[7]

THE LEGACY OF ART AND COMMUNITY

When looking at the longer legacy of community that Hip Hop culture draws from, we see its intellectual and cultural roots in the Harlem Renaissance's "Niggerati" movement and the Black Arts Movement. The aforementioned Nina Simone is one of many exemplars in the Black Arts Movement. "Simone helped people survive. . . . She captured the warrior energy."[8] Her song "To Be Young, Gifted, and Black" helped cultivate a consciousness of self and the situation for Blacks. It went on to be designated by the Coalition of Racial Equality (CORE) as the Black national anthem.[9] This song and others helped redefine "Blackness" as a desirable attribute, the ultimate sense of belonging. This pride and energy from one's social identity is tethered to one's individual-level identity as well. Self-consciousness, esteem, and efficacy are embedded in these cultural narratives. These

[Black] Power and Arts movements are similarly tethered to contemporary Hip Hop culture, as sense of community and social identity remain prominent features of contemporary Black America.

REFLEXIVITY, BELONGING, AND PRIDE

Consistent reflexivity and within-culture existential moments are some of the most potent and unique aspects of Hip Hop culture. These are opportunities to build awareness and critique, not only of others but also of oneself—to look inward as much as outward. These are opportunities to share a sense of belonging, to enhance solidarity, and accentuate cultural strengths and assets. These are opportunities to support or contest cultural narratives. For example, in an interview with NPR, Nas reflected on how A Tribe Called Quest helped embed a street credibility and "coolness" to being Afrocentric.[10] As the Black Arts Movement has done in the past, Hip Hop culture continues this tradition of fostering a sense of community and introspection.[11]

BETWEEN-COMMUNITY TENSIONS: SAME THING MY NIGGA ELVIS DID WITH ROCK 'N' ROLL

Authenticity, as it relates to perceived cultural outsiders, is often connected to perceptions of misappropriation and co-optation of the culture.[12] J. Cole's lyrics on "Fire Squad" speak to this, as he talked about Elvis, Eminem, and Macklemore appropriating rock and Hip Hop. He ends with, "White people have snatched the sound. . . . Watch Iggy win a Grammy as I try to crack a smile."

Iggy Azalea, in the meantime, has been embroiled in her own bit of between-culture tension. Despite her incredible mainstream success in Hip Hop, as a White woman from Australia some people in the Hip Hop community labeled her a cultural outsider. Fellow Hop Hop artist Azalia Banks lashed out on Twitter at Azalea shortly after the Eric Garner decision in late 2014 for being insufficiently vocal about perceived injustices affecting the Black community. Azalea responded directly by encouraging Banks to focus her efforts on advocacy.

In an effort to quell the firestorm and offer Azalea some [Hip Hop] cultural context, Hip Hop legend Q-Tip, formerly of the group A Tribe Called Quest, offered his own response on Twitter. His writing appeared to be neutral in tone, geared toward increasing awareness of Azalea's situation. He seemed to have a goal of both cross-cultural (i.e., Black/White and US/Australian) and within-culture (i.e., Hip Hop culture) solidarity. Azalea's response did not seek to build bridges; she instead took offense and was resentful. At the same time, she gave some insight into her perspective on Hip Hop culture and her role in it. She stated she is "influenced by" Hip Hop; however, she is "blending musical genres" to produce "pop rap albums."

WITHIN-COMMUNITY TENSIONS

Along with any community's cultural pride and resiliency are the potential for tensions, dilemmas, and dialogues about circumstances, causes, symptoms, and solutions. It is these within-culture narratives that are particularly powerful when looking closely at the intersection of Blackness and Hip Hop culture. Here we find debates about identity, social environments, history, coping strategies, and ultimately the future well-being of Black America. It is the "Did you hear 'Black Skinhead' by 'Ye?" or, "What did you think of 'The Blacker the Berry' by Kendrick?"

The idea of belonging, instilling a sense of community, and strengthening solidarity is also of particular salience in the Black community because of a powerful within-culture tension of authenticity and "selling out" to further personal gain at the expense of the Black community.[13] One of Hip Hop's most ardent supporters accused his eventual partner of this at the onset of their relationship. "You're one of those handkerchief-head house Negroes. . . . You ain't got nothing to do with us Black Folks," a young Larry "Kris" Parker (later to be known as KRS-One) said to his eventual friend, Boogie Down Productions (BDP) co-founder Scott Sterling, AKA DJ Scott LaRock.[14] At the time, Sterling was a young social worker working at one of the shelters and group homes where the often-homeless Parker spent his time. Shortly after, after being dissed by Marley Marl of Queens, KRS-One and BDP embarked on creating two of the most community-centric anthems in Hip Hop history. BDP's "South Bronx" and "The Bridge Is Over," written in response to Marley Marl and MC Shan's "The Bridge" and "Kill That Noise," two classic odes to their own Queensbridge, New York community, will live forever in Hip Hop history.

TRILL (TRUE AND REAL) HIP HOP OR MINSTRELSY?

Tensions also exist around the overall intersection of Hip Hop culture and Black culture. Are the depictions, stylings, and caricatured representations of Blacks simply modern day minstrelsy? Remember, producers and patrons of minstrel shows that mocked and debased Blacks asserted "characters, songs, and dances were based on 'real' Black folkways and culture."[15] In minstrel-era productions, "Whites were mesmerized . . . as though they were on safari, journeying through a jungle world filled with Black half-human and half animal-like creatures who were as "savage" as they were sad."[16] It was these caricatures that were celebrated and sold to Whites (and non-Whites) nationally and internationally as authentic blackness.[17] In Hip Hop today, it is important to be aware of the similar risks within (perceived) empowerment via today's multicultural audiences interacting with Hip Hop's encoded messages and imagery. Even when repurposing imagery for empowerment and strength, the net result is still negative when those in positions of power and influence use them for dehumanizing purposes as Whites persisted to do with minstrelsy as part of popular culture in America. These tensions were captured thematically in Spike Lee's film *Bamboozled*, Little Brother's album *The Minstrel Show*, and Lupe Fiasco's video for the song "Bitch Bad."

(THEY DON'T KNOW) WHO WE BE: COMMUNITY CHALLENGES, STRESS, AND RESILIENCE

In his song "Who We Be," DMX included the audience in his authoring of the inner city Black experience, with the inclusive "They don't know who we be." He made it collective, especially with the choral call and response-like repetition of the phrase throughout the track. The song gives urgency to the need to add clarity about the social reality of Black life. Tracy Murrow's debut album, released in 1987, was the first Hip Hop record to have a parental advisory label. It followed in the tradition of Schoolly D., who many claim was the first truly explicit hardcore Hip Hop artist. The most popular single by Tracy Murrow, also known as Ice-T, was "6 in the Morning." The track shined a light on experiences and details that many residents of Black neighborhoods around Los Angeles could identify with—from the LAPD to the battering ram, street violence, prostitution, and jail.

As common, traumatic, and desperate as conditions often are, they rarely rise to a level of awareness that provides any impetus for change. According to William Cross, who tries to keep the details of these experiences in perspective, "Even though the lyrics of numerous Hip Hop songs try to convey the Faustian predicaments in which many Black males [and females] find themselves in everyday life, it often takes a particularly horrific event to raise the consciousness of the broader society."[18]

FEATURE: REVISITING THE MATTERING OF BLACK LIVES

The horrific event that inspired Cross's words above was the death of Derrion Albert in 2009. On that fateful September afternoon in Chicago,

Albert was killed during a fight sparked by youth affiliated with two different gangs. Although gang affiliation does not warrant assault or death in and of itself, Albert was not associated with any gang activity.[19] This event did register on the radar of broader society. In the wake of the public outcry and attention came a citywide mentoring program meant to help three thousand "at risk" youth in school and out of school.[20]

Another recent and tragic event may have been the tipping point, after a sequence of events to eventually raise the consciousness of broader society. On July 17, 2014, four New York Police Department officers forcibly apprehended unarmed 43-year-old Eric Garner in broad daylight. One officer used a chokehold forbidden by the department while the other three officers wrestled and pinned him to the ground. Garner repeatedly yelled, "I can't breathe" at least eleven times after being wrestled to the ground. He died minutes later. The New York City Medical Examiner's Office ruled Garner's death a homicide because the officer's actions were intentional in causing his death from "compression of neck (chokehold), compression of chest and prone positioning during physical restraint by police."[21] All of this was caught on video by an acquaintance of Garner on a cell phone.

Garner was reported by bystanders and himself to have just finished breaking up a fight on the street. Officers reported that they were responding to a report that he was selling loose cigarettes on the premises, a charge Garner denied. The footage, with clear audio and video, was circulated widely on television media and on social media. The grand jury decision was announced December 3, 2014, not to indict officer Pantaleo, who applied the chokehold that led to Garner's death.

THE DEVIL MADE ME DO IT

The Eric Garner grand jury decision came just a week after a similar decision for another nationally followed case of an officer involved shooting of an unarmed Black man. Michael Brown was eighteen years old when killed in Ferguson, Missouri. In this case, police officer Darren Wilson reported fearing for his life after an altercation inside his police vehicle where Brown had his hand on the officer's gun. Describing the incident to the grand jury, Wilson stated, "The only way I can describe it is I felt like a five year old holding on to Hulk Hogan." Wilson continued, "He looked up at me and had the most intense aggressive face. The only way I can describe it, it looks like a demon. . . . It looked like he was almost bulking up to go through the shots."

These types of descriptors are similar to what is called a "superhumanization bias." In their research, Adam Waytz and colleagues consistently found White respondents to show an implicit and explicit bias associating Black people with superhuman descriptors (e.g., ghost, paranormal, spirit, wizard, supernatural, magic, and mystical) in comparison to White people. At the same time respondents also reported Blacks less capable of performing everyday activities in comparison to Whites.[22] Finally, and relevant to the interaction between Wilson and Brown, these biases were also associated with the tendency to view Black people as experiencing less pain than Whites. In the study, this diminished recognition of pain was elicited by questions like "Which person is more likely to have superhuman skin that is thick enough that it can withstand the pain of burning hot coals?" Again, the grand jury decision was not to indict Darren Wilson for the death of Michael Brown. The United States Justice Department echoed the decision not to indict Wilson, citing a lack of evidence for criminal intent in their independent investigation.

The details of the Brown case are much less straightforward than the Garner case, with no video and a number of conflicting testimonies. However, critics said first and foremost that less lethal force could have been used as the unarmed Brown stood eight to ten feet away when the final shots were fired. Further, there was concern from the beginning about the ability of the district attorney to oversee the case fairly. The belief was that, at the very least, a possibility existed that the officer's actions were not warranted, something that could only be explored fully in a court of law.

Cases like those above and like that of unarmed Walter Scott, shot in the back and killed by a South Carolina police officer, must be understood in the context of an epidemic of police officer-involved killings of Black men and women.[23] These cases continue to pour salt in the collective wounds of the Black community. Wounds exist from the long-term legacy of killing and violence directed toward the Black community as well as the short-term as the country has yet to heal from the July 2013 failure to convict George Zimmerman in the death of seventeen-year-old Trayvon Martin. Martin was unarmed when Zimmerman, a self-appointed community security officer, shot him, saying that it was out of self-defense as he feared for his own life.[24] The premise of this case was supported by the state of Florida's "Stand Your Ground" law, which says there is no duty to retreat when one is under imminent threat of danger and that the use of deadly force is permissible. And although not involving an officer per se, the Trayvon Martin case was also very close in the collective memory of the Black community.

What made the Brown and Garner cases so unique and palpably unsettling in the wake of Martin's death was that their killers did not have to

stand trial. The take away from these cases for many, especially those identifying as part of the Black diaspora, was literally that Black lives do not
matter in the United States. This collective sentiment spawned widespread
support for the hashtag "#BlackLivesMatter" on Twitter. The moniker
Black Lives Matter and a new wave of protests, disruptions, and "die-ins"
have echoed around the United States as a mantra and bona fide social
movement to help raise awareness about the (new and old) Black experience in the country and spur meaningful change.

SPRINKLE SOME CRACK ON THEM

In the Black community, the contentious and potentially fatal relationship between law enforcement and Blacks has been a constant. It has been
explored in comedy, from Richard Pryor's 1979 *Live in Concert*, where he
talks first about how "[Police] don't kill cars, they kill 'nigg'ars" and follows
with "police got a chokehold they use out here . . . they choke niggas to
death," to Dave Chappelle's "sprinkle some crack on them" bits about fear of
the police during his 2000 *Killin' Them Softly* performance.

This subject has been explored in Hip Hop, from N.W.A.'s 1988 single
"Fuck tha Police" to the 2014 Michael Brown-inspired "Don't Shoot" by
The Game, Diddy, Rick Ross, 2 Chainz, Fabolous, and others. In 2015, after
the death of Freddie Gray, a young Black man, while in the custody of Baltimore's police department, Jasmine Sullivan created a stirring rendition of
Nina Simone's song "Baltimore." Prince recorded his own track "Baltimore"
also in response to the Gray death. An accompanying video to Sullivan's
version shows footage from Simone herself talking about the duty of artists
to give voice to the contexts within which they exist, footage from Civil
Rights–era tensions, and footage from Baltimore today.

Between Michael Brown's death and the recent death of Sandra Bland at
the hands of the criminal justice system, the Black Lives Matter movement
has emerged as a powerful voice against inconsistencies in law enforcement.
Between these bookends about law enforcement involved deaths, there has
been consistent attention to the disproportionate–involvement of the Black
community in the criminal justice system. Yet, these issues are often not
framed as system-level issues in broader society; they are framed as personal level failures that warrant excessive punitive and disproportionate
outcomes. Individual effort, behavioral discipline, violent tendencies, and in
some instances cognitive and intellectual deficits anchor the majority of
narratives around existing disparities in the criminal justice system.[25]

Hip Hop's ability to tap into these disparate trends for Blacks and the
criminal justice system, within a collective memory and narrative available

to the Black community, makes this an easy continuation of a cultural dialogue. It has the ability to both be cathartic and an opportunity to revisit an ongoing discussion with fresh eyes, distinct to a contemporary place in time. It is as much current as it is historic, and an activation of prior memories and images of Emmett Till, Malcolm X, Dr. Martin Luther King Jr., Trayvon Martin, and specifically those killed by law enforcement: Fred Hampton, Amadou Diallo, Oscar Grant, Kimani Gray, Sean Bell, Tamir Rice, Mike Brown, Eric Garner, Walter Scott, and Freddie Gray—to name just a few. Hip Hop culture provides context in a way that statistics alone cannot, in a way that privileges cultural knowledge, and in a way that taps into youth culture.

COMMUNITY RESILIENCE: NOW WE'RE HERE

Again, a sense of community and the associated feeling of belonging can exist from a wide range of social identities. For example, take the story of one young man who started from the bottom, similar to the personal narratives of resilience discussed earlier. In this instance, it was not just he alone; it was he and his whole team. Now, he and his whole team are here. Identifying where "here" is for Aubrey "Drake" Graham, or anyone else can be elusive. Yet for most it conjures up a similar idea and feeling of *making it*, that "come up" that James Peterson speaks of.[26] For each individual, this will look different, and his or her "team" will look different. It could be family; gender; friends; a team, club, or social group; a neighborhood; a spiritual community; or other interest group. For people identifying as Black, overcoming adversity is part and parcel of existence in the United States as members of the African diaspora.

Interestingly, Drake's narrative resonates even though his racial identity differs from the traditional Black U.S. citizen. He is from Canada and identifies as multiracial, with a Black father and White mother. In an interview with Jay Smooth, he responded to inquiries about his racial identity and why he identifies as "mixed" as opposed to "Black": "I think Canada's very accepting. But at the same time I get a lot of love everywhere in the world for just being diverse, instead of just being straight out [one thing]. I'm all mixed up and people embrace that." Regardless of Drake's racial identity, people can identify with the universality and urgency of *making it* while overcoming challenges.

Many in the Black community who feel persecuted in the United States link their identity to a history of slavery, disenfranchisement, and contemporary social and political oppression. The proverbial *bottom* is an appropriate moniker for how many people personally identify their circumstances, especially in lower-income communities. In fact, the label "bottom of the pyramid" is often given to those living in absolute poverty.[27] Poverty is one of the most common types of adversity reflected upon in Hip Hop, as are the challenging experiences connected to living in poverty.

However, this bottom can also be an emotional space exploring mood, workplace and employment struggles, school circumstances, community violence, law enforcement harassment, and family life (e.g., single parenting/home instability). All the cathartic "war stories" ring sweeter when there is a positive resolution. People respond quite differently to risk, stress, and adversity and there is no guarantee that things will turn out well.[28] Power exists when people respond to stress and adversity with success. At an extreme (traumatic adversity) this manifests as post-traumatic growth. Some people do well, while others do not. To be able to state that one weathered the storm and emerged with positive outcomes is significant. To be a part of a community that is weathering storms consistently prompts a desire for the storms to stop. It is from this point where change often begins.

Hip Hop's discourse on these issues does not have to be a grand sociopolitical commentary; they simply have to be relevant to the individual and their life stories. Listeners can connect, visualize, and reflect upon the similarities. They can be "transported" in their own unique ways.[29] Hip Hop taps into an array of life experiences, ups and downs, struggle and adversity, but also coping and triumph.

THE CANON, PAST AND PRESENT

Hip Hop's musical canon includes community narratives that capture the spirit of community solidarity, pride, strength, and power, along with collective coping and resiliency. As with all narratives, risk must be considered amid empowerment. Older Hip Hop tracks, as mentioned earlier, include songs like Kool G. Rap's "Streets of New York," Tupac and Dr. Dre's "California Love," N.W.A.'s "Straight Outta Compton," Public Enemy's "Rebel Without a Pause," Common's "The People," DMX's "Ruff Ryder's Anthem," and others like "Brooklyn's Finest by Jay Z and Notorious B.I.G., "Hip Hop Hooray" by Naughty by Nature, and "On My Block" by Scarface.

Tracks like "Life Is Good" by Mos Def/Yasiin Bey, "Black Girl Pain" and "Get By" by Talib Kweli, "I Used to Love H.E.R." and "The Corner" by Common, and "Family Tree" by Bone Thugs-N-Harmony are tracks that highlight group identities and collectivity while seeking to balance empowering and risky elements. Other tracks following these patterns include, "Harlem Streets" by Immortal Technique; "Mathematics," "Fear Not of

Man," and "Umi Says" also by Mos Def/Yasiin Bey; "My Clique" by Kanye West and guests; and "Empire State of Mind" by Jay Z and Alicia Keys. Newer tracks that are not yet part of Hip Hop's canon but reflect community themes include: "Some How Some Way" by Jon Connor, "Till I Die" by Machine Gun Kelley, "Every Ghetto" by Talib Kweli and Rapsody "Where I'm From" by Jezzy, and "The World" by Rapsody. To contrast, newer tracks with community narratives but higher-risk content include "Lifestyle" by Young Thug and Rich Homie Quan; "My Niggas" by YG, Jeezy, and Rich Homie Quan; and "We Dem Boyz" by and Wiz Khalifa.

THE HEALING POWER OF COMMUNITY

Although Hip Hop culture values individualism and allows people to represent themselves in uniquely creative and personal ways, it is as much about the cypher as it is the battle. Hip Hop culture values authentically representing your community, whatever it happens to be. Community narratives focus on collective experiences; they shift the focus from "me" to "we" or "you" to the collective "you all."

These narratives capture the way communities get their needs met. More specifically, they discuss unique traditions, skills, and activities that help its identifying members (1) grow, (2) overcome challenges and adversity, and (3) work toward change. Immense pride and a reinforcement of identity often takes place with this awareness. Worth noting is that these communities often magnify growth (*and* risky) experiences. While accountability increases for one's thoughts and behaviors, it is in the context of group experiences (e.g., What is my role as daughter in this family, as a quarterback on this team, a Black male in society, or as a member of this neighborhood?). These narratives encourage critical analysis of community histories to understand pathways needed to achieve better conditions.

Sometimes, along with this sense of belonging and collectivity comes a desire for better. Sometimes, community conditions are perceived to be unfair, or obstacles are found to stand in the way of these communities being at their best. However, awareness is only the first step. The major questions become "So what? What are you going to do about it? What role do you play in actual change?" Hip Hop has never been silent on issues of change, and shifting from solidarity and awareness to pressure for collective improvement is explored in the next chapter.

CHAPTER 7

A Change Is Gonna Come: Calls for Better across Black Communities

In an open letter to WorldStarHipHop.com creator Lee O'Denat posted online at Davey D.'s Hip Hop Corner, Universal Zulu Nation (UZN) Information Minister Quadeer Shakur took a stand for Hip Hop:

> Mr. O'Denat, the followers of your site are impressionable young men and women who "follow" you for a reason. As salacious as you may want your site to be, our youth are looking for answers and solutions to the many problems that plague our communities. The young people use your site as an outlet to escape the world they are living in, only to find that you place them right back at the starting point.

Ultimately, UZN's goal was to assert its pride in Hip Hop culture. It was also to affirm the boundaries of what it felt was a healthy representation of the culture. However, the organization also wanted to support efforts toward the long-term improvement of community conditions, not escapism. UZN identified a perceived injustice but also a vision for a new and better future for both the Hip Hop community and youth. It ended with a demand.

We are asking with all due respect that you include a disclaimer at the bottom of the front page of your website concerning your company and Hip-Hop Culture. A great footnote on your site should be: "World Star Hip-Hop is in no way affiliated with real Hip-Hop Culture or its founders or the Universal Zulu Nation. This site [is] solely for entertainment purposes, and does not promote Hip-Hop Culture."

Only follow-up and momentum can sustain these efforts by UZN to preserve aspects of Hip Hop culture; however, it is one step that others who feel the same about can choose to support, follow, and build upon. Change starts with taking a stand for collective improvement.

Hip Hop culture, following in the footsteps of earlier social movements, has a rich legacy of artists taking leadership roles in protesting, pressuring, and being advocates for social justice. Artists, from chart toppers to regionally specific independent artists, have taken the mantle to pressure for systematic improvements in psychological and material conditions at the root cause. These efforts contrast with short-term solutions of escapism. This chapter will touch on this range of artistry and narratives and highlight a few of the many prominent issues providing the impetus for change in the Hip Hop community, including community violence, disparate treatment by the criminal justice system, and the misogynistic treatment of women and girls.

AWARENESS VS. ACTION

The classic Hip Hop song "The Message" is infamous for its vivid details about community conditions so desperate that change feels like the only acceptable option. However, as noteworthy as the recording is, it was actually rejected by Melle Mel at first. "Preachy. . . . Don't nobody want to bring their problems to the disco," he said about the track in a 1992 interview with NPR before returning to say, "Man I got a verse that seems like it just go right with that record." The rest is history. People recite the first couple of verses, but it is the fifth verse that encapsulates the life course that ensnares so many Black youth. It begins with "God is smiling on you but he's frowning too. . . . Because only God knows what you'll go through," and continues to lay bare many of the challenges. In retrospect, that these issues were articulated so explicitly, emotionally, and consistently with today's longitudinal evidence about childhood risk and long-term well-being should make the best social scientists flush with envy.

But as much as "The Message" is referenced as a hallmark of consciousness in Hip Hop, the track is actually more about being aware of problematic conditions and less about change per se, exerting pressure, or direct action to change the root causes of these conditions. The first overtly "political" rap song affirming the Black community is believed to be Brother D and Collective Effort's 1980 track "How We Gonna Make the Black Nation Rise?"[1] It included lyrics like, "Unemployment's high, the housing's bad, and the schools are teaching wrong. Cancer from the water, pollution in the air but you partying hard like you just don't care." The track ends with verses filled with affirmations and racial pride and ultimately a call for collective action for change. Fast-forward several years to Public Enemy's "Fight the Power" and later "Shut 'Em Down," we hear different narratives, of protest and actual pressure to address disparate relations in the system.

This is where and why Hip Hop's narratives about the development of a social interest, a sense of belonging to communities, are essential. These are scaffolding on top of growth, because skills alone are limited in both Hip Hop and in life. A social relationship, service, mentorship—Hip Hop's value of "each one teach one"—are the pathways to community betterment. These are the narratives that bridge person and environment, *me* and *we*.

ME AND/OR WE? I AM NOT FREE UNTIL WE ALL ARE FREE

Revisiting Davey D. and KRS-One's 2005 dialogue about the almost unwritten contract between artist and listener about how to and what to appropriate from an artist's material is compelling, especially as it relates to narratives of change. KRS-One introduces a level of complexity about change, with simultaneous artist *and* listener change. Both artist and listener are on their own life-course growth timelines. This simultaneous maturation has yet to be formally introduced into the literature on the relationship between Hip Hop and well-being. How should listeners interact with art of artists when the artist is also seeking self-improvement on their own subjective scale of change, especially when their content reflects this development? KRS-One described his own journey using an analogy of matriculating through the U.S. educational system.

He stated that material from his early career, released during Hip Hop's so-called golden era, was the equivalent of first grade and learning his ABCs—necessary, but not sufficient. He equates his current artistic material and growth, including roughly 17 years of metaphysics, spiritual development, and knowledge attainment, as preparing for college and graduate school. KRS-One added that he is seeking empowerment by studying all of what life has to offer (e.g., across religious texts and philosophies), learning every day, and learning from everything. He emphasized that this personal growth is not at the expense of his commitment to Black people or his lifelong kinship and embodiment of Hip Hop culture, "I'll go to any hood and tear up anyone that claims to rep Hip Hop."

One example of KRS-One's maturity is his *Hip Hop Lives* project, a 2007 collaboration with producer Marley Marl. Remember, the track "South Bronx," officially released as a single in 1986 and featured on Boggie Down Production's debut album *Criminal Minded*, sparked the infamous conflict between the group Productions and Marley Marl's Juice Crew. When the song "The Bridge" came out in 1985, KRS-One felt his community of the Bronx was being slighted. He believed MC Shan was calling Queensbridge the birthplace of Hip Hop, as opposed to the birthplace of Shan and the Juice Crew.[2] In response, KRS-One came out with "South Bronx" and "The Bridge Is Over." Twenty years after the infamous "Bridge Wars," the collective growth and maturity of KRS-One and Marley Marl enabled them to put an end to one of Hip Hop's most famous conflicts.

In their conversation, KRS-One pointed out to Davey D. that individuals need to demand better lives for themselves and to say "I don't belong here in this situation" for their lives to improve. Davey D. responded that while some feel it is enough to personally "be free," he takes an alternative view, saying, "I am not free until we all are free." Davey D.'s challenge captures the difficulty of trying to balance the priorities of identity, growth, and community simultaneously.

THE STRUGGLES OF CHANGE: BLACK AND HIP HOP

The Black community and members of the Hip Hop community share a common struggle. Each struggles to reconcile its history in the United States while maintaining integrity and clarity about what desirable change looks like. Next is determining who is accountable for authoring these details and determining what to be proud of versus what to feel shame about. Is the strategy "by any means necessary" in response to the severity of the struggle? Or, is there greater value in taking the moral high ground in order to help anchor one's integrity?

Further, who do we support as leaders and why do we support them? For every ardent Black supporter of Barack Obama, there are Obama haters and detractors. For every Oprah Winfrey fan is an Oprah critic. For every Jay Z and Snoop Dogg fan is another that thinks it hypocritical to celebrate either of these men.

In the same way, the television show *Empire*, immensely popular in its first season, is lauded by many as a dynamic modern day soap opera—with a Black cast—but derided as stereotypic and buffoonery by others.[3] Its 5.1 rating made it the top show on the Big 4 networks in the important 18–49 demographic, averaging 13 million viewers, the best first season on any network since *Grey's Anatomy* in 2005. But even these numbers are misleading, as viewership has risen each week, and the show finished with a 6.9 rating and 17 million viewers, according to the Nielsen Company.

Similarly, since the earliest social movements working toward positive change for the Black community, for every advocate of non-violent civil disobedience is another suggesting change cannot come without a more direct and radical disruption of the system. Some were more vocal supporters of Reverend Dr. Martin Luther King Jr., some were more vocal supporters of Malcolm X, and some were more vocal in support of the Black Panther Party for Self Defense. Of course, there were also those who straddled the middle and found the commonalities among these change agents.

What is considered right, just, and authentic in the Black community varies widely depending on the audience. Honest critiques can be shunned as simply airing dirty laundry at one end of the spectrum. At the other end of the spectrum it may be considered blasphemous words out of the mouth of an Uncle Tom betraying the race. There are profound racialized fault lines within the Black community, and consequently Hip Hop as well.

HIP HOP NARRATIVES OF CHANGE: INNER AND OVER VIEWS

A long list of artists have spoken out on behalf of positive change within and for the Black community, and again for Hip Hop as a culture. Their goal has been to inspire better material conditions (i.e., positive and supportive relationships as much as equitable policies, procedures, treatment, and opportunities) for the Black community and the wider African diaspora. In some instances the target of change is the environment or system, while in other situations the target is the people. This is akin to the over view–inner view labels given to Chuck D. and Rakim respectively. As we consider how change narratives have operated in Hip Hop culture, it is wise to view them as both a progression of artistry over time and related to the four other dimensions of empowerment. Together, esteem, resilience, growth, community, and change are core values of Hip Hop culture—values that give the culture direction and purpose.

WE GON' BE ALRIGHT: HIP HOP'S NEWEST CHANGE AGENTS

While some might argue Hip Hop has lost its way, there is a need to look at both the artistic progression since the earliest waves of artists and the advancement in cultural identity within the music. Contemporary artists mastered the manipulation of Hip Hop's artifacts and continued to innovate in lyricism and production. However, these artists also learned and built upon the embedded values and narratives that allow the full exploration of knowledge of self as well as self and community improvement. These artists feel empowered as individuals, as members of the Hip Hop community and as part of the Black community. While still balancing society's tendency to rely on only two categories of Hip Hop (conscious vs. gangsta), these artists have continued to create material that falls all along a rich spectrum of empowering content. These newest artists are introspective as much as they critically analyze their environments. They allow themselves to be vulnerable and strong.

Lupe Fiasco, who hit the broader public radar in connection with his fellow Chicago native Kanye West, is a Hip Hop artist regularly mixing personal themes with social and political commentary. He has an incredible catalog of tracks that speak to each dimension of empowerment, along with powerful inner and over view-oriented change narratives. His second album, *Lupe Fiasco's The Cool*, follows the story of a young man with an estranged father who is raised by "the streets" and "the game," a personification of the situation that too many young people find themselves in. His most recent album, *Tetsuo & Youth*, is a brilliant piece of work, each track with layers of depth and complexity. It is as much a textbook as it is an artistic piece. Its depth and complexity may challenge its mainstream appeal, but its artistic, cultural, and empowering relevance is immense. From a change perspective it tackles both the inner and over view. Inner view issues like identity and coping exist alongside over view issues like the prison industrial complex, community violence, systemic changes in employment opportunities, arms trafficking, and the social welfare safety net.

On "Deliver," Lupe synthesizes the many issues associated with community need within "the ghetto." Now of course one would have to define and identify with "the ghetto" or "the hood" to embrace this narrative as relevant. Lupe states, "The ghetto is a physical manifestation of hate, and a place where ethnicity determines your placement . . . reminds you niggas your placement is the basement, white people your place is the attic." Like Jay Z once said about Public Enemy's records decades before, "You could name practically any problem in the hood and there'd be a rap song for you."[4]

Rapsody, a North Carolina emcee, has been in the game since 2006 with her original group Kooley High. She released her first solo mixtape in 2010, *Return of the B-Girl*, after signing with 9th Wonder. Another North Carolina native, J. Cole also joined the ranks of Hip Hop's stronger voices of change after being co-signed by Jay Z early in his career. Each of his three studio albums has reached the No. 1 spot on the Billboard Top 200 chart.

His third, *Forest Hills Drive*, debuted at No. 1 and was certified platinum within the first five months of its release in 2014.

This wave of more mainstream artists, and there are many more who are less mainstream, embody the best of Hip Hop's cultural gifts, respect for its artifacts and its values. The result is that in terms of pure Hip Hop artistry, late 2014 and 2015 has seen the continued release of culturally empowering albums: *To Pimp a Butterfly* (Kendrick Lamar), *Forest Hills Drive* (J. Cole), *Beauty and the Beast Deluxe Edition* (Rapsody), *An Album About Nothing* (Wale), and *Tetsuo & Youth* (Lupe Fiasco). These artists balance attention to the inner and over views, speak honestly and confidently about working to be at their best, but remix the strategies of their Hip Hop predecessors in innovative, individualized, and authentic ways. These artists have set the table for the incredible pool of New(est) School emcees like Dizzy Wright, Joey Bada$$, Mick Jenkins, Jidenna, Jon Connor, Chance the Rapper, and Oddisee.

THE INDEPENDENTS

As suggested, amid the different generations of Hip Hop's cultural change agents have been a bevy of independent artists who have not enjoyed as much mainstream success but have been critical to the continuity of the spirit of change buoyed by prior generation's political and social movements. James Peterson chronicles this spirit of the "underground" in Hip Hop culture well in his book *The Hip Hop Underground and African American Culture*. From OG-era groups discussed earlier, to more recent veteran artists like Immortal Technique, to newer independents like Jasiri X, Dee-1, John Connor, Mick Jenkins, and Rapsody today, an impetus for social change to improve the conditions of Black communities is clear.

Regional Emcees and Activists

Artists like Jasiri X, Rebel Diaz, and Tef Poe balance artistry and activism. Hip Hop culture is a passion and a vehicle for building awareness of disparities and mobilizing individuals and communities to work toward positive change. We will look at Jasiri X and Tef Poe a little more closely below. They are cited here as regional for their interest and actual work in local and regional issues as much as their broader social relevance. For example, on the one year anniversary of Mike Brown's death, both were part of the "Ferguson is Everywhere" concert in St. Louis to help inspire change, along with artists like Talib Kweli, Common, M1 of Dead Prez, Immortal Technique, Rapsody, Bun B., Rebel Diaz, and Pharoahe Monch.

Jasiri X is as much an emcee as he is a community advocate and activist. He is as concerned about excelling at his craft as an emcee as he is in using these skills to help young people develop, to build awareness and pride about Pittsburgh and the larger Black and Brown community, and to inspire others to work toward positive community change. He founded the 1Hood Media Academy to teach youth how to analyze and create media for themselves. In fact, in the spirit of identity, growth, and community, Jasiri X and his 1Hood collective recently made their own version of "Young, Gifted, and Black."

Similarly straddling the line of emcee and community activist, Kareem Jackson hones his craft while shedding light on the circumstances surrounding the Ferguson, Missouri, case of Mike Brown and the larger issue of injustice as it relates to law enforcement and the criminal justice system. Jackson, known as Tef Poe, emphasized the intersections of Hip Hop culture, change, and his individual role as person and artist: "I would personally consider myself a sellout if I didn't contribute something greater to the situation. . . . Hip-hop sets the tone for the hood. In certain pockets of St. Louis, I have more power than Barack Obama, so I have a responsibility."[5]

The Wisdom of the Elders and Young People's Energy

"No one can win the war individually, we need the wisdom of the elders and young people's energy," Common points out on the Grammy Award-winning song "Glory," his collaboration with John Legend that connects the Civil Rights Movement with present day social justice efforts. Following in the footsteps of the Student Nonviolent Coordinating Committee and its pioneering youth leaders like Julian Bond and Diane Nash, the current generation's youth-driven movements such as Black Lives Matter, Dream Defenders, and the Millennial Activists United (MAU) share a common underlying component. These organizations insist on immediate collective action for change, with younger people playing a prominent role. Ideas like disruption, disobedience, energy, and tangible results are prominent in their strategies, where the underlying sentiment is that the status quo is no longer acceptable and that present conditions must be changed.[6]

MAU is a Ferguson-area organization bolstered by an insistence for perceived justice in the wake of the death of Michael Brown as well as an emphasis on the intersection of gender in civic engagement. As MAU activists explained to The Feminist Wire, this women-driven movement seeks to integrate strategy and tactics from prior generations with a millennial voice and style for today's unique challenges. Implicit in this and what they seek to draw from is not only what the prior generation had to endure but also the "movement" background and mindset, while also appreciating the instrumental role of women. After a meeting between young activists and President Barack Obama, MAU co-founder Ashley Yates expressed her satisfaction that youth voices were being heard, that they could share the experience of being Black in an America that seemingly does not value their lives and criminalizes them. However, she also highlighted the urgency for meaningful policy changes, the Ferguson Action website reported.

However, some critics pointed out a disconnect between early and present generations of activists, specifically noting that in early Ferguson-related work Reverend Al Sharpton was never on the ground with Ferguson youth and neglected to speak with them when given the opportunity.[7] Sharpton and his National Action Network (NAN), who rejected these critiques, were also criticized during the National Justice for All March/Rally in Washington, DC, on December 13, 2014, for not providing sufficient opportunities for youth voices and youth organizers to be heard.[8] These generational divisions mirror Student Nonviolent Coordinating Committee (SNCC) and Mississippi Freedom Democratic Party (MFDP) tensions in deeply segregated Mississippi, with state-sponsored murder, assault, terrorism, and economic discrimination against Black residents.[9] These types of generational divisions also mirror Harlem Renaissance-era tensions between the perceived Old and New Negro.[10] Finding that balance of knowledge and spirit alongside the constant specter of respectability politics is a continual task in change efforts.

WHO YOU CALLING A BITCH?

"Don't be calling me out my name . . . U.N.I.T.Y. means a Unity," Dana Owens, also known as Queen Latifah, said on her track "U.N.I.T.Y." With these words and with the literal title of "Queen," she ushered in a new era of positive focus on women in general, but Black women more specifically. The track was about disrespect in calling a woman a bitch, but the track was also about male-initiated intimate partner violence, and female-on-female violence. Although filled with anger and resentment at the perceived suffering girls and women had to endure, the track was also a bit of an olive branch with a vision toward positive collective change among young men and women.

Latifah was the archetype within mainstream Hip Hop for the feminist, political, and culturally empowering Black women image during the so-called conscious era of Hip Hop. At the time of "Ladies First" many Hip Hop crews had a female member. Many, including MC Lyte, Roxanne Shante, and Yo Yo had agendas championing power and strength, while some had community-oriented and explicitly race and culture-promoting identities like Isis and Ms. Melody. Depending on the cultural identity of their crew, women differed in their public gendered and racial identities. For example, X-Clan had Isis, who had a decidedly Afrocentric orientation, and Boogie Down Productions had Ms. Melody with a more U.S.-oriented nationalism. Despite many women being affectionately called queens in the Black community, there was only one Latifah, and she did her best to put "Ladies First." Other classic tracks championing women and solidarity in Hip Hop's canon include Lauryn Hill's "Doo-Wop (That Thing)," Eve's "Love Is Blind," and "Ladies Night" by Lil' Kim, Angie Martinez, Left Eye, Da Brat, and Missy Elliott.

Young, Female, and Black for Change: Fists Up, Fight Back!

Girls and women may be showing up for distinctly disruptive efforts in dealing with present struggles for change. In an interview with Al-Jazeera, Erika Totten, a Washington DC-area parent and activist suggested, "For actions that are actually being disruptive, and shutting things down, its Black women that are organizing, planning, and leading these actions." She cites the potential for less ego, better communication skills, and a more collective spirit among women to be important ingredients for their effectiveness. "We can connect with our sisters in knowing that this is my sister. What happens to her, happens to me," Totten said, sounding a little like Davey D. in his discussion with KRS-One mentioned earlier.

In 2004, a Spelman College student group's concern about Nelly's "Tip Drill" grew from a mild whisper of consternation to a loud roar across the nation. Spelman College is a historically Black college for women, and its protest of the song and video was connected to the track's overtly explicit and exploitive messages and images about women. The protest led to a boycott of Nelly's bone marrow drive event at the college. Interestingly, he has since been vocal about his resentment of their protests, saying in an interview with the Huffington Post that the mission of the bone marrow drive, including a match for his sister, was of greater priority than what he believed to be the objectives and merit of the protest.

Shouting from the Margins

Many conversations about the female community in Hip Hop culture take a back seat to conversations about Black males. In fact, at times it appears that to assert freedom and positive changes to the welfare of the Black community, ignoring and thus reifying oppression and exploitation of

Black women is necessary.[11] But there are real concerns specific to women and girls in general, and Black women and girls specifically, reflected in contemporary voices for change. And many contemporary voices continue the traditions of Hip Hop feminists like Queen Latifah and Toni Blackman. They follow in the footsteps of the black blues queens and clubwomen like Ma Rainey and Bessie Smith. These women lived by the principle "Lift as We Climb" so that sharp gender-nuanced protest and critique exists within the same vision of growth for all.[12]

Joan Morgan helped crystallize this for the Hip Hop generation in her quintessential inquiry into the age-old debate around examination of feminist ideals within Hip Hop culture that is ripe with oppressive and marginalizing representation of women and girls, writing that "Hip Hop and feminism are not at war but my community is. And you [Hip Hop] are critical to our survival."[13] She views black-on-black love to be the fundamental principle that links an effective agenda that simultaneously privileges and prioritizes the well-being of Black women and the Black community and Hip Hop culture as a vehicle for reclaiming hegemonic spaces and reframing identities and communities on her/your/our own terms.

#AllWomen

The newest generation of change agents have broadened the list of priorities to use Hip Hop culture and Hip Hop culture-inspired cultures as vehicles for all women of color and all perceived marginalized communities, anchoring efforts in global change. For example, Natalie Crue and Nora Rahimian engage in their own personal and professional work linked to social good, but they also collaborate on a project called #CultureFix. Crue has a strong history of social justice work and community activism.

Iranian-born Rahimian, who saw social struggle firsthand, affirms Hip Hop culture's ability to help negotiate social identity, not least her own. Speaking on The Starting Five Live show on Rap Station radio, she described #CultureFix as "a network of artists, and cultural producers, and change makers and activists from around the world who are using their art and culture for social change." Although great strides were being made, its followers found that many people around the world were working in silos. Rahimian said that the solution she proposed with Crue was to "create [#CultureFix] a platform where they can support each other's work, share victories, reach out for resources, and just create a globally connected group of amazing people doing really good work." On the state of Hip Hop, both emphasized that Hip Hop culture's most active voices and talents are actually thriving, and that people must not be misguided by limiting their own awareness of the culture to what is presented in the mainstream.

Changing What Exactly? Misogyny and Sexualization of Girls

In its simplest terms, the current circumstances for women and girls are better than ever. The newest young women entering the workforce are better educated than young men of the same age, and also better educated than their mothers or grandmothers at the same age, according to 2013 data from the Pew Research Center. For women ages 25–34, earnings were 93 percent of men's earnings in 2012. Yet at the same time the status quo is unacceptable. The gap still persists for women, which remains a problem in general. However, in 2013 Black women only earned 64 percent of what white men earned and substantially less than White women, according to U.S. Census Bureau data. The intersectionality of gender and race around income helps to pinpoint the need to keep pushing for gender equity in legislation, in our media and our conversations. The systemic inequities present in policies, media representation, and cultural norms are deeply troublesome. Hip Hop has been a constant reflection of these person-environment dynamics since its earliest days.

Tupac's "Keep Ya Head Up," released in 1993, was the perfect example of the intersectionality of race, gender, and class, but it privileged gender as the vehicle to get the conversation started and validate the uniquely female experience. It came in the wake of the 1992 Los Angeles riots and the killing by a female Korean American store clerk of Black fifteen-year-old Latasha Harlins, whom the video was dedicated to. Stevenson deftly argues that although racial and social tensions in South Los Angeles have been high since before the 1965 "riots," the Harlins case was the underlying spark to the 1992 unrest.[14] But "Keep Ya Head Up," from its dedication to Harlins, shined a bright light on the experiences of, more than the abstract statistical presence of, female-headed households, welfare recipients, harassment, victimization, sexual assault, and the right to choose (abortion). Ultimately, it is a plea to endure the cumulative stressors and to be resilient.

The concept of misogyny, or the systematic degrading, exploiting, and sexualizing of women and girls is not a Hip Hop issue but a societal issue. Thus, initiatives to improve conditions for women and girls and to eliminate misogyny must begin with wider society. The GrassROOTS Community Foundation (GCF) understands this and commits its work toward public health social action so that women and girls can enjoy the best social environment possible to live, work, and play. GCF, co-founded by Dr. Janice

Johnson and Tariq "Black Thought" Trotter (of Hip Hop group The Roots), focuses on communities considered to be at a disadvantage because of higher rates of poverty, food insecurity, crime, female-headed households, and health disparities. Its work includes educating and translating important public health information, supporting meaningful wellness initiatives, supportive community-based volunteering and organizing, and advocacy with local stakeholders and policymakers to improve the community.

A healthy, inclusive, and equitable social environment improves the odds of individual-level health and well-being. It is within this context that uniquely Hip Hop initiatives can promote well-being inside and outside of Hip Hop culture. Legendary emcee MC Lyte's Hip Hop Sisters Foundation bridges these two worlds to promote "positive images of women of ethnic diversity, bringing leaders from the world of Hip Hop, the entertainment industry, and the corporate world," according to the foundation.

The American Psychological Association (APA) Task Force on the Sexualization of Girls examined theory, research, and clinical practice to better understand the influence and prevalence of media and cultural messaging that sexualizes girls. The issue of sexualization of women and girls is a major concern among Hip Hop's most vocal critics. At the lesser end of the spectrum, sexualization is "sexualized evaluation," and at the most extreme end is sex-related trafficking and abuse. Concerns exist about the psychological impacts of increased sexualization of women and girls, such as self-objectification or internalizing a need to be evaluated by others. Concerns about sexualization exist for boys and men as well, as the resulting attitudes and behaviors can influence every aspect of and type of relationship, from friendship, to intimacy, to partnership, to satisfaction with partners, according to an APA report.[15]

Complexions

Across the landscape of Hip Hop culture, the voices shedding light on exploitive lyrics toward women are often masked. They are hidden underground. However, evidence suggests that exposure to pro-social or "pro-equality" lyrics in music can help improve attitudes and behaviors toward women.[16] Thus any suppression of these messages, deliberate or not, perpetuates inequity and bias. One of the more lyrically potent contemporary artists wearing a badge of femininity on her sleeve while expressing the need for change is the artist Rapsody. Despite being on the scene for more than eight years, her biggest mainstream buzz has come from appearing on a verse on uber-popular emcee Kendrick Lamar's album *To Pimp a Butterfly*.

In her verse on the track "Complexion (A Zulu Love)," Rapsody not only gives a nod to Tupac's homage to Black women in "Keep Your Head Up," she makes a powerful statement about colorism and skin tone, an issue that is prominent between races and ethnicities as it is within them. Hip Hop has many precedents on the issues of identity and appearance, including specific attention to complexion and appearance such as Black Star's "Brown Skin Lady" and Dead Prez's "The Beauty Within."

More rigorous research evidence of color and skin tone bias has emerged as it relates to differential treatment within schools and other settings, when before it was only anecdotal and accepted as conventional wisdom by those most directly affected.[17] In an interview with BET.com about her track with Kendrick Lamar, Rapsody shed light on her thinking about the issue:

We, Blacks, are still suffering the effects of slavery when it comes to colorism. There is divide within our culture between darker and lighter Blacks that says if you're lighter, you're thought to be smarter and more attractive. If you're darker, you're not as smart or beautiful. There are millions of Blacks around the world, not just here in America, who are purchasing bleaching cream to fit into the European standard of beauty. . . . It's important for everyone still struggling with it today, and so the ones coming up hopefully won't have to deal with it.

RISKS INHERENT IN CHANGE: NOT ALL IDEAS OF POSITIVE CHANGE ARE CREATED EQUAL

John Huppenthal, Tucson (Arizona) Unified School District's superindendent of public instruction, filed a Notice of Noncompliance against the district about the use of songs by musicians Rage Against the Machine and KRS-One in the school's curriculum. The letter argues that these materials promote the overthrow of the United States government, resentment toward a race or class of people, and ethnic solidarity. Huppenthal cited an Arizona law created in 2010 to prohibit ethnocentric courses, such as Mexican/Chicano studies and African American studies. The legislation in question is House Bill 2281, Sections 15–111 and 15–112. Section 15–111 states: "The legislature finds and declares that public school pupils should be taught to treat and value each other as individuals and not be taught to resent or hate other races or classes of people."

There is much to critique about the assumptions and implications of the legislation, but that is beyond the scope of this book. However, at its most basic, this challenges efforts that seek to strengthen a sense of community and build opportunities to critically analyze communities and societies for identifying areas in need of change. Legislation section 15–112 continues to state: "A school district or charter school in this state shall not include in its program of instruction any courses or classes that include any of the following: (1) Promote the overthrow of the United States government, (2) Promote resentment toward a race or class of people, (3) Are designed primarily for pupils of a particular ethnic group, and (4) Advocate ethnic solidarity instead of the treatment of pupils as individuals."

Complicating things is that these are subjective interpretations of course content, adding to the complexity of how to interpret another person's interpretation of lyrics as a component of coursework. Further, if a range of perspectives are offered in a course—as text to critique and analyze—how should this be evaluated? Further, if the other elements are there but there is no existing organized movement toward the overthrow of government, does it matter? If a component of identity development involves assessing one's situation historically and in the present where the evaluative result is resentment of other's behaviors believed to play a role in this situation, how does this factor into education? The legislation is supposed to exclude a critical analysis of oppressive societal conditions, but the aforementioned conclusions may be the results of this critical analysis.

Rejecting elements of culturally responsive education when research highlights its effectiveness is a challenge. Racial and ethnic solidarity, along with gender solidarity, familial solidarity, and school athletics and team sports, are each an opportunity to build a sense of belonging and to reinforce positive development. Each of these dynamics are highlighted in research for its own sake and also as a buffer within systems perceived as alienating and oppressive.[18] Thus this type of legislation has many challenges in the face of existing social science research.

If uncontested, it is a precedent that challenges Hip Hop–integrated strategies within education because it limits the types of artists and art used, it is inconsistent with culturally responsive and critical pedagogies, and it conflates solidarity with divisiveness and disorder. Educators should be able to have significant flexibility in use of content but ensure that critical analysis is always a core feature of the pedagogical process. This should be the case in general, but it specifically relates to cultural responsiveness as well. We will discuss this in more depth in Chapter 10 (Hip Hop and Education), but a significant part of more culturally inclusive teaching includes bringing in more of student's cultural and social environment as pathways to learning. The conflation of solidarity with divisiveness and disorder will be discussed more in the following section.

"YOU GUESS I'M JUST A RADICAL"

Historically, concern about predominantly Black groups expressing solidarity and a desire for self-determination have been associated with surveillance and group infiltration in the United States, such as the FBI's COINTELPRO counterintelligence program, which targeted so-called Black nationalists. Since the early 1900s, they were either truly perceived as or framed as gangs, extremists, and hate groups. Most notably, Marcus Garvey, the Nation of Islam, Clarence 13x (founder of the Nation of Gods and Earths) and the Black Panther Party for Self Defense promoted nationalist ideals in the last century. All of them were seen as dissidents, and government-sponsored counterintelligence operations were waged to deliberately disrupt or extinguish these groups. Documents from the FBI specifically said the program was to "expose, disrupt, discredit, or otherwise neutralize the activities of . . . organizations and groupings, their leadership, spokesmen, membership and supporters and counter their propensity for violence and civil disorder."

Like education that promotes solidarity and self-determination, Hip Hop culture's history of protest and social change, which follows in the footsteps of nationalist ideals and the Black Power and Black Arts movements, bear the scarlet letter of suspicion and surveillance. Despite similarities in racial pride, attention to cultural strengths, the desire for better, and strategies of protest for change, nationalist efforts are most often contrasted with more active cross-cultural bridge builders like Reverend Dr. Martin Luther King Jr. However, Dr. King too was targeted and investigated. In 1999, after the U.S. Department of Justice stated there was insufficient evidence for criminal charges, the Circuit Court of Shelby County, Tennessee, found otherwise in a civil case. The local, state, and federal government, along with the mafia, were found to be deeply involved in the assassination of the Reverend Dr. Martin Luther King Jr. The jury found Loyd Jowers participated in a conspiracy to do harm to Martin Luther King Jr., with others, including governmental agencies. Evidence suggests that the Department of Homeland Security is similarly monitoring the Black Lives Matter movement and leadership as in these earlier change efforts.

THE CANON, PAST AND PRESENT

The tracks continually being added to the canon of Hip Hop music seek to capture the spirit of critical analysis, awareness of opportunities for improvement, and action toward creating better community conditions. These voices of change are directed within at fellow community members and externally toward system level changes. Again, a wide range of social identities and communities are prioritized in these songs. Tracks like "Fight the Power," "Shut Em Down," and "Can't Truss It" by Public Enemy, "Self Destruction" by The Stop the Violence Movement, and "We're All in the Same Gang" by the West Coast All-Stars paved the way for later tracks like "Changes" and "Keep Your Head Up" by Tupac, "Stakes Is High" by De La Soul, "Point of No Return" by The Geto Boys, and "It's Bigger Than Hip Hop" and "They Schools" by Dead Prez. Further still are tracks like "Point of No Return" by Immortal Technique, "Why?" by Jadakiss and Anthony Hamilton, and "Respiration" by Black Star featuring Common, that, like "Changes," deftly capture the connection between community and change.

Over the last several years, tracks included "Words I Never Said" and "Around My Way" by Lupe Fiasco, "HiiiPower" by Kendrick Lamar, "Dear Chicago Summer" by Chance the Rapper, "Eyes Wide Open" by Rapper Big Pooh, "Don't Let Them Get Away With Murder" by Jasiri X, "Don't Shoot" by The Game and Various Artists, the nontraditional "Be Free" by J. Cole, and the *Selma* movie-inspired "Glory" by Common and John Legend.

THE HEALING POWER OF CHANGE

Hip Hop's change narratives are about how people can use their voices and talents with others to make their communities the best they can be. They not only capture how community challenges are experienced but also the perceived causes and strategies for improvement. The full range of these narratives is used for empowerment so that individuals can take on a leadership role to improve conditions in their communities. There is recognition of organizing, planning, and using teamwork to achieve the desired vision of change. These narratives identify sources of inspiration and support for efforts toward change; often they are embedded in examples of community resilience and prior civic engagement.

Even though identity and culture are integral to personal development, health, and well-being, it took much longer to be recognized as such in formal professional circles. Seeing the arts as a component of both culture and well-being also took time, and Hip Hop specifically took even longer. Individuals who have used Hip Hop's artifacts and values to propel self and community improvement have created a foundation for current efforts. Hip Hop's cultural ambassadors of today lead professional efforts in physical health, education, out-of-school time (OST) programming, and mental health that help to both create and realize Hip Hop's healing power. Their groundbreaking efforts and their extraordinary voices will be explored in more depth in the following chapters.

CHAPTER 8

From Emotions to Learning and Growth: New Models for Understanding Hip Hop

The integration of Hip Hop culture into structured efforts to promote well-being can be summed up with two basic questions individuals can ask themselves: What can I learn? How can I grow? Learning can refer to anything from academic concepts and ideas to healthy nutrition and physical activity tips. Growing can mean identity development or it can mean an increased sense of belonging. As we move from understanding "what" Hip Hop culture is and how its values of improvement and getting "better" can be achieved through the use of Hip Hop's artifacts, we can turn to the specific settings and specific measurable outcomes we expect to see. At the same time, we can hear some of the voices intimately involved in bringing those outcomes to life.

The following four chapters review these settings and accentuate these voices from the perspectives of some of Hip Hop's new cultural ambassadors. First, however, it is necessary to revisit what we have covered and provide proper context for these settings and voices. The initial chapters provided an overview of Hip Hop culture, its artifacts and values, Black identities, the ascension of Hip Hop into the mainstream, and its history as a renewable, natural resource for well-being, including its developmental narratives. The subsequent chapters explored these narratives of esteem, resilience, growth, community, and change through the lens of Hip Hop culture's musical canon. These narratives and the vast library of material spanning decades embody Hip Hop's cultural values and have been shown to be empowering forces for self and community improvement.

The range of theoretical approaches, interdisciplinary perspectives, and general interest in music and well-being have generated a crowd of voices in this field.[1] To help anchor the remainder of the conversation in this book and unify some of the ideas about music and well-being, four frameworks will be integrated: (1) Brynjulf Stige's version of "health musicking" in dramaturgical terms, (2) Stefan Koelsch's framework of music-evoked emotions,[2] (3) Raphael Travis and Anne Deepak's (2010) individual and community empowerment (ICE) framework,[3] and (4) Raphael Travis and Tamara Leech's (2014) empowerment-based positive youth development (EMPYD) perspective.[4]

To help understand how music (and other elements of Hip Hop) helps trigger learning and growth, these perspectives are represented by three main concepts (Figure 8.1): Music Interaction, Music-Evoked Emotions, and Well-Being.

The first concept of music interaction, also discussed as "health musicking," is shown by the contexts of interaction—everyday listening, self-health, and professional situations—as well as how these contexts intersect with Hip Hop's narratives of esteem, resilience, growth, community, and change.

MUSIC INTERACTION: HEALTH MUSICKING AND HIP HOP

First, Stige's version of "health musicking" in dramaturgical terms uses the experiencing of and interpretation of music in sociocultural contexts. He defines health musicking as "the appraisal and appropriation of the health affordances of: arena, agenda, agents, activities, and artifacts."[5] It is important to recognize that these musical opportunities can be empowering or risky in their individual level experiences or in their systematic

Figure 8.1. Musical Pathways to Well-Being

appropriation.[6] Finally, Stige's caution about overemphasizing the "conscious goals" or "cognitive aspect" of musicking is a perfect segue into the value of the second concept of music-evoked emotions.[7] In other words, evocations of emotions are not always from deliberate experiences or the purposeful appropriation of art.

MUSIC, EMOTION, AND HIP HOP

The second part of the model is Koelsch's framework of music-evoked emotions.[8] The breadth of its conceptual applicability contrasts with other models about mediating mechanisms that arouse emotion, such as the BRECVEMA framework from Patrik Juslin and colleagues.[9] Instead, this framework is based on interacting with (creating or responding to) music in (1) everyday, (2) health-musicking, and (3) professional therapeutic situations. More specifically, the framework is about understanding the evocation, modulation, and termination of emotions and moods in these musical interactions.

Guiding the framework are seven principles of how people interact with music, recognizing that it is not deterministic and that people have a role too in how it is appropriated. The principles include: *evaluation, resonance, memory, expectancy/tension, imagination, understanding,* and *social functions. Understanding* and *social functions* of interacting with music are two principles not found in other frameworks.[10] Each of these principles is especially valuable for considering the mechanisms involved in receiving and producing Hip Hop's powerful narratives, and the complex skills needed to engage Hip Hop's artifacts.[11] Although discussed discretely, these principles likely overlap in their evocation of emotions.

Evaluation is whether or not one believes the music helped achieve the goal of its use. Did it meet its perceived functional value? Its favorability is therefore context-specific and depends on if it "worked," often in relation to emotional regulation.[12]

Resonance refers to listeners mirroring the emotional experience that they perceive cognitively and physiologically. This includes feelings like happy and sad, along with more complex ones like empathy.[13] This principle connects directly to the hallmark characteristics of Hip Hop's narratives, which are the brilliant presentations of people's stories and the ability to give voice to the voiceless. The resulting narratives give people a safe emotional space to identify with and explore sensitive issues.

Memory is the principle that speaks to nostalgic and autobiographical memories that are often evoked through musical interactions.[14] In Hip Hop, while applicable to all dimensions, these have particular relevance to the esteem, resilience, and community narratives where stories and identities are such a critical feature.

Expectancy and tension are the specific sonic musical properties associated with certain emotional responses. This has to do with acoustics, continuity, structural inconsistency, rhythmic balance, and the ability to predict subsequent sounds. These sound features, beats, and overall musicality within Hip Hop are believed to have independent influences on how people experience music.[15]

Imagination has to do with the emotional effects of thinking outside the box.[16] Consider songs in Hip Hop's musical canon like "If I Ruled the World" by Nas and "I Wonder if Heaven Has a Ghetto" by Tupac. We can label one facet of the imagination component as the *Hook Gestalt* because of our ability to create an entirely new meaning for a song by imagining ourselves within our own unique story, anchored by our subjective interpretation of the song's hook (or chorus).

Imagination extends beyond the emotional mirroring of resonance because of the activation of imagery or mental movies. This principle is relevant to Hip Hop's narratives of esteem, resilience, and community for its "story" to resonate. However, imagination is also applicable to growth and change narratives because listeners are imagining what the best versions of themselves and their communities can be, impacting self and community improvement. Resilience narratives are applicable as well, as listeners entertain ideas of thriving as opposed to constantly being in survival mode.

Understanding is one of the two new principles introduced by Koelsch, along with social functions. The understanding principle may mean recognizing moments in the music's structure, such as the resolution of tension, or in the case of Hip Hop, recognizing samples and breaks, or comprehending metaphors and similes. It can also be an understanding of the overall theme, intent, or motive behind the song. These moments of clarity and understanding are associated with feelings of reward.[17] From the standpoint of Hip Hop's narratives, these moments of understanding can correspond to any pairing of the music themes with goals of improvement, which happens when the listener makes an emotional connection that opens a pathway to becoming better.

Social Functions are the powerful emotional elements found in engaging music. The need for connection and belonging by people is aided by music. At its most basic, music can be social via listening or music-making with others, including coordination and cooperation.[18] Each Hip Hop narrative is relevant here, but of particular interest are esteem, growth, and community. Esteem refers to narratives of seeking to experience fun and joy. Growth is built on attempts toward self-improvement, including making connections with others and developing a greater sense of community belonging. Community is that sense of greater belonging, the feeling of solidarity, and collective pride and strength one feels in a social group.

THE BETTER PRINCIPLE AND EMPOWERMENT-BASED WELL-BEING

The third part of the model is the individual and community empowerment (ICE) framework and the empowerment-based positive youth development (EMPYD) model. The ICE framework recognizes five dimensions of empowerment that shape the musical experience and the functions and goals of engaging Hip Hop culture, whether it is in everyday life or in learning and growth settings with professionals. As they have been since Hip Hop's origins, the value-driven dimensions of esteem, resilience, growth, community, and change can be empowering to individuals and the communities they are a part of.[19]

The EMPYD model represents well-being, or the operationalization of self-improvement. It is measured by seven interrelated dimensions (Figure 8.2). These are indicators of healthy development. The key features of this model are its interrelated dimensions, specific reinforcing pathways that also coalesce into unique features of well-being like mastery and morality. On top of this is the critical role of belonging and community that amplifies each of these domains that already exist within feedback loops.[20] The empowerment dimensions of the ICE framework and the youth development indicators of the EMPYD model have specific conceptual connections that allow excellent opportunities for measuring health and well-being implications.[21]

When combining these models, we have an incredibly robust opportunity to explore experiences with Hip Hop culture in everyday life, as a technology of self, and in a range of professional settings. We can pay attention to what is empowering and what is risky. We can look closely at the specific mechanisms, both physiological and cognitive, of how emotions and other short-term reactions are produced, as well as implications for longer-term health and well-being.

REVISITING THE MUSICKING EXPERIENCE

Artifacts

In general, individuals (agents) use artifacts for musicking or experiencing music.[22] In this book, we are concerned with how people engage with Hip Hop's cultural artifacts, categorized before as primary, secondary, and

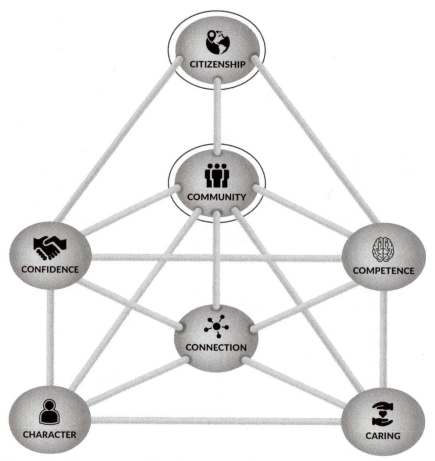

Figure 8.2. Empowerment-Based Positive Youth Development as an Indicator of Well-Being

tertiary. This does not mean one group of artifacts is more or less important. They are just different. In summary, the first group of artifacts available for use are the material grist for the mill used by Hip Hop's five elements: the microphone, turntable, DAW, break, sample, paint, stencil, and other singular items creatively manipulated. Secondary artifacts are the aesthetics of the culture that guide its potential energy, such as the cypher, battling, sampling and looping, flow, layering, remixing, digging, call and response, and communication and language.

Tertiary artifacts are produced within the culture but can themselves be reorganized in the same manner as primary artifacts—through the aesthetics of the culture—to create newer, more complex and creative pieces that contribute to knowledge of self and improvement. These include beats, hooks, lyrics, mixtapes, throw ups, pieces, and [dance] moves. These are collectively the tools of engagement in Hip Hop culture, allowing for a complex array of opportunities for experiencing music. Specific artifacts have particular connotations but are interpreted in myriad ways, which help guide what, where, and how things are appropriated and experienced.[23]

Arena

The arena is the context in which musicking, or engaging of artifacts, occurs.[24] This may be a part of everyday listening or take place within a professionally led setting. Even in everyday listening, one can experience music in different contexts: at home, in a vehicle, at work, outdoors, or in a shop of some sort.[25] In the following chapters, we add the professional arenas of education, out-of-school time (OST), physical health, and mental health to everyday listening and health-musicking (Figure 8.3).

Everyday listening and health-musicking can also merge with each professional arena as outside musical experiences can reinforce professional mediated experiences and vice versa. Similarly, each arena can overlap with other arenas. For example, when interdisciplinary objectives are sought, such as *learning and growth*, it occurs through an overlap between education and mental health arenas.

Agents

Agents include any person involved in the experiencing of music, from an individual listener to a helping professional.[26] This book is concerned with how individuals interact with music—particularly youth and Hip Hop—and the range of professionals that help with these interactions in education, physical and mental health, and out-of-school time (OST) settings. For example, to help in the area of mental health, these professional agents might be social workers, music therapists, counselors, or psychologists.

Agenda

The agenda is the "evolving issues, goals, and themes as conceived consciously and unconsciously by the participants" of the musicking experience.[27] In relation to Hip Hop culture, this includes the overarching value of improvement and its dimensions of esteem, resilience, growth, community, and change as discussed in prior chapters (Figure 8.4). The underlying val-

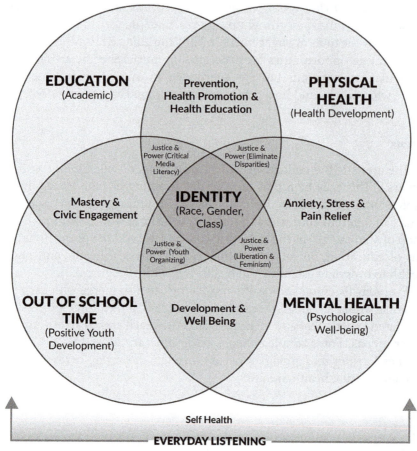

Figure 8.3. Contexts and Goals (Arenas and Agendas) for Music Experiences

ues and themes—including individuality, authenticity, survival, mentorship, unity, and resistance—are all manifest in the agenda.

Activities

Activities are the ways in which people engage with the music, whether active or receptive, creating or listening/interpreting.[28] In relation to Hip Hop culture and this overarching model, this refers to any form of engagement with Hip Hop's cultural artifacts. It could be in the form of digging for samples, blending "C.R.E.A.M." by the Wu-Tang Clan and "Can't Tell Me Nothing" by Kanye West in a mix, battling in an emcee cipher at the

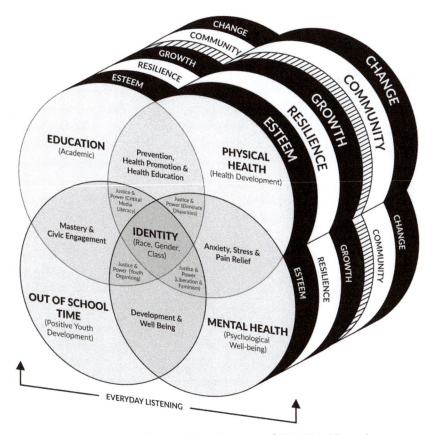

Figure 8.4. Intersection of Music Experiences and Hip Hop Narratives

J.U.I.C.E. youth program in Los Angeles, creating a science-inspired rap for the Science Genius B.A.T.T.L.E.S. project in New York, interpreting and processing through lyrics to Blue Scholars' "Oscar Grant [Shoot the Cops]" in a Beats, Rhymes, & Life youth group after learning about the Walter Scott death in South Carolina, or creating a graffiti mural that memorializes either the late Sandra Bland or Sean Price.

The following chapters embrace the idea of using musical experiences, emotions, and cognition as pathways to learning and growth. Informed by the Hip Hop specific model of individual and community empowerment, and the culturally specific model of empowerment-based positive youth development, the next chapters will examine how the newest generation of Hip Hop's cultural ambassadors integrate the culture within physical health, education, out-of-school time, and mental health contexts.

CHAPTER 9

Hip Hop and Physical Health: Healthy Environments to Live, Work, and Play

When considering the full healing power of Hip Hop culture in relation to physical health, the goal is not necessarily to identify an illness and determine how Hip Hop can provide the cure. While other forms of music have been studied for their value before, during, or after medical procedures, Hip Hop's history of use has been in disease prevention, health promotion, and health education with regard to HIV/AIDS, cardiovascular disease, and violence. Many newer efforts that integrate Hip Hop culture build on the evidence that using music and art can help people build and sustain healthy lifestyles.[1] These strategies to improve physical health use a person-centered perspective that encourages healthier lifestyles for whatever one's present physical condition is and for wherever one lives, works, and plays.

PHYSICAL HEALTH AND MEDICAL SETTINGS

Music is most often discussed with regard to physical health for its value in reducing stress, protecting against disease, and pain management.[2] Music, through both passive listening and more active interacting, is used to treat chronic illness, cancer, and cardiovascular disease. Recent research using randomized control trials found that the most commonly measured outcomes for these treatments are for psychological or mental health well-being.[3] Inhibition of pain is also a common outcome measure.[4] Furthermore, among these trials only the cancer study used a music therapist and went beyond patient-driven listening. In general, results suggest that music therapy has the largest effect on quality of life as opposed to actual physical health outcomes.[5]

When looking at chronic and acute pain among hospital patients, music is often used before, during, and after surgery. Results suggest that the best outcomes are associated with patient-centered strategies that allow patients to select the music, when it is played, its volume, and how much is played.[6]

SETTING THE STAGE FOR HEALTH DEVELOPMENT PATHWAYS: SHIFTING ENVIRONMENTS

One Step Forward, Two Steps Back: Post–Civil Rights and Well-Being

Considering community improvement and social justice values embedded in Hip Hop culture, there remains significant room for bringing attention to existing health inequities and the contributing social and environmental factors at the intersections of race, class, and gender. To the extent that music engagement facilitates attention to community change, this can translate to healthier environments, thus truly contributing to life course health development (LCHD).

The LCHD model is helpful for conceptualizing the ultimate desired outcome of health and well-being. The key elements of the model and its applicability to understanding music's value in promoting health are that health develops continuously over the life course, it is an emergent set of capacities and potential, it is sensitive to the timing of environmental exposures and experiences, and it is adaptive with strategies to promote resilience and plasticity amid environmental changes and challenges.[7] Within this framework we can appreciate Hip Hop culture's value to health and well-being, how it has been used, and how it can be used.

W. Michael Byrd and Linda Clayton capture the promise of the heart of the Civil Rights era and the fabric that binds the social environment and health so tightly by citing health and well-being gains for U.S. residents:

The Civil Rights Act of 1960 and 1964; the Voting Rights Act of 1965; initiation of President Lyndon Johnson's multifaceted Great Society and War on Poverty programs; the formation of a predominantly White student-led counterculture protesting against the Vietnam War; a Native American civil rights movement; Hispanic American activism; seeds of a gay liberation movement; and a soon-to-become-prominent feminist movement. From a health care standpoint, the desegregation of most of the nation's hospitals, the enactment of Medicare/Medicaid, and the beginning of the neighborhood health center (NHC) movement by 1967 represented the first national efforts in a century to open the health care system to Blacks and the poor.[8]

This did not last long. Byrd and Clayton continue:

> By emphasizing ending the Vietnam War, muzzling and controlling counterculture, deemphasizing individual civil liberties, downsizing federal government, slowing down or obstructing the implementation of civil rights measures, focusing on a new and diverse international order superimposed on the Cold War, and shifting the judicial system toward the Right, Richard Nixon in 1968—leading the new Republican, conservative, and Christian Right—forever altered America's political landscape.[9]

As of March 2015, the percentage of Americans without health insurance decreased to 11.9 percent due to the Affordable Care Act, the most sweeping health reform since Medicaid and Medicare.[10] In late 2014, the percentage was 18 percent. Health disparities—differences in health outcomes that are closely linked with social, economic, and environmental disadvantage—are often driven by the system of care but are also linked to the social environment in which individuals live, learn, work, and play.[11] Among Blacks, the most common health-related measures capturing these disparities are life expectancy, morbidity, risk factors, and quality of life.[12]

Racial and ethnic disparities exist in access to and quality of care to prevent, treat, or ameliorate major health problems. These trends exist for physical and mental health concerns among adults and children.[13] When focusing on outcomes, the biggest contributors to disparities in life expectancy between Blacks and non-Hispanic Whites are cardiovascular disease, cancer, homicide, diabetes, and perinatal conditions. Four cross-cutting health care areas are related to these factors affecting mortality: (1) maternal and child health, (2) lifestyle modification, (3) functional status preservation, and (4) rehabilitation and supportive and palliative care.[14]

Contributors to Morbidity and Mortality

According to the National Research Council report *A Common Destiny: Blacks and American Society*, "Who will live and who will die and how much handicap and disability will burden their lives depend in large part on conditions of education, environment, and employment as well as access to adequate medical services. Health is not only an important 'good' in itself, it is also a determinant of life options during the entire life."[15]

When we look at Black health and well-being, it is important to examine contributors to morbidity and mortality, and their underlying lifestyle and environmental correlates. For example, the most prevalent issues by race (and contributing factors) include: cancer (smoking), cardiovascular disease (nutrition), chronic kidney disease (nutrition, diabetes, and hypertension), diabetes (nutrition), HIV and AIDS (risky sexual behavior and injection drug use), and homicide (community violence, poverty, education, and family stability).

However, contributors to health outcomes are more complex than simple linear connections like the relationship between physical activity and obesity. This is not to ignore common contributors like physical activity, but it is to recognize other factors such as income, availability of healthy foods, safety of community spaces for physical activity, and cultural factors. For example, lower income residents report fewer average healthy days. Residents of states with larger inequalities in reported healthy days also report fewer healthy days on average. This relationship holds true at all levels of income.[16]

NUTRITION AND PHYSICAL ACTIVITY

The main risk factors for heart disease are high blood pressure, high LDL cholesterol, and smoking. The lifestyle factors that lead to the presence of these risk factors are nutrition (unhealthy diet), physical activity (low levels), and excessive alcohol and tobacco use.

A major part of the story of Black well-being in the United States and health equity relates to how the social environment is shaped, both intentionally and unintentionally. The line of intentionality is often fuzzy, and this is why scrutinizing the ascension of the more risky elements of Hip Hop culture warrants attention.

Healthy Foods

An area of concern that continues to be explored is the disproportionate prevalence of less healthy food options for Black communities and lower-income communities. Concern exists because of the toll this could have on nutrition and physical activity, especially since being overweight and obesity are major predictors of cardiovascular disease. For example, evidence of neighborhood oversaturation of fast foods is a public health concern.[17] In both urban and rural settings, there tend to be fast food and convenience stores disproportionately located in majority Black and lower-income communities.[18] Contributors to fast-food consumption are especially difficult to combat when cost and availability are also top barriers to consumption of fruits and vegetables.[19]

The African Americanization of Death: Blacks and Menthol Cigarettes

In another trend beginning in the mid-1960s, the tobacco industry marketed a high-risk product among segregated Black communities under the guise that it was healthy. Prior to then, mentholated cigarettes were marketed to the general population as an alternative, healthier option when smokers had a cold or cough that made smoking regular cigarettes unpleasant.[20] Substantially higher rates of targeted marketing on television and in Black publications like *Ebony*, coupled with their supposed health benefits, helped the skyrocketing sale of menthol cigarettes in the late sixties and early seventies. Coupled with these advertising trends were the association with the word "cool," popular in the Black community, and its links to Black popular culture and music. The proportion of the Black community smoking Kools, which had the highest tar levels among the most popular menthol cigarette brands, jumped from 14 percent to 38 percent between 1968 and 1976.

This African Americanization of menthols is significant because evidence suggests that menthol use has uniquely damaging effects on the body and is addictive.[21] For example, menthol slows the rate of nicotine metabolism, allowing it to remain in the body for a longer period of time.[22] Presently, among Black smokers, 70 percent smoke menthols. Although Kool has been unable to replicate its marketing successes to wider audiences, it did include a decidedly Hip Hop–oriented Kool Mixx campaign that was only marginally successful.[23]

The premise of the campaign was based on much of what is known in contemporary research about the power of music. An internal 1981 RJ Reynolds document specifically states how "music is the framework or building block for a deep emotionally resonant theme."[24] Music was the vehicle to "nostalgia, a reflection of desired moods, and group identification."[25] Its vision of success for these music campaigns was to create, "A strong desire to be in the places envisioned, near the action, and see the scene in which it is taking place. A feeling or mood of pleasure, relaxation, or excitement depending on one's need at the time. Cues and symbols which permit the target to personally identify with the experience and feel that it accurately reflects their desired lifestyle, values, and status."[26]

In a more recent study of Black men and women in Los Angeles, not only were they overwhelmingly more likely to smoke menthols—80 percent were either menthol only or menthol and regular smokers—they were significantly more likely to believe menthols have medicinal value and to have other menthol smokers in their social network.[27]

HIP HOP AS A HEALTH RISK: RISKY CONTENT

Early efforts to use rap music to promote healthy living competed with early "music effects" research that consistently paired rap music and heavy metal/rock music with risky and delinquent behaviors and poor school performance.[28] Following concerns about exposure and risk, researchers like Denise Herd and Brian Primack began to specify and measure music's risky content in greater detail, while others continued to explore the relationship between rap music exposure, including videos, and risky behaviors.[29]

Concerns about entertainment in the mainstream and popular culture are about the amount of risky attitudes and behaviors in content. For example, a study measuring the survival rates of artists performing on any album in the all-time top-1000 rock, punk, rap, R&B, electronica, and new age albums found they had a significantly higher mortality rate than the general population of North America and Europe.[30] Also of concern is North American music stars dying earlier post-fame, with the disparity beginning about three years after onset of fame. Further, a disproportionate amount of their mortality was related to alcohol and drug use.[31]

Labeling certain mainstream genres of music as "good" or "bad" and associating music exposure with negative outcomes for listeners has dominated research over the last thirty years. Rap music continues to be investigated for its potential to elicit high-risk attitudes and behaviors. In some research rap music preference has been associated with risky behaviors such as substance use.[32]

An in-depth analysis of alcohol use and brand referencing in rap music between 1979 and 1997 found that mentions of alcohol increased from 8 percent to 43 percent of songs, while favorable mentions jumped from 43 percent to 73 percent.[33] Specific name brand mentions increased from 46 percent to 71 percent.[34] Think Busta Rhymes and P. Diddy's 2002 "Pass the Courvoisier," which reports indicated a jump in profits for the liquor's parent company Allied Domecq of 4.5 percent in the first quarter of 2002, reaching double digits shortly after.[35] This appeared to be a trend at the time where marketing spiked. In 2002, *Source* magazine founder and CEO

Dave Mays reported that cars took up three pages of advertising in the magazine the year before. He continued, "This year . . . the publication will have 35 pages of car ads by the end of the year."[36] These increases in brand mentioning among a culturally specific audience and the residual profits for large corporations echo back to the targeted menthol cigarette marketing campaigns described earlier, prompting concerns over the commercial-like nature of certain songs.

One of the most recent studies by a leading research lab keeping tabs on the prevalence of high-risk messages in commercially popular music focused on alcohol prevalence in the songs that youth were most often exposed to between 2005 and 2007.[37] They found that alcohol was mentioned in 20 percent of the songs, often with actual brands, and the consequences of use were framed as significantly more positive than negative. Alcohol was associated with wealth, sex, and luxury objects more than fifty percent of the time. In other instances, still in the thirty to forty percent of the time range, alcohol was connected to partying, other drugs, and luxury vehicles.

Specific to rap music and based on the premise that marketers prefer this type of brand placement as a cheaper alternative to marketing, an experimental study assessed the potential influences of musical preference, artist image, and product/brand familiarity on product liking.[38] The study used a made-up brand, manipulated conditions for the artist's image (half read a negative news story while the other half read a favorable one), and manipulated product placements (half had product placement while the comparison group did not). Short-term attitudinal effects were found, where youth that preferred rap music and positively endorsed the artist were more likely to have positive attitudes toward the brand. These effects persisted even with low brand recognition. Again, much of the critiques on the content of music have been that music primes antisocial attitudes and behaviors, and facilitates scripting of risky sexual attitudes and behaviors, both where social learning can occur.[39]

HIP HOP AND RISKY OUTCOMES

Looking to simple exposure/risk studies in the last decade, a significant and positive relationship was found between listening to rap music and both substance use and aggressive behaviors.[40] A year later, a study found that when Black females perceived more sexual stereotypes in videos, they had a more negative body image and engaged in more risky behaviors such as binge drinking, marijuana use, and multiple sexual partners.[41]

However, introducing mediating variables or other potential causal factors has helped move the debate beyond simple exposure and causal arguments about the influence of rap music. A study looking at "problem music," a labeling problem in and of itself, found little evidence of a causal relationship between listening to rap music and self-injurious thoughts or behaviors, once mediating variables were accounted for.[42] Self-esteem, delinquency, and conservatism better accounted for variability in self-injurious thoughts and behaviors than did exposure to "problem music" including rap music, with self-esteem the most prominent influence across factors.[43]

Similarly, there is alternative evidence that includes positive and healthy outcomes associated with listening to Hip Hop. Youth who prefer Hip Hop and are more avid listeners often experience greater depth in meaning. These listeners develop more prosocial and empowering experiences with rap music.[44] Similar ideas were found in a study on club scenes, where individuals with higher levels of enjoying listening to Hip Hop music were significantly more likely to report higher condom use.[45] These potentially health-music(king) examples contrast to the formal interventions where Hip Hop culture is used as a culturally sensitive approach to improving health outcomes.

PHYSICAL HEALTH AND EDUCATION: PREVENTION, HEALTH PROMOTION, AND HEALTH EDUCATION

"When we say 'Let's' y'all say 'Move.'

'Let's!' 'Move!'"

This quintessential call-and-response, a hallmark of Hip Hop culture, is shouted back and forth between the self-proclaimed "World's Greatest Entertainer" Doug E. Fresh and a crew of schoolchildren, joined by MC Easy AD of the legendary Cold Crush Brothers. The track is called "Let's Move." It is but one of nineteen songs on the album *Songs for a Healthier America*. Although not all Hip Hop–oriented, the tracks and an accompanying curriculum are focused on health education and inspiring youth and families to embrace healthful nutrition and regular physical activity.[46]

Hip Hop Public Health (HHPH), a Columbia University obesity prevention program and research project, spearheads the program along with Partnership for a Healthier America. Its partners include musicians, physicians, public health researchers, entertainment industry professionals, health advocates, and schoolchildren.[47] Such prevention and health promotion activities are especially helpful because current physical education programming in schools is under intense scrutiny, and from different directions. One side is looking at content and potential ways to innovate because of the continued rise in obesity and diabetes. The other side is looking at ways to narrow offerings because of testing pressures.

HHPH seeks to address existing health disparities through the well-documented pathways of nutrition and physical activity with a culturally sensitive approach using elements of Hip Hop culture. They approach disparities as an issue of health literacy. A recent evaluation of one of their projects was for "Hip Hop Stroke," a three-session, three-hour program. Results indicated that youth ages 8–12 were able to learn and retain relevant stroke information and demonstrated an intent to call 911 when necessary 15 months post-intervention.[48]

A second program, Hip Hop Healthy Eating and Living in Schools (Hip Hop HEALS) is what helps ground its participation in the *Songs for a Healthier America* project. It "incorporates Hip Hop music into multimedia health messaging including short animation films to enhance a didactic curriculum designed to reduce the incidence and prevalence of childhood obesity.[49] Their "Old School" project is an elementary-school-based educational program aimed at demystifying concepts of aging, dementia and Alzheimer's disease, and impaired memory.[50]

SMOKING, NUTRITION, VIOLENCE, AND HIV/AIDS

In the mid-1990s, more prevalent notions of cultural sensitivity within health initiatives emerged. Thus prevention and interventions sought to use music as a cultural resource for tailoring messages to increase knowledge, improve attitudes, and promote prosocial behaviors that would ultimately lead to improved health and well-being outcomes. Rap music's potential as a uniquely better resource stemmed from its massive popularity among youth in general and youth of color in particular.[51]

Early efforts to understand the health effects of Hip Hop culture were not consistently investigated empirically, but a few studies offer a glimpse of these early attempts. A 1995 study examined the use of rap music in smoking prevention videos to determine if the rap video would be more effective than a traditional video presenting smoking prevention material or a discussion-only model. No change of intent to smoke was found over time and there was no difference when compared to the traditional video or discussion-only control.[52]

A year later, another study compared a rap video to a traditional video offering nutrition information for a group of pregnant Black teens, finding

no significant difference in its effectiveness.[53] However, in 1999 James
Tucker and colleagues tested a rap-integrated health promotion video as
a strategy for violence prevention alongside a more commercial video, a
video of trauma resuscitation, and a facilitated discussion. The commercial
video and rap video were the most successful for participant retention of
material, problem identification, and perceived impact.[54]

MULTIMODAL HEALTH STRATEGIES: HIV/AIDS

Several studies used a similar theory of rap music/Hip Hop culture
as a source of culturally sensitive health promotion, but as part of a cluster of strategies. Much of this work has been connected to HIV/AIDS
prevention. Blacks have the most substantial burden of HIV and AIDS
among U.S. populations, including 44 percent of new infections
each year.[55] Compared to Whites in the same categories, the prevalence
rates are almost seven times higher among Black men, 20 times higher
among women, and 45 times higher among men that have sex with other
men.[56]

Beginning in 1988, Renetia Martin and Florence Stroud helped connect
ideas of cultural sensitivity to HIV/AIDS work.[57] They described the value
of projects occurring in San Francisco that were culturally and linguisti-
cally appropriate, meaningfully facilitated by Black individuals, and within
the Black community. Later studies evaluated similar efforts. For example,
in 1997 in South Africa, Keller found that a rap music contest helped produce health promotion materials for HIV prevention. Young people who
heard the winning song or saw the winning video were significantly more
likely to use contraception. The study also found greater effectiveness when
health promotion messages were paired with other media (music, television, radio).[58]

Torrance Stephens and colleagues introduced a Hip Hop–integrated
music model for health promotion with a focus on HIV/AIDS, discussed it
in the context of music therapy, albeit with a health promotion emphasis,
and also speculated on its broader applicability.[59] A close examination of
the model's protocol demonstrates significant similarity to later therapeutic discussions of rap and Hip Hop therapy.[60] Researchers investigating
HIV/AIDS therapy among incarcerated male adolescents in Brazil found
traditional methods ineffective. However, when they became more collaborative and integrated adolescent interests, results improved dramatically.[61]
Adolescents were substantially more enthusiastic about interventions using music, Hip Hop arts, graffiti, and the creation of an album of HIV/

AIDS prevention music. Intervention efficacy was not measured, but the program was nationally awarded and the album was adopted by several other prevention programs and aired on the radio. Health promotion themes were linked to substance use, violence prevention, human rights, and solidarity.[62]

Building upon prior initiatives, rap music and Hip Hop continue to be an effective part of HIV/AIDS prevention initiatives today, especially among the Black community.[63] Hip Hop 2 Prevent Substance Use and HIV (H2P) was a substance use and HIV prevention program for youth ages 12 to 16 that incorporated Hip Hop culture to increase knowledge about healthy behaviors, increase refusal skills, and increase accuracy of perception of peer norms. While significant increases in knowledge, skills, and awareness (especially about the risks of marijuana use) were found at the conclusion of the study for the intervention group, little difference existed from the comparison group.[64]

MULTIMODAL HEALTH STRATEGIES: NUTRITION AND PHYSICAL ACTIVITY

The multimodal obesity prevention strategy Hip Hop to Health Jr. was introduced in 2002, with its results eventually published in 2005.[65] Despite its name, the clear links to Hip Hop culture were vague in this randomized controlled trial. When describing the program model, there was reference to exercise for both parents and preschool children and a group rhyming component for the children. One can speculate that perhaps these components used rap music or beats in the background, but there was no clear link to Hip Hop culture.[66]

The model was grounded in cultural sensitivity, including tailoring messaging, activities, information, and dietary considerations to the unique psychosocial realities of Black and Latino families. Results were promising in that the intervention reduced BMI increases in the intervention group two years post follow-up.[67] However, little difference was noticed from the control group on measures of fat calories, saturated fat, frequency of physical activity, or intensity of physical activity. A later group-randomized study replicated the intervention but it focused on Latino Head Start centers. The intervention was well received but showed no difference between the intervention and control groups for BMI, dietary intake, and physical activity.[68] Currently, a program is modeled on its successful BMI reduction strategies for three- to seven-year-olds.[69] It includes literacy activities and the use of a music CD called *Happy Healthy Kids*.

DANCE

When Hip Hop dance was compared with aerobics, ice-skating, and another body conditioning activity among high school and undergraduate students, Hip Hop dance and aerobics demonstrated the most significant increases in positive well-being and a reduction in psychological distress.[70] A similar study of Hip Hop dance in conjunction with gym-based activities and behavior modification strategies for improving nutrition and physical activity with elementary schoolchildren found improvements in blood pressure, "bad" cholesterol levels, and waist circumference.[71]

On the non-intervention side, akin to the health-musicking side of music is both the training and injury/recovery side of dancing that contributes greatly to physical health. As outlined by b-girl Sophie on her b-boy/b-girl blog, the shoulder, spine, hip, and ankle are but a few of the potential and common injury areas for dancers. Her organization, Urban Dance Health, takes a physiotherapeutic approach to helping dancers stay at peak performance and recover from injuries as healthily as possible when necessary.[72]

Formal research integrating elements of Hip Hop–related dance are still in early stages. The UK's *Project Breakalign* offers an example of how these types of research agenda can be established. This partnership exists between higher education and community members with a team of b-boys and b-girls, physical therapists, and researchers at the Institute of Sport, Exercise, and Health in London. The project conducts research on fatigue, weight distribution, ground reaction force (wrist and shoulder), and muscle activity.[73] Thinking in an interdisciplinary capacity, additional measures of nutrition, mental health, and well-being would be excellent supplements to this project.

THE GOOD DOCTOR SPEAKS

Did you know Arkansas had a public service announcement campaign with rapping for health promotion and prevention known as Health Raps? Did you know that April 13, 2004, was the date that Nelly canceled his bone marrow drive at Spelman College after objections and planned protests by a vocal group of students? Did you know that on June 1, 2007, legendary producer Marley Marl, KRS-One's adversary in "The Bridge Wars," suffered a heart attack? Did you know that just three short months later "The Hip Hop Doc" Rani Whitfield had a regular series of posts dealing with healthcare disparities among the Black community on Allhiphop .com? Dr. Whitfield has a health-related timeline on his website that includes this type of information alongside information about his work, past and present.

He has been on a range of national outlets as a public health advocate seeking to increase awareness of important health issues especially prominent in the Black community like HIV/AIDS, obesity, cardiovascular disease, and substance abuse. Two music projects include: first, Dr. Whitfield's collaboration with emcee Dee-1 on driving under the influence.[74] A second project, *Get on the Bus*, tackles issues that include teen pregnancy, prescription drug abuse, and childhood obesity.[75]

HEALTHY IS THE NEW GANGSTA

In his online article "7 Ways to Eat Good While on a Hood Budget," Stic of Dead Prez tries to help readers understand the life course perspective to health in its simplest terms, "bottom line always remember, we can pay now or pay later (in suffering and doctor bills, etc.) when it comes to our dietary discipline and choices."[76] Stic also authored a book, *Eat Plants Lift Iron*, with full recipes and exercise regimens based on his own experiment engaging in a plant-based diet and weightlifting regimen. His goal was to maintain his distance running and active lifestyle while gaining twenty pounds and moving to a fully plant-based diet. The book helps make mind-body connections by taking readers on the psychological journey he went through during the process. Rounding out the book's content is information about nutrition, physical activity, and general mentorship.[77]

The tag line for Stic's movement is "Well Rounded Well Being" and the front of one of its latest T-shirts is emblazoned with the slogan "Healthy is the New Gangsta." Stic said that the movement "recognizes the urgency in our communities in general to revolutionize our priorities as it relates to health." The movement's website and materials champion Hip Hop values, as Stic embodies everything he promotes. He is as much "about that life" and an authentic participant in what is promoted as he expects his audience to be.[78]

Speaking of exercise regimens, music can even help improve less desirable environments during physical activity. One study of music's potential found that using portable music devices could make even the least desirable environments more enjoyable when participating in everyday physical activities.[79] Going for a jog or bike ride in a busy or noisy area? Bring your headphones!

PHYSICAL HEALTH AND MENTAL HEALTH

Much of the literature related to physical health and health settings over-laps substantially with mental health because of the outcomes measured. Even when researching issues like music's influence on chronic illness or a condition like cardiovascular disease, the prioritized outcome measures include a mental health variable like anxiety, mood, stress, or depression.[80] However, music-evoked emotions that we value (like happiness) are not simply outcomes in and of themselves.[81] Rather they have corresponding physiological responses that we do not fully understand but that are none-theless meaningful. Recent research shows significant cross-cultural agree-ment about how emotional states are experienced as body sensations, mapped as distinct areas of the body.[82] Specific to music though, for exam-ple, when music is associated with nostalgic memories that bring joy and happiness, these feelings of joy and happiness correspond with other mean-ingful neural and biomedical changes.[83] In this respect, we are just begin-ning to understand the elements of why and how.

HEALTH OVER THE LIFE COURSE: CUMULATIVE STRESS, PTSD, AND ALLOSTATIC LOAD

We have seen in prior chapters how Hip Hop's developmental narratives often capture the uniquely stressful reality of being Black in the United States. These aspects of Black life are important because there are macro-level triggers and residual effects from issues of social inequality and racial discrimination. For example, individual events (e.g., Hurricane Katrina, the deaths of Trayvon Martin, Eric Garner, Walter Scott, Tamir Rice, Freddie Gray, and Sandra Bland) and structural challenges including resi-dential segregation, employment stability and poverty, law enforcement in-equity, and education quality are social and environmental challenges. These social and environmental challenges are often the adversities, stress-ors, and traumatic experiences associated with an accumulative physical and mental health burden that predicts ongoing and later life depression, anxiety, and PTSD.[84]

The aforementioned challenges interact with individual biology down to the intracellular level and manifest psychologically and physiologically throughout the human body. To the extent that these processes do not allow the body or mind to recover, it results in wear and tear on the body. Research is consistent that this buildup of wear and tear over time, or "allostatic load," results in poor health development. Ultimately this shows up as poor health outcomes including illness, reduced brain health, and lessened cognitive abilities.[85] We see the significant role of socioeconomic stressors, as the immigrant health advantage—foreign-born people are healthier—disappears when controlling for SES.[86] The role of income cannot be overstated, as people over twice the poverty level are three times more likely to report psychological distress.[87]

VIOLENCE AND THE CRIMINAL JUSTICE SYSTEM AS PUBLIC HEALTH ISSUES

Socioeconomic disadvantages also exacerbate other concerns, such as community violence, availability, and exposure to narcotics and weapons, and excessive criminal justice supervision and involvement. These present major stressors to individuals and families. Aside from allostatic load, the magnitude of stress may equate to traumatic stress, which has its own emotional, physical, and behavioral health challenges.[88] Simply as a health factor, homicide is the second leading influence on the difference in life expectancy between Black and White males.[89] At 46 percent of all homicides in the United States, the relative rate difference for Blacks was 650 percent higher than for Whites. The greatest risk exists for individuals between the ages of 15–29.[90]

Greater concentrated poverty, especially in relation to shifting labor markets where employment opportunities shrink, is related to increases in homicide victimization among Blacks.[91] Poverty, combined with a lack of economic investment, also increases access to narcotics and weapons in neighborhoods. Public policies such as Stop and Frisk, Special Weapons and Tactics (SWAT), and mandatory sentencing have added to the mix, contributing to an environment of police hyper-surveillance in these communities. It is an environment where tensions, anxiety, and trauma run high because of the significantly increased opportunities for oppressive and dehumanizing encounters with law enforcement, victimization by excessive force, and potential involvement in the criminal justice system.[92]

On the flip side, economically and socially marginalized environments provide fewer economic and educational opportunities; safe green spaces for exercise, recreation, and play; healthy eating options; and secure living-wage employment opportunities. Investments have to be made in these health-enhancing opportunities and spaces if youth are going to grow to be as healthy as possible.[93]

It is within these spaces that Hip Hop's core values of empowerment emerge and contest the environmental pressures and obstacles to healthy living. From Stic's attempts to change the narrative on healthy foods and physical activity to Kendrick Lamar and Wale's efforts to confront Black-on-Black homicide on "The Blacker the Berry," and "Pessimist" respectively, to J-Live's impassioned plea against police violence on "I Am a Man," Hip Hop continues to confront physical health challenges.

Today's cultural ambassadors pay attention to opportunities to create safer spaces and healthier development within the social realities of contemporary living. Efforts must continue to capitalize on formal Hip Hop–integrated opportunities to promote optimal physical health, but also through everyday listening, and self-health strategies. The following chapter looks closely at Hip Hop and education, including several key cultural ambassadors setting the pace and vision for how to maximize growth and learning opportunities for youth.

CHAPTER 10

Hip Hop and Education: Engagement, Equity, and Excellence

We have finally reached the point where we no longer explain phenomena in a vacuum, where we no longer blame the victim, and where we do not automatically link need or adversity to personal failings. Right? We finally embrace the volumes of research that paint a consistent picture of individual outcomes resulting from a complex relationship between the environment and individual attitudes and behaviors. Right? And lastly, we have been able to apply these understandings in classrooms so that we ensure education occurs for all students in a consistent manner, capitalizing on their gifts, talents, and diversity using the best available tools for learning. Right?

Not exactly. Substantial disparity exists in how Black youth experience education in the United States. However, for the first time in history, high school graduation rates reached 80 percent, with gains largely driven by a 15 percentage point increase for Hispanic students and 9 percentage point increase by Black students since 2006.[1] Amid these gains have been efforts to integrate Hip Hop culture into education (i.e., Hip Hop pedagogy) in a variety of ways. This chapter highlights the contextual realities of education for many Black youth, contemporary thinking on Hip Hop informed pedagogies, and how promising aspects of these strategies intersect with other strategies of betterment.

"NOBODY CAN EVER TAKE THAT FROM YOU"

The belief that Black youth come to class armed with ways of thinking and acting that hurts their ability to learn was a favored theory in earlier research seeking to explain disparities in educational outcomes.[2] Yet, since the earliest periods of slavery in the United States, evidence shows that even in the most challenging situations, the Black community, as a culture, have looked to education as an important path forward.[3] Many parents hold the belief that what makes education so special is that once gained, it can never be taken away. Evidence suggests that this line of thinking has been right on track. Research shows that based on data dating back to slavery, education has been one of the most prominent mediators of racial inequality because of its substantial impact on wages and wealth accumulation as well as the significant influence of local politics on educational policies, including funding provision.[4]

The belief that widespread opposition to formal school-based education exists, and that it is a self-sabotaging cultural norm producing existing disparities, has been shown to ring hollow.[5] Pockets of opposition to success within educational spaces exist across all cultures, but these have more to do with [a lack of] social engagement, perceived differences in treatment, unequal access to resources, and differences in cultural behaviors.[6] In fact, current research shows that when compared to White students, Black and Hispanic students reported more positive attitudes toward school.[7] Black youth also come to class with unique ways of thinking and acting that help their ability to learn.[8]

Black youth have been shown to persist with favorable, pro-school attitudes in the face of significant adversities. Yasser Payne and Tara Brown's research with Black men between 16 and 19, who identify as street-life-oriented, echoes this. Findings among this heavily stigmatized group suggest these young men have positive attitudes about what formal education can do for them but negative attitudes about actual past and current school experiences.[9]

We have a better understanding of the unique educational experiences influenced by family, community, and school environments, resulting in different educational outcomes. Some realities increase risk, while other realities are protective of favorable school outcomes. Newer research helps pinpoint these contributors to Black student excellence and academic success. For example, research consistently shows that the best-performing students reported high levels of class/school (academic and social) engagement, a climate of fairness and safety, neighborhood unity, substantial prosocial out-of-school time opportunities, and high standards and expectations.[10] Chris Emdin and Ian Levy spend significant time connecting Hip Hop's aesthetics to class and school engagement. Emdin's Reality Pedagogy is similarly anchored in helping the best version of students show up in classrooms to learn.

EARLY AND ENDURING SUCCESS

All evidence points to the fact that early academic success tends to endure. Students who perform well in middle school are significantly more likely to graduate high school regardless of school quality. Furthermore, the top Black students who enroll in the most selective colleges and universities consistently graduate at rates similar to their White counterparts, at rates of 85 percent and higher.[11] Back at the high school level, a recent Washington, DC, study looked closely at the intersection of academic performance and school quality. The highest-performing (top quartile) students entering high school were able to perform above the state average and graduate on time at over 85 percent of schools, regardless of quality. However, consistency in academic success is not absolute, as in the five lowest-performing schools, student potential could not override the contextual challenges. A 69 percent difference in on-time graduation rates existed between lowest and highest quality schools for students entering in the top quartile of eighth grade performance.[12]

EDUCATIONAL CHALLENGES AND THE BLACK COMMUNITY

When looking closer at national trends in the school experience for Black youth we are able to see how school culture may contribute to an environment of distrust among students and inhibit the development of ingredients for student success. These trends in policy, exclusion, and bias suggest that these are the pathways for how social and academic engagement declines, how the school climate feels unfair and unsafe, and how low expectations are normalized.

Suspensions and expulsions, or involuntary disengagement, have increased dramatically at all levels, from preschool through the high school years. When examining zero tolerance policies, the increases stem from a school's criminalizing of minor disciplinary infractions often coinciding with increased police presence and enhanced school-wide security measures.[13]

Nationally, Black students are three times more likely to be suspended and expelled in comparison to White students.[14] These differences in treatment start as early as pre-school, where Black children are 18 percent of enrollment, yet 48 percent of children receiving more than one out-of-school suspension. For White students it is 43 percent versus only 26 percent respectively.[15] Black students are also much more likely to be referred from school *directly* to law enforcement intervention. Evidence exists at the national and state levels showing how these disparities in suspension and expulsion are exponential, start early, and persist when controlling for severity of offense.[16] Further, for Black students suspension percentages rise by grade, by gender (male), and when there is a disability.[17]

Newer research angles have dug even deeper to look at differences in treatment according to skin tone, or lighter versus darker shading of skin, adding to the complexity of the Black educational experience. When looking at suspension rates, the odds of suspension were about three times greater for young Black women with the darkest skin tone compared to those with the lightest skin.[18] Part of the challenge in eliminating bias is that much of it is implicit, occurring outside of consciousness or deliberate willful differences in treatment. Although, recent research on executive functioning more specifically identifies the degrees of cognitive control over bias in decision-making.[19] Acceptance of accountability to existing biases is not yet a cultural norm among teachers or education students of any race or ethnicity.[20] Besides the influence on school culture and academic engagement, suspensions and expulsions are associated with a greater likelihood of repeating a grade or dropping out altogether, and ultimately substantially lower chances of upward mobility and long-term income generating prospects.[21] When we move past these most blatant of exclusionary practices, suspension and expulsion, we can focus on what actually helps engagement and how Hip Hop fits into the picture.

HIP HOP AND ACADEMIC ENGAGEMENT AMID FEAR AND BIAS

Chris Emdin helps us understand how the presentation of self can simultaneously affirm the worst of society's biases to the uninformed, while being an empowering force to others when discussing the "ice grill."

The ice grill instilled fear in older folks and people from other neighborhoods, and when my friends and I wore it, people clenched purses tighter and avoided making eye contact with us. From the looks on the faces of the older people who wore business suits and demeanor meant we were bound for a life of failure and regret . . . another group of young Black males with a scripted and bleak future. To my friends and I, our projected image meant we were thinking a little harder, were a little bit sharper, and were a little more prepared than anyone else for any surprises life offered. We were Hip Hop. . . . Mine remained on my face as I walked through the school building and into my classes. In those fields I sat and listened to the teacher speak, wanting to be a part of the discussions, hoping to share my ideas, but feeling as though what was going on was completely removed from who I was and who people like me were.[22]

Emdin also talks about the importance of democratizing educational spaces, a task with many dimensions. At its most basic it means making classroom learning accessible to all. The young, engaged, yet not engaged effectively by the teachers, must be helped to feel the classroom learning is about him or her and the communities and people he or she values. Engagement of this type includes being participatory, hands-on, active, and project-based. Persistence in these more active learning styles have been especially helpful for, but not limited to, Black males.[23]

Expanding accessibility also includes allowing out-of-class knowledge inside the classroom, and even privileging culturally relevant experiences and knowledge that is often inhibited within traditional educational spaces.[24] The dynamics of teacher-student interactions becomes especially important, as does how the educational climate is framed and transformed over time. Breaking down these barriers, welcoming individuals in their entirety, and respecting their intelligences creates full participants in learning. The proverbial "ice grill" or callous disinterest can melt into active engagement, social and academic. Repeatedly, research shows us that little opposition to school exists; rather, an opposition exists to school climates that are perceived as systematically assaulting one's identity.

What makes Hip Hop culture unique is the constant attention to person and environment, its cultural familiarity, its participatory nature, and its potential to engage all senses. These characteristics exist whether creating or interacting with the art. It is also instinctively social. Hip Hop's role in education is anchored by these facts and the direction offered through the culture's value of self and community improvement. The introspective question of "Who am I?" is always present in Hip Hop as is prioritization of context and exploration of knowledge of self, akin to emancipatory learning.[25] The constant negotiation of self, within society, is a hallmark of the Black experience. Similarly, the constant negotiation of self is also a hallmark of Hip Hop culture.

Newer Hip Hop–integrated pedagogies in education build on these commonalities to include identity sharing, connection, and linkages to issues and communities considered important to young people.[26] Learning is essentialized as a life skill, not just a skill for the classroom. Further, some of the unique tools of Hip Hop, often called the aesthetics of Hip Hop like digging, sampling, layering, and remixing, lend themselves nicely to achieving educational objectives. These shared tools and values and assumptions among individuals who embrace Hip Hop culture are the basis for steadily increasing interdisciplinary practices using Hip Hop culture to advance education, physical and mental health, and out-of-school time strategies with youth.

HIP HOP'S THREE CLASSROOM LENSES

The integration of Hip Hop culture into education was discussed by Marc Lamont Hill as falling within one of three major categories, or pedagogical approaches: [Being] *Of* Hip Hop, *About* Hip Hop, and *With* Hip Hop.[27] These are useful heuristics for thinking about what is being leveraged from the culture and what aspects of the educational process are being privileged with its use.

Of Hip Hop

Hip Hop's secondary artifacts are on display here, as the style and aesthetics of Hip Hop culture influence the style and aesthetics of the learning experience. From cyphers to remixes, Hip Hop itself is front and center in the education process. Truths are embedded within any aspect of the culture and help reorganize traditional ways of knowing and understanding. At its best, these cultural artifacts and ways of relating challenge traditional educational strategies and knowledge, and introduce innovative new ones. It pushes toward new ways of teaching and learning.[28]

At its most basic, Hip Hop culture includes ways of speaking, acting, and relating that are inclusive rather than exclusive to cultural adherents. For example, what is learning and education supposed to look like in a classroom that integrates a Hip Hop worldview?[29] Hill noted how one student professed the value in something as simple as speech, "It's easy to speak here, even you speak this way Mr. Hill," taking note of the comfort level embedded in African American Vernacular English.[30] The honest contradictions of contested meanings within the culture must be a part of this.

Emdin's five C's of reality pedagogy is fully "of Hip Hop," offering a multitude of opportunities for Hip Hop truths to manifest, in aesthetics as much as text. For example, the cypher is a facilitator of ideas, sharing, and democratic participation. As important is the sense of camaraderie, active engagement, and interrelated specificity, like in battles, which function as facilitators of competitive growth and constructive criticism.[31] His approach is also a gateway to supportive peer socialization, and creating a community of learners that support and reinforce one another—shown to be especially valuable for Black students—where both identity and mastery collide to propel youth forward.[32]

FEATURE: SCIENCE GENIUS

"Don't tell nobody, but we're gonna solve DNA hereditary molecule under our name."[33]

This song, one of many Science Genius-inspired tracks from the project that launched during 2012 and 2013 across New York is an academic exercise to help convey the acquisition of academic knowledge in chemistry. The goal of Science Genius is to increase engagement of students in science with the same fervor as many engage Hip Hop culture.[34] The project, the brainchild of Dr. Chris Emdin, with a hefty cosign and contributions from GZA of Hip Hop's legendary Wu-Tang Clan, and integrates the full gamut of Hip Hop culture within science education. The Science Genius B.A.T.T.L.E.S. (Bring Attention to Transforming Teaching, Learning, and Engagement in Science) competitions bridged the battle and cypher elements of Hip Hop to spur innovation, creativity, fun, participation, and unity while learning. During the first two years, there have been an average of 10 schools and 30 students involved.[35]

Incidentally, the Watson and Crick DNA song is based on the melody and structure of the Kanye West, Big Sean, and Jay Z Hip Hop track "My Clique." However, looking closely at these lyrics, one cannot help but imagine the songwriter(s) "trying on" these personalities of two incredibly skilled scientists, confident allies, on the cusp of a major scientific breakthrough.

This is part of the Science Genius criteria that allows full engagement: (1) the main topic/concept of the rap must be referenced in different ways at least three times in the verse; (2) be creative in your expression of the science (e.g., envision yourself either as somebody involved in the scientific process or an object undergoing the scientific process and draw connections between your real world experiences and the concepts themselves); and (3) information must be scientifically accurate and verifiable.[36]

The above students recognized the significance of blazing their own trail, not out of naïve ambition, but from substantive theoretical positioning, experimental testing, and, ultimately, a willingness to change. This is fully engaged learning made possible through the style and aesthetics of Hip Hop culture.

About Hip Hop

The second cluster of strategies is all about Hip Hop. Preexisting artifacts (e.g., a known song) can be used or new materials can be created. However, the preexisting material is usually an individual activity-specific prompt; not necessarily a fully developed curriculum or immediate link to an educational standard. Educational spaces, any type, are the educators, and students become cultural critics, analyzing, critiquing, and even producing their own Hip Hop artifacts or texts. It can be a standalone artifact-driven activity, or an integration of Hip Hop artifacts (preexisting materials) into an "ordinary" curriculum. It is in these spaces that James Peterson's ideas of educational elements of *consciousness* and *search and discovery* are most germane.[37]

One of the mechanisms where this emerges is when an outside program comes in to "take over" a classroom. Often, this starts as an introduction to Hip Hop culture and an introduction to Hip Hop's primary artifacts and core elements—maybe even with the learning of skills associated with each element (e.g., emceeing, or deejaying/production). There are then the residual learning/growth opportunities above and beyond the skill development, which often includes learning about oneself and the community. The potential topics and themes are wide ranging and touch on all aspects of student's social context and lived experiences.

Common themes that emerge include issues of identity and social justice.[38] Education may also have a more implicit social justice orientation through the contextualization of reality, without being explicitly justice-oriented in the tradition of critical Hip Hop pedagogy.[39] Asheru talks about the importance of teachers in this process, "The work comes in when teachers come and put material into context. How does it fit with your reality?" However, as mentioned by Hill about education and Amy Donnenwerth about therapy, considerable care must always be shown about disclosure anxiety, and when addressing sensitive topics and issues of trauma.[40]

The goal of these activities is not to be measured against or validated against the traditional canon of knowledge. It is not comparing Tupac to Shakespeare. It is Tupac's material independently as text. It is beat-making and production in general. It is cultural understanding and exploration with educational benefits. This is Hip Hop *first*, then school-linked outcomes. These successful early forays into productive use of content and material allowed specific links to curriculum and standards and courses.

With Hip Hop

Care is warranted in strategies "with Hip Hop" because here it is not really "about" Hip Hop at all; it is about the curriculum. Educational spaces are the educators, and subjects are connected directly to traditional curriculum standards.[41] The goal is concrete; a serious advancement of academic achievement outcomes. The aim is to use Hip Hop culture strategically to motivate, to "transmit traditional subject matter," for example, by being directly linked to the common core and to encourage lifelong learning.

Sometimes, this occurs in a very trivial way with Hip Hop as a novelty trick to promote learning or memorization, what Sam Seidel refers to as "using Hip Hop via the peanut butter and the pill" strategy.[42] However, the range of subject matter to which this applies is actually extensive. As with subjects like health—nutrition, physical activity, and the social determinants of health—or the hot contemporary topic, criminal justice and law/public policy, it is time to pay attention to systematic, comprehensive, and in-depth pedagogy in Hip Hop culture.

For example, B. Lee Cooper and Rebecca Condon have written extensively about the educational disciplines whose curricula can be enhanced through the use of music in general.[43] I write out these disciplines because it is at this level of specificity where true innovation in Hip Hop integration must occur. The opportunity to contribute to learning environments is vast and rubrics must be developed with detail and breadth across each of these disciplines. Disciplines include:

- Cultural (e.g., Black or Latino/Hispanic) Studies,
- Business and Economics,
- Criminal Justice and Law/Public Policy,
- Education,
- Geography and Environment,
- Public Health,
- Health Care and Wellness,
- History,
- Language and Linguistics/Language Arts (Writing),
- Mass Media and Communications,
- Philosophy and Religion,
- Psychology,
- Science/Technology/Engineering/Math (S.T.E.M.),

- Sociology and Anthropology,
- Social Work,
- Urban Studies, and
- Women's/Gender Studies.[44]

If we extrapolate music to the multitude of artifacts within Hip Hop culture, then we have an incredibly rich template from which to enrich learning within contemporary curricula.

When education is at its best, the wisdom and experience of educators interacts with the intellectual depth and richness of Hip Hop.[45] More substantive strategies include standards alignment, but they also explore content in-depth. For example, Marcella Runell and Martha Diaz's *Hip Hop Education Guidebook, Vol. 1* is one of the more comprehensive efforts to specifically link Hip Hop texts, activities/lessons, and academic content standards.[46] These can be units, or a more comprehensive arrangement of units organized as a full curricula. This is where the quality of teaching is paramount. Educators can connect the dots to traditional educational objectives easily, while also using Hip Hop's transformative potential to transcend basic objectives into something bigger, better, more relevant, and life-long.[47] Measurement of desired strategy outcomes is especially important here. A priori objectives in curricular standards must be established.

INNOVATIONS IN PEDAGOGY INTEGRATING HIP HOP

Emery Petchauer and Marc Lamont Hill coined the concept "Hip Hop Based Education" to encapsulate all things Hip Hop with education, echoing the sentiments of others on moving beyond Hip Hop as text-centric strategies, to accentuate Hip Hop aesthetics as tools for accessing a wide range of educational disciplines and material; for accessing all the artistic forms; and by including a wider range of voices beyond those indoctrinated within the culture.[48] This work also emphasizes authenticity and context, where student knowledge, skills, and life experience outside of the classroom is privileged and honored inside the classroom. These new directions are but a glimpse of the potential for moving education and allied fields forward in practice, and developing robust studies to understand the influences of Hip Hop–integrated educational strategies on academic and well-being outcomes.

A wide range of education driven initiatives have integrated Hip Hop as a way to engage youth. For example, Music Counts is a piano-driven math skills program that uses an array of music stylings to engage youth and build math skills. We have to move toward more nuanced measurement and evaluation to determine the depth of traditional student outcomes coupled with any outcomes related to other opportunities for learning or growth that are embedded. Below are several other examples, including strategies that embed social justice learning.

FEATURE: SOCIAL JUSTICE MATH

Social justice math is an example of unpacking and contextualizing specific concepts and learning within traditional educational domains. It allows you to use math to facilitate understanding of social justice issues but does the reverse as well, allowing you to learn math from studying equity and justice topics within society.[49] Edna Tan and colleagues write about similar ideas of integrating student history, culture, and social need into coursework through math and science.[50] For example, when looking at economic and social issues, several specific issues to investigate mathematically include: (1) Prisons, racial profiling, the legal process, death penalty; (2) Poverty, minimum/living wage, sweatshops; (3) Housing, gentrification, homeownership; (4) War, defense budgets, military recruiting; (5) Public Health, AIDS, asthma, health insurance, diabetes, smoking; (6) Educational access, funding, testing, achievement gaps; (7) Environment: pollution, hunger, food and water resources; (8) Welfare, TANF; and (9) Immigration.[51]

The goal of exploring these issues and issues like financial education is not necessarily to dwell on existing social disparities but rather to understand problems and emphasize the use of math in the identification of solutions to existing problems. In an ideal situation, this process would inspire people to learn additional math skills and to become active and engaged citizens working on solution-oriented projects. An annual conference about math education and social justice, Creating Balance, is also held to explore such issues. Critics of social justice math fundamentally disagree with the tenets of social justice, believing it is done to indoctrinate youth to a liberal agenda.

FEATURE: WORDS LIIVE

Sage Salvo (also known as Gilbert Perkins), executive director of Words Liive, said the program places an emphasis on "closing a context gap, or Contemporary Language Integration (CLI)." He stated that "if material is not familiar or relevant it acts as a barrier to learning."[52] Words Liive uses the lyrics of urban music, code and computer programming language, social media lingo, and text message language. Salvo explains that not only is Hip Hop music culturally familiar but that it is also a literary text. "[Hip

Hop] as a 40 year old body of work, actually should justly be placed on the spectrum as a neo romantic [literary] period." He adds that the textual volume (i.e., 1000 words per song and 12,000 words per album) is equivalent to any major literary composition. With Words Liive programming these Hip Hop compositions and other "contemporary languages" are critiqued, analyzed, and integrated with traditional classroom literatures as educational prompts within English, history, social studies, and technology curricula.

FEATURE: FLOCABULARY

Flocabulary is an online library of educational Hip Hop songs and videos for grades K–12 to aid teachers (and students) to achieve common core objectives in English/language arts and math. Supplemental materials are also available to promote excellence in social studies and science. The Flocabulary approach capitalizes upon the combination of music (for memorization) and Hip Hop's cultural popularity (for engagement) to help educators and students achieve learning goals.

FEATURE: GUERILLA ARTS INK, AND THE HIP HOP EDUCATIONAL LITERACY PROGRAM (H.E.L.P.)

"Imagine a classroom where a teacher is using the lyrics of Nas to teach a lesson on African American music from the 19th century to present. Or cross-referencing the lyrics of Joni Mitchell, Marvin Gaye, and Mos Def to talk about the global pollution of our water sources."[53] Emcee, and international Hip Hop educator Asheru created his educational literacy program as a culturally relevant, standards driven, Hip Hop–integrated approach to educational excellence. The emphasis is on literacy development standards but also an integration of social justice themes such as poverty, violence and environmental issues. Although an emphasis is on national reading, standards for classroom use, these materials can be used in out-of-school time activities and the home.

> When we created these books I only had three criteria, it had to be vocabulary rich, it had to be relatively clean, and it had to have some type of social justice commentary or messaging that we could spin off. Like Kanye's "Diamonds in Sierra Leone," we talk about conflict resources in Africa, how diamonds are formed, and materialism in Hip Hop. But I'm not going to quote Kanye as any type of authority on how to stop the crisis in Sierra Leone.[54]

Asheru continued on to talk about the fine line that exists in trying to use content that they like to teach literacy and put it into context for their lives, values, and virtues. "I try to find ways to contextualize what they naturally listen to." He founeded Guerilla Arts Ink to promote innovative and culturally relevant education for youth through the arts.

CRITICAL HIP HOP PEDAGOGIES

Widespread support exists for Hip Hop–integrated strategies employing a social justice lens.[55] Marcella Runnell (2007) offers a model of critical Hip Hop pedagogy with three main features: (1) examination of power differentials that privilege dominant groups, whether it is race, class, gender, or other cultural or institutional entities; (2) popular culture is used for critical pedagogical purposes that inspire action toward positive change; and (3) any element of the culture can be used, in whole or part as the main pedagogical tool, or a supplement as long as it is in pursuit of social justice objectives.[56]

For purely academic results, it remains to be seen how much a normative engagement in relevant, critical, and prioritized analyses naturally facilitates empowerment and inhibits stereotype threat. This approach contrasts to *specific interventions* to improve cognitive appraisals of belonging and ability. Evidence suggests both are steps forward. Both can help navigate the hurdles that interfere with effective use of existing knowledge, intellect, curiosity, and competencies that help academic success for Black youth.[57] However, when thinking about more holistic outcomes of development and growth, the potential value of critical Hip Hop pedagogies is promising.

MULTICULTURAL EDUCATION AND CRITICAL HIP HOP PEDAGOGIES: WHAT CAN WE LEARN?

Hip Hop–integrated strategies within education emerged as a strand of multicultural education and also as a strand of extracurricular programming at the margins of formal education.[58] Questions remain. *Can Hip Hop help in the perceived inequality in educational opportunity?* Can Hip Hop help with:

(1) engagement (i.e., point of service, face to face engagement; for knowledge building; grit; mastery; satisfaction with the learning process, improving resources and the environment; grades, creating a community of mastery and peer reinforcement)
(2) continuation (i.e., promotion from one grade to the next, not dropping out, summer learning and excelling/growth mindset)

(3) graduation (completion)

(4) bringing attention to contextual opportunities and challenges (i.e., zero tolerance, police harassment [criminal justice inequity continuum], environmental stress and pathways to positive change);

(5) inspiration to be a voice and contributor to service toward positive changes (civic engagement)?

CRITICAL HIP HOP PEDAGOGY AND MENTAL HEALTH: WHAT CAN WE LEARN? HOW CAN WE GROW?

To best help today's youth, these interrelated strategies must be fully built upon. At a more systematic level, mental health professionals must be allowed to work more directly with educators to help integrate opportunities for well-being into the classroom experience. Chris Emdin and Ian Levy have realized this little-used opportunity and are working on conceptualizing this approach. Raphael Travis and Joshua Childs have written about the necessary collaboration between educators and mental health in the newest #HipHopEd book.[59] Debangshu Roychoudhury and Lauren Gardner discuss their Hip Hop Psychology Liberation (HHPL) model as an important therapeutic and educational justice model that speaks directly to marginalizing educational environments at issue for today's youth.[60]

Collaboratively, educators and mental health professionals can build strategic classroom experiences from the dual-focused questions, What Can We Learn? *And . . .* How Can We Grow? These two questions collectively capture Hip Hop's superordinate value of improvement with an eye toward identity at its core. The classroom and school experience must have clear messages for Black youth: You belong. We want you here. We value your knowledge. We expect excellence. We want this to be a safe environment for you but not oppressive and demeaning. Collaboratively, educators, mental health professionals, and other Hip Hop cultural ambassadors can integrate Hip Hop experiences that transform learning environments into vibrant communities of excellence and healing, where students learn and grow to be at their best.

FEATURE: THE 10 BIGGEST CONCERNS OF HIP HOP–INTEGRATED EDUCATION

Taking a closer and critical look at Hip Hop–integrated strategies in education, there are several concerns, or at least ambiguities, to consider amid the promising aspects in content (ideology and material), pedagogy, and outcome measurement. These are outlined in ten questions:

1. When are risky themes of substance use, misogyny, and violence considered excessive?
2. Will the culture be misappropriated and coopted within the educational system?
3. Will Hip Hop artists be overemphasized as role models?
4. Will Hip Hop be overgeneralized as representative of youth or Black culture?
5. Will activities be stigmatized and problematized; become a distraction or path to discipline?
6. Is challenging the status quo and reform fundamental to Hip Hop–integrated strategies?
7. If reform is targeted, what are the prioritized strategies?
8. What are the optimal credentials and structures for Hip Hop–integrated education?
9. What are the prioritized outcome measures?
10. What is the most promising evidence for the effectiveness of Hip Hop–based strategies?

These concerns must be considered along with how to ensure materials, strategies, and artifacts are youth-centered and not biased excessively by the facilitator.[61]

THE HIP HOP COLLECTIONS AND ARCHIVES: STRENGTHENING CULTURAL RESOURCES

To strengthen the educational value of Hip Hop, there is a need to preserve Hip Hop's artifacts, values, and essential ingredients of the culture. Beginning in 2002, Hip Hop culture took a bold leap forward as the preservation of critical Hip Hop artifacts was prioritized in partnership with institutes of higher education. These repositories of culture are critical to multicultural education and a major resource for varied pedagogies working "with" Hip Hop. Prominent archives include: Harvard University's Hip Hop Archive (notably attended by 9th Wonder as a Hip Hop Fellow and featuring the Nasir Jones Hip Hop Fellowship), Cornell University's Hip Hop Collection, which focuses on the artifacts of the culture (featuring Bambaataa as a visiting scholar), the College of William and Mary's Hip Hop Archive (emphasizing Virginia Hip Hop), and Atlanta's Tupac Shakur Archive. Each archive has its own unique strengths and lenses it prioritizes for exploring Hip Hop culture.

Universities and high schools can improve the scope of their offerings by connecting with and engaging these archives. To be clear, individuals have maintained their own collections and archives since the inception of Hip Hop culture. In fact, as we have noted before, deejays in and of themselves are cultural archivists. Mixtapes, a major Hip Hop artifact, also function as mini archives because they preserve individual tracks, their component parts as beats, hooks, lyrics, and associated samples, and the temporal and sonic presentation of these artifacts. The web-based Mixtape Museum is one of the many champions of both mixtape culture and the value of archiving. We also recognize that any time a larger system is involved in the culture, fears of cooptation arise. However, educational archiving, especially within university settings, has unique value. These archives spotlight the global, the national, and the local, further recognizing the universality of the culture alongside the cultural specificity of the local.

Benefits of institutional archiving, especially in partnership with institutes of higher education, include: (1) being a site of knowledge production; (2) enhancement of the cultural curricula to convey/solidify attitudes about race; (3) ensuring the consistent presence of curricular material on Hip Hop culture and Black culture; (4) ensuring an additional pathway toward equal distribution of time and space devoted to multiple cultures, such as White vs. Black culture; (5) strengthening pedagogical integrity toward effective use of curricular materials across topics (e.g., bias, discrimination, but also pride and resilience); (6) preserving the integrity of data and artifacts for empirical use; (7) access to institutional financial resources (economic capital) for awareness building; (8) access to the social capital of the university, in terms of reputation and social networks; and (9) it builds upon the core elements of multicultural education in higher education settings.

AN EXPANSIVE VISION OF EDUCATION: LEARNING AND GROWTH

Hill correctly pointed out our need for a more holistic interpretation of education and teaching, "an alternate, more expansive vision of pedagogy that reconsiders the relationships among students, teachers, texts, schools and the broader social world."[62] Further, education must consider how to best work in partnership with other disciplines. And as much as we prioritize context as integral to education, the context within which Hip Hop–integrated strategies exist must also be attended to. This holds especially true for Black youth in general, and Black male youth specifically, who because of racial politics are consistently forced to contest a larger narrative and pattern of relationships in education. The narrative be feared, disciplined, and contained.[63] Hip Hop–integrated strategies offer one path forward—for some—because of its relaxation of oppressive cultural narratives; its necessitation of incorporating community contexts; its dynamic and engaging nature; and its cultural consistency, privileging cultural knowledge, attitudes, and skills normally inhibited in traditional school environments.

If Hip Hop–integrated strategies in education are to move forward effectively, it is necessary to develop a comprehensive list of concerns and risks, contingency plans, strategies to mitigate these risks while also validating existing concerns (do not ignore or shame), and models of effectiveness as exemplars (or at least as empirically testable examples). Promising ideas about ideology, content, pedagogy, and outcome measurement for the integration of Hip Hop and education have been put forward.[64] These ideas offer guidance about how to move the culture, its assets, and young people's talents "from the margins to the center."[65]

A similar attentiveness is needed for the actual outcomes as well. This vision must lead to well-being outcomes that are conferred through engagement (to students, to schools, to communities) in ways that are active forms of lifelong learning. Education must occur inside and outside of classrooms, in MK Asante words, with "two sets of notes."[66] And these learning opportunities must not be merely for grades but rather for ongoing learning and connection to real world applicability. New pedagogies, infrastructural support for cultural resources through higher education, reinvigorated attention to archiving the culture, and a new wave of ambassadors to help realize youth potential offers substantial promise for Black youth education.

CHAPTER 11

Hip Hop and Out-of-School Time: Creating New Pathways to Growth and Change

In 1991 Karen Pittman uttered six words to the House Select Committee on Children, Youth, and Families that forever changed the landscape of youth work outside of clinical settings: "Problem free is not fully prepared."[1] So simple, yet so profound in helping us to realize that we cannot treat all youth as though they are broken and need to be fixed. Pittman elaborated,

> We are trapped in a very dangerous form of linear thinking; a form that says we have to fix young people before we can contribute to their development. We will continue to assume that, with the exception of education, the other kinds of things that have to happen to prepare people for adulthood happen by osmosis.[2]

In other words, even if we were to pin down the common yet elusive problems of youth like substance use, risky sexual activity, and violence and "fix" them, it will not necessarily help young people to be healthy and thrive in society. But she did not end there. She asked the committee an important question, "Are we trying to build better youth to ensure the support and safety of our communities, or are we trying to build better communities to ensure the support and safety of our young people?"[3]

This led to an equally compelling phrase popularized shortly after, "Fully prepared is not fully engaged."[4] From a policy standpoint, all of her points were attempts to conceptualize how to best invest in the types of community experiences that will help young people achieve their potential and be "ready for college, work, and life."[5] This is one of the hallmarks of out-of-school time (OST) strategies because it moves deliberately to preparing youth for and engaging youth in life, with or without academics. It allows room for those who do not fit neatly into the status quo of the educational system. It is a safety net to prevent youth from falling through the academic cracks. It opens the door to new types of mastery that can be leveraged for their future. When employed correctly, OST provides community spaces that augment other opportunities for learning and growth.

This chapter first looks closely at OST strategies that incorporate Hip Hop. In these instances, the programs are primarily about Hip Hop elements and help promote youth well-being. The chapter concludes by focusing on several programs that act as *communities of change* to promote both self and community improvement. These initiatives exemplify Hip Hop's narratives of *growth, community*, and *change*. They are also real world examples of how positive youth development characteristics reinforce one another. Throughout, we hear the voices of Hip Hop's new cultural ambassadors who anchor these initiatives and highlight Hip Hop's empowering values that are embedded in their programming. The results demonstrate the types of well-being objectives that correspond closely to empowerment-based positive youth development.

This chapter also recognizes the ongoing personal uses of Hip Hop (i.e., health-musicking) by youth participants in these programs, and their link to esteem, resilience, growth, community, and change. For example, youth activists indicate how they use Hip Hop to regulate emotions, cope with the stresses of everyday life, and as a form of motivation to sustain their focus on personal responsibilities (like school) and their activism.[6]

FULLY PREPARED THROUGH HIP HOP: HIP HOP, GROWTH, AND COMMUNITY

In the same manner that cultural sensitivity and moving beyond the deficit focus was promoted within health promotion and clinical mental health strategies, there were ideas in thinking about the community as a whole. Efforts to build upon the unique strengths of communities for both youth and community development existed alongside the realization that cultural assets were relevant to any of these initiatives.[7]

Mazi Mutafa of Words, Beats, & Life, Inc. (WBL) helps crystallize the connection between Hip Hop's *knowledge of self* and what it means for mastery and the positive development of young people. Mutafa is another Hip Hop cultural ambassador who travels internationally, such as to Senegal in 2015 to help spread the empowering elements of Hip Hop culture and broaden cultural connections. When reflecting on the work of WBL, he places mastery of one's future and *growth* skills within the context of the creative economy and as an ingredient of knowledge of self. He cites four types of mastery as core programming objectives for youth participants in WBL that allow them to transcend circumstances and situate themselves well on track for healthy development over the life-course:

> The creative economy potentially allows you to create your own job, not seek a job, but create it; to provide for your family and yourself. With our after school program we promote four outcomes, skill set mastery, employability, pursuit of post-secondary education, and self-mastery. . . . These constitute . . . the mastery of future. The idea that you can be the driver of what is possible for your life.[8]

For WBL, the foundation is how skills are nurtured, cultivated, and used as leverage for long-term development. Mutafa also speaks to how WBL is not youth-centered but "community-centered," again capturing the relationships among developmental characteristics.

FEATURE: ALL ABOUT HIP HOP (AAHH)

All About Hip Hop, a southeastern Unites States program that lives and breathes the idea of a community of change through Hip Hop culture, includes community-based programming and therapy groups in its work at regional detention centers. Natalie Davis, the organization's executive director, described how its leadership is intentional about making strong connections between staff and youth, creating a sense of community and engendering a sense of responsibility among participants to be active and engaged citizens who are concerned about developing solutions to problems in society.[9]

For AAHH, Hip Hop culture is the vehicle by which growth and development toward these objectives emerge. Its activities introduce Hip Hop culture: its elements, history, and philosophies. The culture of the organization is relationship-driven and aims to build supportive relationships with young people, acknowledge the advantages of being successful as a student, and to impart the discipline and skills to help them both in and out of the classroom. AAHH then encourages civic interest and the qualities of leadership to its youth. Davis captures these ideas,

> The ultimate goal is to turn all of those things into something that will feed you, feed your family, and feed the community. . . . We are not a program, but a community. We want to build strong connections with students. We create a community of support that is intergenerational, self-reflective, and solution-oriented.[10]

Similar to WBL, Davis and AAHH seek to expand awareness among youth of the many ways that they can use their Hip Hop skills in their communities.

> Many youth are creative. Helping them understand how their creativity can be put to use is important . . . deejaying skills, b-boy and b-girl skills, urban arts skills. One of our functions is to expose them by introducing mentors that are professional working artists. One of our priorities is ensuring that they see examples and models of how to do it in a way that is community-focused, professional, thoughtful, and critical.[11]

FEATURE: TODAY'S FUTURE SOUND

Today's Future Sound (TFS) brings mobile music production and deejaying to schools, community centers, and a range of youth-centered events. The objective is to use the power of music to transform and inspire youth to create positive change in their personal lives and communities. TFS activities are educational, allowing youth to master skills related to industry quality music production, S.T.E.M. (science, technology, engineering, and math) knowledge, and communicating digitally and on the web. Its activities are also therapeutic in their facilitation of youth expression and voice. Finally, TFS activities are developmental in their ability to promote confidence, creativity, prosocial peer and intergenerational relationships, the skills mentioned above, and a community interest.

Dr. Elliot Gann, TFS executive director and lead instructor, was part of the U.S. State Department's Next Level cultural exchange program with Senegal in 2015. Reflecting on aspects of TFS that stand out, Gann echoed Davis's enthusiasm and commitment to creating community spaces where relationships are the core of program experiences. It is not only that kids relate positively to instructors from the community that they can identify with, it is also his ability to develop a rapport with them. "It is the ultimate rapport building device, especially as a White male. It helps make me less threatening so that the expressive, cathartic, and therapeutic relationship can happen."[12] He adds how masculinity and self-efficacy are valuable components of the organization's work.

> As men in Hip Hop there is thing about masculinity. . . . We have men who are masculine and who are good role models. . . . They're modeling that you can be a strong male figure and go out and help the community. . . . [These relationships] give kids skills and experiences that they can incorporate into themselves and then perpetuate—from generation to generation. It is also helping youth to experience themselves as having efficacy, as creators and artists. Now you're a producer. It builds an identity, so important for a positive self-regard and self-esteem. The idea of mastering something [is important], especially if it is valued in a community. We have created a community, a space, a cypher . . . an audience and a culture where kids are recognized.[13]

FEATURE: #HIPHOPED

#HipHopEd has progressed from a good idea to a staple for Hip Hop culture in educational spaces. It began as a weekly Twitter chat on Tuesdays with a topic for discussion moderated by a core group of its leadership who include Timothy Jones and co-founder Chris Emdin. Recent topics include: *It's Been a State of Emergency* (on Freddie Gray, Baltimore, and the Black Lives Matter movement); *Teaching* [Kendrick Lamar's] "*To Pimp a Butterfly*"; *International Hip Hop*; *The Impact of Health Disparities on Hip Hop and Its Ability to Influence Health Disparities*; and a three-week series titled *Women In Hip Hop*, commemorating Women's History Month. The chat has transformed to an even larger platform with a wider web presence, more tools for engaging professionals and individuals seeking to advance connections between Hip Hop culture and education.[14] There is even a record label seeking to help spread awareness of the incredible artistry identified through Hip Hop–integrated educational initiatives.

Also an emcee, Timothy Jones reflected on his own involvement with #HipHopEd and what emerged as a vision for the movement. It started as simply an alignment with the things he liked and was good at as an emcee, as a longtime worker in positive youth development, and as a visionary.

> #HipHopEd is a technical freestyle. My wife said . . . "It captures everything that you love to do. You like to write (but you don't like

writing long), you like to talk (and it's quick), you're engaging people, and you get to talk about things you love—which are education, Hip Hop, and young people. A no-brainer." . . . [We thought] let's take this chat to a level that is touching everybody. Even those who are tenured PhDs were Hip Hop before that. Those [Hip Hop] sensibilities are how you make those connections that are able to be transformative in the lives of young people.[15]

While #HipHopEd is an "education"-oriented space, because of the quality and depth of information shared and the sense of belonging instilled, it actually functions as more of a developmental community. By leveraging knowledge, best practices, and relationships across generations, #HipHopEd has emerged as a true community of growth and change.

Chris Emdin spoke about its future in the context of maximizing the relationship between research, teaching, and the exploration of ideas.

My eyes light up and my spirit lights up when I think of #HipHopEd. It is this accidental identity that has the ability to transform what we can do as academics. . . . An entity that fuels itself, that allows us all to have a model for what it looks like to take our work to the next level. Where we're able to take it from the Ivory Tower to the streets, and then right back to the Ivory Tower. #HipHopEd is everything. It becomes the vehicle by which all of the work gets done. It is the trigger where people say "let's take this work and run with it."[16]

These are but a handful of the new spaces in which Hip Hop culture plays a prominent role in transforming lives.

OPPORTUNITIES FOR GROWTH AND CHANGE: FROM ME TO WE

The early 2000s were a time during which renewed attention was paid to positive youth development. In the initiatives that ascribed to this model, youth were treated as leaders and partners in reshaping communities. The objectives were to involve youth in opportunities to improve the environments in which people and families "live, work, learn, and play."[17] It was not only the belief that youth could transcend adverse conditions but that they could be change agents themselves so that other youths in their communities would not have to battle similarly adverse conditions.[18]

Theorists, researchers, and practitioners entered this discussion with different terminologies and nuances to their perspectives, but they had many overlapping ideas about strengths, culture, the roles of young people, and justice. Fundamentally, they felt young people could no longer be marginalized; that adults and youth must recognize the range of social, economic, and political influences pervasive in young people's lives; that youth must be partners (as resources/assets) in recognizing community strengths and improving conditions that need to change; and that innovation, culture (including youth culture), and media/technologies must be prominent.[19]

Some of the distinct but related terminology for this work include: social justice youth development, youth organizing, community youth development, youth activism, active engaged citizenship, civic engagement, Hip Hop development, empowerment-based positive youth development, community social work, and youth-led community organizing.[20]

RACIAL AND ETHNIC IDENTITY, HEALING, AND CRITICAL CONSCIOUSNESS

While there is tremendous overlap across civic-minded initiatives, there has also been a divergence in the meaning of engagement. Some theorists and practitioners are much more explicit about the integration of non-dominant group status (e.g., Black and Latino racial and ethnic) experiences and the cultural legacies of liberation, freedom, and healing from uniquely oppressive forces.[21] Identity-oriented objectives have been most consistently associated with youth organizing, social justice youth development, and critical youth empowerment.[22]

For example, social justice youth development is clear about the long-term goal of healing, critical consciousness, and action across the individual, community, and global levels. Awareness occurs in three stages: first, is an awareness of the self, which facilitates identity development. In the second stage, alongside community organizing and its related strategies, is social awareness, a precursor to actual solutions for increased equity and justice. The third stage is global awareness and connection to the struggles of other communities. The goal of all stages of awareness is to promote well-being at the individual and community levels.[23] Essential for the achievement of these objectives is an ongoing analysis of social dynamics and an ability to engage in specific opportunities to contribute to specific social change. For example, Los Angeles's Youth Justice Coalition, and also the Community Coalition with its youth-driven group South Central Youth Empowered for Action (SC-YEA), has been vocal about the importance of solidarity among the Black and Latino communities in the wake of the highly publicized cases of officer-involved deaths of Black citizens and the Black Lives Matter movement. Community Coalition Executive Director Alberto Retana says, "If we are to truly deal with racism in America impacting Latinos, we need to understand what is happening right now with Black America. . . . And in fact, there are many Afro-Latinos in our community that experience both narratives first-hand."[24]

There is a difference between *identity-integrated* youth organizing and *identity support* programs. While the latter celebrates culture and facilitates critical education about race, ethnicity, and gender, it does not engage in direct action for improving conditions.[25] Melvin Delgado and Lee Staples distinguished between *adult- and youth-led* organizing efforts, with the latter referring to efforts that had youth determining the level and nature of collaboration with adults.[26]

THE ISSUES

Looking specifically at what research uncovered about the most common issues youth rally around in the United States, there are systemic issues that affect youth and those that are intergenerational, as well as issues that affect the individual and those that affect the community. These "root cause" issues are much more closely connected to health and well-being, and have implications for the entire lifespan.[27] The top issues for more than a third of the initiatives were, in order: (1) educational justice, (2) racial justice, (3) environmental justice, (4) health justice, and (5) juvenile justice. Many campaigns are also multi-issue and intersecting. For example, health campaigns often include environmental work, food justice, and reproductive health and rights.[28]

Age-related issues for young people stem from being labeled a minor, a child, youth, or kid in the United States. It is the lived experience and interpersonal dynamics of being a young person and not having power in a wide range of daily activities including finances, mobility, nutrition and physical activity, and the many political, social, and economic policies influencing parents and neighborhoods.

DESIRE, OPPORTUNITY, AND QUALITY OF CIVIC ENGAGEMENT

The desire for young people to help is not the same as actually helping, and opportunities for them to engage are not equal. A young person's ability to engage in social analysis and have self and collective efficacy sets the tone for action toward social change.[29] These civic attitudes are not meaningful without tangible opportunities to engage in actions toward change. If specific pathways to engagement do not exist, then youth are being underutilized as resources, and their opportunities for personal development are being muted.[30]

Youth organizing programs enjoyed a resurgence in the United States in the late 1990s and early 2000s, after the vacuum created from the breakup of many youth organizing and social justice groups from the Civil Rights era.[31] During the Civil Rights era, youth had very visible roles on the frontlines for change, and they were active in protesting injustice and contributing to community development. The renewed efforts were a direct legacy of organizing in the 1960s and represented the thinking, ideologies, and practices of past efforts. The principles of the Black Power and Black Arts movements, and of individuals like Saul Alinsky and Paulo Freire, remained strong. However, signs suggest that at least in some major cities those gains have once again diminished. For example, Tim Eubanks, supervisor for the Austin Healthy Adolescent program in Austin, Texas, talks about the decline in youth activists and his role in reversing this trend:

> For me it is part of working with older youth, especially older youth of color in Austin. I'm coming to it from a loss of youth leadership programs. We used to have Young Scholars for Justice, we had the Youth Mobilizers, and we had the activists with Out Youth . . . all of these strong programs so that if you were 17 or 18 years old and you lived in East Austin, you had a choice of different things you could be involved in that were really about changing the city in the ways you wanted it to be changed. . . . Let's create programming that allows young people to express themselves, but let's not shy away from what we want to see changed.[32]

GROWTH, CHANGE, AND HIP HOP

The best of today's contemporary civic engagement strategies integrate innovative and culturally sensitive strategies, and they consider youth culture, racial-ethnic culture, Hip Hop culture, and other regionally specific cultural strengths in their programs. The immediacy of Hip Hop culture; its potential to be youth-driven; its multimedia potential; and its ability to be verbal, auditory, visual, and physical while addressing, issues relevant to both people and environment, allow it to be an incredibly rich asset for achieving youth organizing goals. Further, Hip Hop's value of protest and its unflinching willingness to speak to political, economic, and social issues invites an expanded definition of good citizens and engaged citizenship.

Historically, tension has existed around the meaning of engaged citizen-ship. Is the ideal citizen one who volunteers within the confines of the status quo; one who is aware and involved in the latest current events; or someone who is oriented to equity and justice, contests the status quo, and stays involved in current events?[33]

PAYING IT FORWARD

The emcee and community health peer educator Darrion "Chi" Borders talked about his personal transformation as an individual and artist via the path leading to his current role as an engaged citizen and professional. He is a living embodiment of the young people Davis is committed to helping in AAHH programs discussed earlier. As a reminder, the goal of AAHH is to try and help youth grow into the best versions of themselves. Chi started out in high school with a program called the Cipher, modeled after Chris "Kazi" Rolle's *The Hip Hop Project* in New York. Chi understands commu-nity needs and believes in his ability to be a change agent. Much of this is anchored by his own growth and resilience. He sees his current role as a form of "paying it forward."[34]

> Cipher showed me how to think outside of the typical. All they knew was that I would freestyle. I came to them with an open mind. I was like, think greater than the typical. For some youth, it wasn't their thing. After other youth dropped out, I was still there. It kept me grounded. I learned I could work with people. I could build with oth-ers. It showed me minds together is very powerful.[35]

Recent research points to the short- and long-term developmental ben-efits of civic engagement in adolescence. For example, Wing Yi Chan and colleagues found that civic engagement in adolescence is related to higher life satisfaction, civic participation, and educational attainment, and it is related to lower rates of arrest in early adulthood.[36] These are the individual successes that suggest youth development is possible amidst community development and that effects may endure across the lifespan.

The benefits of community arts programs include facilitating resilience and youth development through increased self-efficacy, skill-building, and building prosocial relationships.[37] Hip Hop–specific efforts have shown similar promise. For example, performance arts–based workshops, with the development of health promotion–oriented Hip Hop songs, were seen to improve relationships among community organizations and build support for public health initiatives.[38]

The city of Philadelphia has several high-profile examples of programs that intersect community arts and public health. First, the City of Philadelphia *Mural Arts Program* enjoys tremendous popularity and recently celebrated its thirty-year anniversary. It began as an anti-graffiti campaign in the mid-1980s. With its constellation of murals throughout the city, it now stands as a beacon of pride and resilience driven by art. The second project, the *Building Brotherhood: Engaging Males of Color* public art program, is a Hip Hop–driven program geared to engage men of color around mental health. The goal is to increase awareness of mental health issues; to encourage discussion of needs and mental health concerns among Black, Latino, and Asian men; and to enable easier access to services when needed.

These two Philadelphia initiatives are public health initiatives specifically linked to Hip Hop culture. The construction of murals may not be considered in the exact same manner as spray painting walls or trains surreptitiously in the dark of night—part of the reported excitement of the culture. However, as part of the creative economy, aside from individual-level learning and growth, it is a pathway to legitimate employment and a generator of positive emotions for many in their communities.

FROM CIPHER TO THE CITY: CHI AND AUSTIN'S HEALTHY ADOLESCENTS

The second example from Philadelphia bears some similarity to the work being done in Austin. The city's health services department has a Hip Hop artist and peer educator who is working in communities across the city to help provide peer-to-peer education and health promotion opportunities. As a skilled emcee, Chi is a gifted communicator, able to engage others with skills inaccessible to many other peer educators. Further, his source of inspiration is as much from the evidence of community need as it is embodying the emotion of personal transformation: "After our first album [*The Cipher*] . . . I was like 'my momma is listening to it!' I was a junior in high school. I stopped doing sports and went straight to the music. It showed me a new area in life that I could achieve, ever since, I've been writing . . . and reaching people through my voice," Chi said about his transformation from student to youth leader and health educator.[39]

Tim Eubanks hired Chi and helped expand the vision of optimal health to life in Austin through youth-led and peer-to-peer initiatives. "Chi is an incredible artist and hasn't given up yet. I'm trying to increase the number of youth organizing projects and community organizing projects in Austin. And Hip Hop is one way to do that because of the history in Austin with

Zel Miller III connecting with young people (through Hip Hop) from the late 1990s until today," Eubanks said.[40]

I AM (NOT) HIP HOP

KRS-One is infamous for his quotes about *being* Hip Hop, and Hip Hop being something one *lives*. However, if we are to bring our attention back to truly distinguishing between youth culture and Hip Hop culture for young people, we must recognize differences in time and place. Contemporary youth culture exists at a unique temporal position in the history of Hip Hop culture. Hip Hop culture, and rap music in particular, are one part, albeit an immensely popular part, of the overall popular culture landscape and subject to the forces of the commercial entertainment industry.

There has been the demise of what was simultaneously commercially successful and socially critical.[41] The year 1988 saw the release of Public Enemy's *It Takes a Nation of Millions to Hold Us Back* and N.W.A.'s *Straight Outta Compton*. The latter firmly entrenched the "gangsta" era, but it was also socially critical. What was distinct about the content of Public Enemy and N.W.A. was, albeit to varying degrees, a simultaneous attention to cause and effect. Through these artists, issues such as the devastating effects of substance use and community violence, federal and state legislative policies (e.g., the war on drugs), funding decisions, and the criminalization of entire communities, moved from awareness only within the Black community to the broader public.

Today's youth may or may not feel Hip Hop sufficiently speaks to their immediate concerns on youth rights or broader community issues that influence their lives. They may not feel that music exists as a social force or that it is a viable social justice and youth organizing resource. Much of this has to do with how music is now commoditized and distributed.

For example, in MK Asante analysis of what he dubs the post-Hip Hop generation and social change, he captures the words of a twenty-one-year-old woman: "I want to be a part of the generation that's going to rebuild this city and fight against the officials in this city who are trying to keep us out. I love Hip Hop, but if the Hip Hop generation ain't about doing this kind of work, then we need something else."[42] He continues with his own perspective:

Many young people who were born into the Hip Hop generation feel misrepresented by it and have begun to see the dangers and limitations of being collectively identified by a genre of music that we don't even own . . . [a] lack of ownership that has allowed corporate forces to overrun Hip Hop with a level of misogyny and Black-on-Black violence that spurs some young folks to disown the label "Hip Hop generation."[43]

EMBRACING HIP HOP BEYOND PEDAGOGY AND STRATEGY

Despite pessimistic sentiments and general malaise about the effectiveness of Hip Hop culture in speaking to the needs of today's youth, there remains a rich history of examples and a vibrant core of Hip Hop–integrated spaces in education, in out-of-school time, in mental health and physical health settings, working toward both (youth) development as mentioned in the prior sections, and (community) change. This starts with honest critiques of the varied manifestations of Hip Hop culture, holding commercialized Hip Hop accountable, increasing the visibility and appropriation of change-oriented Hip Hop narratives, and recognizing the many examples of Hip Hop activism, both big and small.

ACTIVISM AS SIMPLY BEING YOUNG AND ACTIVE

In the same manner as the Millennial Activists United organizing approach described in Chapter 7, Andreana Clay highlights how many youth use a *virtual activism-mixtape* approach to change, and "sample" inspiration and strategies from a variety of sources and reformulate them to suit their personal sociopolitical awareness, mobilization, and direct action needs.[44] This can be helpful in situations where growth *and* action must be personalized, where there is no absolute desire to be a part of a traditional leadership-driven movement.

The use of Hip Hop in these instances is often a part of creating new understandings, shaping new narratives, and remixing messages. Sometimes the target is social change, but sometimes the target is simply personal resilience, excellence, and contesting marginalizing treatment or narratives from parents, teachers, peers, or institutions. The net goals are understanding the social determinants of their well-being, simply being active in partnership with their peers experiencing similarly discriminatory and biased contexts, and creating lanes within which other youth can navigate these environments. They are not disempowered from being geographically isolated from larger activist movements, from leadership that may not appreciate their values or tactics, or from a preoccupation with activism toward major policy changes.[45]

HIP HOP ACTIVISM AT THE NATIONAL LEVEL

Bakari Kitwana has been a consistent figure in efforts to integrate Hip Hop culture and community empowerment. He has been a bridge between theory and actual on the ground practice and his book *Hip Hop Activism in the Obama Era* has documented five of the major recent forces linking Hip Hop and social change: the League of Young Voters, the Hip Hop Congress, the National Hip Hop Political Convention, the Hip Hop Caucus, and the Hip Hop Summit Action Network.

GROWTH, CHANGE, AND THE YOUTH AGENDA IN HIP HOP

It is important not to make the lazy assumption that *youth culture* is synonymous with Hip Hop culture.[46] The premise is not to suggest a post-racial agenda, but it is about not being naively Hip Hop–centric at the expense of recognizing racial heterogeneity among Black youth.

The creativity, enthusiasm, and high energy of young people are in-fused with aspects of youth culture. . . . The particulars may vary, and "youth culture" can encompass a broad range of scenes. For example, the Hip Hop activism of street-smart kids, the high-tech games of computer geeks, the service learning projects of middle-class subur-ban students, the sports competition among high school jocks, the violence of urban gangs, the music of metal heads, and the religious activities of evangelical Christian youth.[47]

Stereotypes aside, Delgado and Staples show that the best developmen-tal outcomes for youth (and their communities) come from creating op-portunities to engage and act in the settings in which youth feel comfortable, a sense of belonging, and empowered to make direct contributions.[48]

ME AND MY COMMUNITIES OF CHANGE

Aspirational narratives that are the lifeline of Hip Hop culture permeate out-of-school time opportunities for youth. They manifest as inspiration for personal mastery and being the best version of oneself. They manifest in agency, to be of service to others and to actually facilitate material im-provements in their communities. These narratives offer hope in situations where hope may be grim, or simply where youth have been marginalized and feel disempowered. These narratives help guide intergenerational co-operation, understanding, and commitments to excellence.

Jeff Duncan Andrade highlights the importance of these counternarratives in his discussion of a research-based summer seminar that was a type of hybrid of education and OST. He recognized that raising awareness of social and environmental challenges through critical analysis could be stressful and depress mood levels. Thus, he emphasized the role of youth as change agents, through giving voice to such challenges, developing resources for the education of others, and the development of proposed solutions to challenges. The students' final video projects were filled with self-selected Hip Hop narratives from classic change-oriented artists of the time, like Tupac, Dead Prez, and The Roots.

Today's cultural ambassadors understand the power of Hip Hop culture and are undeterred by myopic representations of the culture in the entertainment industry. They use the range of tools, the life-course scope of its direction, and the empowering nature of its narratives to help youth transform. Today's cultural ambassadors are also undeterred by societal challenges, recognizing youth as assets with abilities to transform society. Youth can be entrepreneurs, having skills that can be cultivated regardless of academic trends and the limitations of the educational structure. Today's cultural ambassadors use and are integrated with technology, allowing them to be intergenerational as much as global, with initiatives like #HipHopEd. They are identity-oriented as much as they are bridge-builders across races and ethnicities.

CHAPTER 12

Hip Hop and Mental Health: Emotions, Coping, Identity, and Growth

Using music as a tool to improve mental health can range from regulating moment-to-moment well-being, to coping with a serious mental health disorder. Health-musicking, self-health, and everyday appropriation of music for self and community improvement has been well documented.[1] These are opportunities for people to grow emotionally, physically, or socially, even when in response to episodic adversity. Certain periods of life are more developmentally sensitive, yet again, these are not necessarily problems or deficits in individuals and should be viewed as opportunities to build assets and potential instead.

Several theoretical orientations guide Hip Hop–integrated strategies relating to mental health, and a deficit vs. asset tension is evident. This chapter explores Hip Hop and mental health, with an emphasis on identity, cultural context, and coping. It continues to build on assumptions of why and how music helps mental health by taking a closer look at self and professionally mediated strategies using Hip Hop. It concludes with the renewed emphasis on strengths, voice, and empowerment promoted by today's new mental health professionals. In these discussions is the understanding of Hip Hop's value for mental health, both with and without the help of a professional—through self-health and everyday listening. However, structured integration of Hip Hop and empowerment *with* helping professionals like social work-ers, counselors, and psychologists strengthens the cultural armor available to help Black youth cope and excel despite challenges in their social environments.

MENTAL HEALTH AND HIP HOP CULTURE

The benefits of music for mental health range from relaxation strategies and emotional regulation among individuals experiencing anxiety and stress, to substantial improvements in mental functioning and quality of life among individuals coping with severe mental illness.[2] Professional interventions and structured uses of Hip Hop culture include both broad strategies and specific techniques or activities.

To determine an overall strategy, professionals draw from specific theo-retical orientations and concepts. The techniques and activities profession-als use are the structured ways people are guided to interact with music or artifacts. Theories involve assumptions about people's thinking and behav-ior and the sources of life challenges. Theories also include ideas about how to best achieve desirable outcomes for such challenges. For example, is the source of the problem primarily the individual's thinking about a situation, or environmental conditions? Alternatively, is it a roughly equal combina-tion of both? Professional Hip Hop-based strategies mostly use the culture as a vehicle to operationalize pre-existing theoretical perspectives, akin to Hill's "*with Hip Hop*" perspective in education.[3]

Hip Hop in mental health is sometimes just a resource, not its own theo-retical premise. At its most basic it is used to build rapport and open the door to further conversation. Timothy Jones, CVO of #HipHopEd and Di-rector of Healthy Connections for Washington, DC's Martha's Table, talks about rapport building in therapeutic spaces in general. In particular he is pinpointing the elephant in the room among many youth work spaces when he says, "You're in your car listening to it. I'm in my car listening to it. Why, if we come together—can't we talk about it? I wanted to know, how are the messages in the music influencing adolescent development?"[4]

Similarly, psychologist Cendrine Robinson talked about rapport-build-ing in her work with youth involved with the criminal justice system and rethinking the assessment process.

I was so happy that I had Hip Hop Therapy at my fingertips. I had several clients who had no interest in talking to me. None. They were court ordered to be in therapy, and then we were meeting in the pro-bation office. Just distinguishing myself from a probation officer was so much effort. For the majority of them, it allowed conversations to happen. They were able to talk about the disturbing things in their lives. Before, because they were mandated, they had learned they could come in and say nothing and get away with it. Finding the right song or artists that would connect with them also helped avoid the mental health stigma. It is not boring clinical questions. It allowed them to let their guard down and just start talking.[5]

Alternatively, at its most comprehensive, Hip Hop–integrated mental health strategies are a part of the entire architecture of the therapeutic experience. For example, Tomas Alvarez's Beats, Rhymes, & Life, Inc. uses teams of trained clinicians, teaching artists, and peer mentors to deliver Hip Hop Therapy using therapeutic, youth development, and social justice frameworks. These therapeutic groups use Hip Hop writing, dialogue, team-building activities, and performance over the course of twelve to eighteen weeks.[6]

BLACK MENTAL HEALTH

Among older Blacks, social inequality and racial discrimination were the largest contributors to mental health problems.[7] Blacks are 20 percent more likely to report having serious psychological distress than non-Hispanic Whites.[8] The proportion of adults with feelings of sadness, hopelessness, worthlessness, or that everything is an effort, all of the time, was approximately double that of Whites as well.[9] When looking at gender, in 2009 the death rate from suicide for Black men was almost four times that of Black women.[10]

Youth are especially vulnerable to stress and trauma in their social environments. Black male students were more likely than White students to feel unsafe in their neighborhood and have difficulty trusting and relying upon neighbors.[11] Stress from perceived discrimination is also salient, as research on Black males suggests discrimination in teen years can be associated with depression at 20 years old.[12]

Moving from depressive symptoms to suicidal ideation, trends suggest that suicidality differences in youth by gender are less about differences in thinking about suicide and more about lethality of strategy and actual follow-through. Black girls of high school age are more than twice as likely as similarly aged boys to seriously consider suicide (18.1 percent vs. 7.8 percent), while attempts are much closer (8.8 percent vs. 7.7 percent) across gender.[13] Even if stress does not manifest as depression or suicidal ideation it warrants concern. Ongoing stress contributes to physiological responses in the body, including wear and tear and serious deterioration of health over time.[14]

BEYOND THE BLACK–WHITE BINARY

Too often statistics fall into a Black and White binary, which does a disservice to understanding the distribution of health. It neglects multiracial individuals, and it neglects the African diaspora in the Black community, including the increasing numbers of foreign-born Blacks in the United States. It also neglects the wide range of national identities present in the Latino and Hispanic communities. For example, health status and trends tend to be better for individuals born outside the United States, but these health benefits decrease the longer they are U.S. residents.[15]

When we look closely at national mental health trends, we see that certain trends, like feeling sad and hopeless, serious consideration of suicide, and development of a plan for attempting suicide, are significantly higher for Native Americans, Latinos/Hispanics, and individuals identifying as multiracial.[16] Actual suicide attempts were highest among Latinos and Native Hawaiian/Pacific Islander youth. The mental health realities of each of these other groups is important, but of particular importance in the context of this book are those considered multiracial. Within the phenotype-dominant social system of the United States, those identifying as multiracial are often socially classified as Black.

ACCESS TO FORMAL MENTAL HEALTH CARE

Whether it is limited access to mental health services, trust in mental health care, uncertainty, or stigma, Black adolescents tend to access mental health care less than other groups.[17] This holds through adulthood where the average is 8.7 percent of adults receiving mental health treatment or counseling. Black women are almost twice as likely as men to receive mental health counseling at 10.5 percent compared to 6.4 percent.[18] For Black adults with a major depressive episode, about half of them received treatment the year prior, compared to more than two-thirds of White adults.[19] Thus, opportunities to engage in activities outside of the formal sector that promote positive mental health and well-being are an essential complement to formal mental health treatment for the Black community.

OPPORTUNITIES FOR THERAPEUTIC CHANGE
AND THE BLACK COMMUNITY

Opportunities to improve mental health in the Black community are substantial if we take advantage of existing strengths. Much of this book has expounded on the importance of thinking about Hip Hop as a cultural strength to draw upon. Research highlights additional strengths in the Black community that can be built upon, including social support, authoritative parenting, esteem, active coping toward resiliency, a cultural history of strengths (inside and outside the United States), collective or community resistance (to oppression), and resilience.[20]

For example, Thompson and colleagues describe the normative availability of extended social supports, firm and appropriately restrictive parents, and robust self-esteem.[21] Mills and Cody-Rydewski similarly distinguish the advantages of extended family ties and social support along with religiosity for improved mental health.[22] Bains echoes these communal and collective-oriented strengths, finding the value of strength of one's inner circle and an active searching for better situations and conditions.[23]

The idea of "grit" has gained a lot of traction in youth work, defined as consistency of interest over time and persistence of effort.[24] We know that resilience is not a character trait but that it is dynamic, temporal, and context specific.[25] However, these characteristics can be meaningful to draw upon during instances of adversity and setbacks to build self-efficacy. Lower self-efficacy is associated with greater suicidal ideation in Black males, but with actual suicide attempts and attempts with injury for Black females.[26] As such, it can be meaningful for youth to know how strengths, grit, and overall resilience have been a regular part of their personal *and* collective culture throughout history.

FROM SELF-HEALTH TO PROFESSIONAL MENTAL HEALTH STRATEGIES

Well before any sustained research about music and well-being, people have turned to music in their everyday lives for their own personal benefit. Everyday listening to one's own, self-chosen music helps to regulate mood and inhibit stress.[27] Professional mental health providers have similarly used music, including rap music and the broader spectrum of arts, to complement less dynamic *talk* strategies.[28]

Music-integrated strategies have been used to improve general mental health and to remediate specific diagnoses. Multimodal strategies have also been especially valuable. For example, a recent randomized and mixed method study by Grocke and colleagues followed individuals with severe mental illness. Over a thirteen-week course, participants were able to sing songs that they preferred as well as write, rehearse, and record their own original songs in a studio. Participants reported a significant improvement in quality of life and spirituality, and a significant difference from the standard treatment group.[29] Recognition of these multimodal benefits is a reason why emcee and high school mental health practitioner Ian Levy has a full studio in his office for his work with youth and is seeking funding for a complement of artist practitioners to help bring a suite of offerings to students.[30]

UNIQUE OPPORTUNITIES, CHALLENGES, AND STRATEGIES: HIP HOP AND MENTAL HEALTH

The standard challenges of working in the field of mental health invites opportunities for innovative new approaches to treatment. Rap music, the broader aspects of Hip Hop culture, and the cultural strengths of Black people mentioned above, including social support, esteem, resiliency, and a cultural history of excellence, are only the beginning.

The active use and reporting of Hip Hop–integrated strategies in mental health have been in existence for roughly twenty years, with substantial work picking up during the last ten years. Much of the earliest work on the therapeutic uses of Hip Hop culture have been built based on the cultural focus of writers in the early to mid–1990s who helped to demystify and legitimize rap music and Hip Hop culture in literature.[31] Writers like Nelson George, Robin Kelley, Tricia Rose, Cheryl Keyes, Eric Dyson, and Todd Boyd soon after, recognized Hip Hop culture's meaning, value, and cultural significance for the Black community, but also the broader American public.

For example, Tricia Rose's groundbreaking work, *Black Noise*, helped bring an unparalleled level of depth to understanding the growth enhancing potential of Hip Hop culture. Cheryl Keyes, although a little later, was able to use a musicological lens to create a bridge to these earlier works. She was able to similarly break down the idea of street consciousness and musicality in a profound and comprehensive manner—that Hip Hop truly is a culture.[32]

Many writers continued in this tradition of analyzing and validating the culture with an emphasis on its relevance in the United States.[33] Still more writers helped continue this cultural generalizability by recognizing that Hip Hop culture's desire for social, political, and economic advancement is being similarly pursued across a range of international communities.[34]

THE FUTURE OF HIP HOP AND MENTAL HEALTH: INTEGRATION OF MIND AND BODY

"Your brain on music . . . is all about connections."[35] What role does the brain play in this association between music appropriation and well-being? A growing body of research offers preliminary evidence of the specific neural pathways by which music evokes affect, motivation, and behavior. Music influences certain brain regions even more than language.[36] Preliminary evidence has developed to show music's relationship to health in four areas with four main neurochemical systems in the brain: (1) reward and motivation [dopamine]; (2) stress, arousal, and emotions [cortisol, serotonin]; (3) immunity [serotonin]; and (4) social affiliation [oxytocin].[37] Music-evoked emotions involve these neural correlates and are often discussed in partnership with "why" people appropriate music. For example, joy, happiness, reward, and dopamine are often connected.

It is this interface with music that Koelsch adds substantively to the conversation, with "how" music evocation is connected to well-being. As discussed earlier, his seven principles of music evocation include: evaluation, resonance, memory, expectancy/tension, imagination, understanding, and social functions.[38] For example, if music creates a soundscape that resonates powerfully with the listener, they may connect more strongly with the emotions in the track. At the same time, no matter how universal a theme is interpreted to be by a professional or third party, it is still the subjective view of the individual that determines meaning and what is evoked. A person's unique background, history, personality, imagination, and understanding, among other principles, are at play.

HIP HOP AND RAP MUSIC STRATEGIES AND MENTAL HEALTH

The first cohort of practitioners and researchers moving into rap music's use as an explicitly mental health strategy, to address a diagnosis or condition, also emphasized its value for enhancing culturally sensitive practices.[39] Hip Hop was introduced to address behavioral problems, health problems, psychiatric disorders, and the people at risk for these conditions.[40] These earliest efforts were still decidedly problem-focused and used medical models to measure outcomes.

In these initial incarnations of rap music use, integration meant sensitivity to music preference (rap music), socialization and communication styles (for people who identify with Hip Hop culture), and a recognition of the unique psychological and social experiences connected to age, racial and ethnic identity, religion, and sexual identity often represented in the music's themes.[41] In other words, using rap music brought a level of relatability and perceived real-world, everyday relevance absent from traditional mental health approaches.[42] The dominant theories emphasized multicultural ecological systems as well as cognitive behavioral and constructivist models.

Although mental health uses of Hip Hop were anchored in references to Black and Latino youth, it can be ascribed to all who identify with Hip Hop culture.[43] These sentiments still apply among many of today's helping professionals. Hip Hop culture can help promote improvements in everyone, but there is a particular transformative potential for members of the Black community.

The earliest Hip Hop–related mental health strategies were tied heavily to what is often referred to as the culture's "golden age" and its legacy. Music from this era's icons include Public Enemy, KRS-One and Boogie Down Productions, Tupac Shakur, and Dead Prez. These artists and their prosocial messages are more readily identifiable, whereas newer therapies and theorizing highlight engagement opportunities from artists and songs that may not be so explicitly prosocial or even known beyond the neighborhood. Newer relevant artists and their song content may simply be favorites of the person. Alternatively, more risk-saturated messages may be used to open the door to therapeutic conversations and residual opportunities for empowerment.[44] For example, Dr. Robinson found in her youth work,

> So many [youth] don't even listen to songs on the radio. They have their own music that's promoted via YouTube that's relevant in their community. For the most part I did use mainstream artists. But sometimes I would let them play songs by their homeboys . . . that made a song and put in on YouTube. Because that was relevant and more of use for them. For some artists like Meek Mill, I was like "really?!" But he made me think more deeply about his struggle and what he's going through and why kids identify with these artists.[45]

CREATION VS. ANALYSIS

Creativity can be expressed in many ways, from lyric composition, songwriting, instrumentation (including production and beatmaking), song selection to musical scrapbooking/creating a mixtape, all core facets of Hip Hop culture. The more active aspect of creating Hip Hop music, especially within groups, is uniquely transformative, especially for marginalized groups, where socially-embedded growth occurs in part by "learning to trust others and coming to feel a sense of mastery" and because "rap music can act as an empowering transformative agent by offering challenges to the politics and ideology of the dominant culture."[46]

In Hip Hop, improvisation bridges two often considered divergent approaches: music centered approaches and music psychotherapy approaches. Creation within Hip Hop culture is a rich, complex, and layered process that touches all the physiological, psychological, and social influences outlined in much of music-centered research. The product is similarly rich, complex, and layered; ready for discussion, interpretation, and analysis from a music psychotherapy standpoint.[47]

In our discussion about mental health and Hip Hop, Ian Levy talked about the interrelatedness of music-centered and music psychotherapy approaches. But he also adds in another layer of how powerful the self-musicking process can be for augmenting this already existing interrelatedness. We spoke just a few short days after the Walter Scott shooting in South Carolina. Scott was an(other) unarmed Black man shot (in the back) and killed by a law enforcement officer. The case resonated in the collective conscience of the Black community like so many other deaths of Black men in situations involving law enforcement officials. Levy's general approach to therapy for youth is to have them create lyrics in a music-centered approach but to eventually process the pieces upon completion. Over time students increase their comfort and skill with this process, and as a result they have a tool that they can use at any point on their own to create rhymes about things and situations they feel are necessary. After the Scott death, Levy shared his consolation in knowing his youth's relative preparation during yet another potentially traumatic period for so many Black youth:

> I know that there are young people who I am working with who have a tool they have been working with all year to sort through their thoughts and feelings, the trauma, their personal experiences, and experiences their families have. With me, and with other individuals that are doing this work, it is just an amazing thing. The fact that I know, is a heartwarming thing in the midst of all that is happening.[48]

The alternative approach uses the music as a starting point, while analysis and talk therapy is the highlighted strategy for growth and well-being. While some approaches are more growth-oriented, others are more directive about the need for systemic changes in socializing communities.

ROOTS OF RAP MUSIC AS THERAPY

The formal introduction to rap music therapy from which many have anchored both practice and research agendas began most comprehensively with Dr. Elligan's Rap Therapy. However, the introduction of rap music as an extensive behavioral intervention, and not simply a media source to analyze or opine about, was as early as 1998 with Stephen's health intervention.[49] The earliest writings about rap music or broader elements of Hip Hop culture for therapeutic purposes were almost universally linked to

Black youth, at-risk populations, delinquency, and psychiatric disorders.[50] These early uses also made pre-existing music the starting point.

Edgar Tyson and Naykeyshaey Tillie-Allen emphasized strengths to a greater degree, with Tyson explicitly discussing the integration of Hip Hop as method for "strengths focused treatments."[51] But overall, in the use of Hip Hop in mental health a largely medical model existed, despite the universal recognition that increased cultural sensitivity was more strengths-oriented because it recognized cultural assets (like Hip Hop culture) within treatment.

To be clear, these were not the only professionals using these strategies. Furthermore, these approaches were created to meet specific needs and challenges in settings that benefited from more culturally appropriate and engaging strategies. However, research and practice builds upon them because these are the strategies written about in peer-reviewed sources, tested early for efficacy, and introduced into the professional literature and narrative for Hip Hop–integrated strategies.

This has been both helpful and harmful. Helpful, because their original intent was to be more culturally sensitive and ultimately more responsive than more traditional approaches. However, it has been harmful in that it inevitably linked Hip Hop–integrated strategies to the most marginalized populations and high-risk groups. The result is that Hip Hop–integrated strategies are often associated with desperation—a last resort.[52]

THE NEW(ER) SCHOOL OF HIP HOP AND MENTAL HEALTH

Again, many in the newer generation of Hip Hop's cultural ambassadors enter the work with a deep appreciation of the transformative power of Hip Hop because of its personal meaning and role in their own lives. For example, Ian Levy spoke about his own introspection and growth via Hip Hop culture. He discussed how he went from being an avid fan to the realization of the depth and substance of content. He was able to hone his skill as an emcee as his own type of health-musicking, finding the process therapeutic in its own right. The result was a validation of Hip Hop's healing power and a commitment to making this skill available for young people in the midst of their own life journeys.[53]

Adia Winfrey developed one of the most comprehensive and substantive mental health interventions integrating Hip Hop culture with the Healing Young People Thru Empowerment (H.Y.P.E.) curriculum. She drew on the origins of rap and Hip Hop therapy to focus on Black boys with a disruptive behavior disorder diagnosis. Although she emphasizes group therapy, she recognizes the rationale for individual therapy at times of crisis, for topical sensitivity, and for some diagnostic categories.[54] Her curriculum builds heavily upon classic cognitive-behavioral and psycho-dynamic theories, augmented by multicultural family systems, Negriscence, and Interpersonal Cognitive Problem Solving (ICPS) theories. She empha-sizes accountability for behavioral change and managing emotions, but with a strong racial identity development component.[55]

To date, this is one of the most comprehensive mental health strategies for Black youth that integrates Hip Hop culture. It includes a strong family dimension, is inclusive of multiple media sources, offers a wide range of rap music styles (eschewing a myopic focus on the proverbial "conscious" rap songs), and offers an accompanying facilitator's guide.

MENTAL HEALTH IN CONTEXT: SOCIAL IDENTITY, GROWTH, AND COMMUNITY

Susan Hadley and George Yancey created an excellent compendium of contemporary uses of Hip Hop culture from a social science perspective, including historical and theoretical perspectives, interventions, measure-ment strategies, and results. The intervention strategies discussed are for both youth considered "at-risk" and youth with specific diagnoses. For ex-ample, in one chapter contributing to advances in theory and strategy for integrating Hip Hop, Vanessa Veltre and Hadley expand on Black feminist theory and academic analysis to describe a Hip Hop feminist approach to therapy with Black adolescent females.[56] Their use of Hip Hop has four objectives: (1) to promote collaboration and the importance of building a strong female community, (2) to explore identity formation and gender-role socialization, (3) to increase self-esteem of young women through em-powering them to develop and honor their voices as female, and (4) to promote social transformation.

Tomas Alvarez III, in the same book, describes his work with youth con-sidered at-risk in the Rap Therapy program of Beats, Rhymes, & Life, Inc. Alvarez built on his graduate student work in pilot intervention to create a form of rap therapy that differed from earlier versions of rap therapy and Hip Hop therapy in four distinct areas. First, as a group modality it is performance-based, it is community empowerment embedded, and co-facilitated by a mental health professional and a teaching artist.[57] Further, youth are viewed as co-creators of change. Youth advocate for their needs and co-construct the interventions necessary to bring about individual and community change.

Alvarez's current perspective is anchored in a strengths-oriented ap-proach, one that facilitates young people's ability to practice self-health and use their own abilities for self-improvement. It operates from the fundamental principle that when a young person's family or community environment has challenges, they deserve to have light shined on what is positive, inspiring, and hopeful, just as much as they are prepared to negotiate the obstacles. "Hip Hop is the rose that grew from concrete. There is resilience, hope, optimism, and creativity," Alvarez said.[58] In an affirmation that this approach is better, he recognized that young people do not see this as therapy but as an avenue to grow and a chance for them to reach their goals.[59]

Felicity Baker and colleagues offer a glimpse into the specialized clinical integration of Hip Hop culture in music therapy with individuals meeting the diagnostic criteria for substance use disorders. In particular, they describe how messages glorifying and messages speaking of the harshness of substance abuse can both be meaningful resources for therapeutic work.[60] The ability of clients to access their emotions and cope in a healthy manner without turning to substances is the underlying goal. Results of the study were positive, showing music to be cathartic, to promote emotional regulation, and to facilitate positive social learning. Results also showed a greater impact on younger populations and the value of private listening over listening to music in public.[61]

DIRECTION WITH PURPOSE: HIP HOP'S THEMES AS A THERAPEUTIC ROAD MAP

Adding to theory and perspective on the potential therapeutic uses of Hip Hop, Tyson and colleagues investigated therapeutically and socially relevant themes in commercially available Hip Hop music tracks. This research team distinguishes their conceptualization of Hip Hop as what others may call rap music: it is lyric and beat-based, with rhyming or talking (not singing) over instrumental sounds or beats.[62] The four main themes elicited were negative behavior criticism, humanistic values, social criticism, and social empowerment. They conclude with attention to the need for an ongoing repository of thematically indexed rap music tracks to assist the collective abilities of professionals using Hip Hop–integrated strategies.

Aaron Lightstone also analyzed themes in music, but with improvised music created by his clients. He found nine more varied themes: (1) authenticity and emotional expression, (2) rapper as critical theorist, (3) boasting, (4) rap battles/insults, (5) drugs, (6) evidence of group process, (7) spirituality (8) violence, and (9) musical wordplay.[63]

Raphael Travis and Anne Deepak's individual and community empowerment (ICE) framework suggests that existing research on themes within Hip Hop can be consolidated into five dimensions: esteem, resilience, growth, community, and change.[64] Raphael Travis updated the earliest research on ICE by integrating these ICE dimensions with the empowerment-based positive youth development (EMPYD) model to form a robust therapeutic model that addresses mental health and overall well-being over the life-course. The model, used in FlowStory's Muzuze materials, is applicable for individual and group work, bridges individual and community, and prior-itizes culture. It also emphasizes the simultaneous presence of potentially risky and empowering music engagement.[65] Aside from Travis and Bow-man's individual and community empowerment Inventory, simultaneously healthy *and* harmful music engagement has only recently emerged as an area of measurement. Another promising leap forward in measurement has been made by Suvi Saarikallio and colleagues, who developed the Healthy-Unhealthy Music Scale (HUMS) to help assess how current music engage-ment relates to potential for depression.[66]

Debangshu Roychoudhury and Lauren Gardner's Hip Hop Psychology emphasizes the integration of Hip Hop and mental health, with attention to authentic expression, the bridging of person and environment, and creating a new type of therapeutic environment. This expressive-based relationship is egalitarian, relaxed, improvisational, and promotes maximum creativity. The objective is to promote the individual goals of clients in partnership with the goals of the communities they value.[67] Roychoudhury, Gardner, and Stetsenko built on this premise of development with their transforma-tive Hip Hop artist-activist stance, not only to promote mental health but also personal development. This is relevant not necessarily as a traditional professionally mediated process; rather, the artist acts as a developing agent, akin to the earlier discussion between Davey D. and KRS-One. However, to the extent that an artist-activist may be involved in a range of Hip Hop ac-tivities that are used therapeutically (e.g., as a resident artist), their role will be more often from a strengths-based and empowerment-driven space (de-velopmental), and less so from a deficit or problem-focused one.

MENTAL HEALTH AS A GROWTH MODEL

The latest generation of individuals looking to promote mental health within Hip Hop culture has moved beyond pre-existing theoretical models. Newer approaches are more contextually grounded, growth-oriented, and attentive to community well-being in partnership with individual well-being. They incorporate the direction of Hip Hop's values of self and com-munity improvement. These strategies privilege identity (including race, gender, and class), voice, and expressivity, with a therapeutic focus on strengths, solutions, and potential. Taking this approach is important for the social and environmental stressors unique to Black youth. Contemporary challenges like discrimination and bias, neighborhood violence, school climate, and the threat of surveillance by law enforcement heighten stress for many Black youth and warrant interventions as much as anything particular to youth.

For example, Dr. Jameca Falconer provided crisis work in the Canfield Apartments of Ferguson, Missouri, the location of Michael Brown's death, shortly after his death. She used Hip Hop therapy as a culturally specific social justice–oriented strategy that could help validate anger and frustration, manage trauma, and provide opportunities for voice and action.[68]

In another example, educational oppression is an assault on confidence and identity, where the opportunity to connect to, engage, and assemble psychological and social supports for success are systematically denied. Roychoudhury and Gardner identify these dynamics as "oppression of [a student's] psyche and an assault on their humanity," a type of psychological violence.[69] Their solution, Hip Hop Psychology Liberation Education (HHPLE), stresses the necessity of mixing mental health and educational disciplines to force learning environments to reduce inequities perpetuated with the educational status quo. It is within this context that educational trends are especially alarming. Approximately 68 percent of high school graduates with appropriate credentials who are low or middle socioeconomic status (SES), "undermatch" and do not attend selective and very selective colleges and universities that they are—on paper—qualified to attend.[70] Lower SES and rural youth are the least likely to attend. According to a recent report, Black students tend to have to achieve at a level *better than the average for a top tier university* to overcome undermatching trends, with a 30 percent increase in likelihood of applying.[71] More research is needed to pin down the complete picture, including our understanding of the short- and long-term benefits among these groups, true differences in student outcomes across school selectivity levels, and more precise accounting of true selection likelihood among these institutions.[72] However, the general economic and social benefits of education across health, mental, and SES are well-established. Further, working toward optimal fit between youth and their environments—and increasing self-sufficiency and ability for youth to shape where they live, work, learn, and play—remains important.

These obstacles to higher education can be helped by educational system policies at the district and school levels, not by student skill-based academic interventions. Equitable norms of engagement must be established for all youth, so that a culture of awareness, high expectations, and pride in academic excellence exists. These norms will boost mental health rather than erode mental health. This culture must coexist with identified admission-related activities that lead to higher education and professional careers, *with* the participation and help of the full range of the country's best colleges and universities.

In the same way that K–12 school climates must be vocal and visible about "wanting" minority youth, institutes of higher education must be vocal and visible about "wanting" minority youth—outside of athletics. The sentiment must be bold and unequivocal toward youth: "We are here! We want you here! And your friends too! You should apply! We value your ideas and your experiences! You can get in! We will help make it affordable! You can handle the work! We support our students! Seriously, we want you here!"

Research supporting the value of health-musicking is also critical, especially for populations that tend not to seek out services. Self-health, health-musicking, and personal appropriation of music in everyday listening is common. But, building on the research of Travis and colleagues, we know that music engagement can be simultaneously empowering and risky.[73] Individuals must recognize their own agency but also their accountability. Professionals can help these efforts by contributing to an ongoing compendium of music, recognizing there will be differences in preferences, that there is increased emotional intensity of self-selected music, and youth culture's tendency to insulate preferred music.[74]

When looking at Hip Hop and mental health, newer cultural ambassadors like Levy, Alvarez, and Roychoudhury and Gardner recognize that formal mental health strategies can benefit from greater integration with broader elements of Hip Hop culture—beyond lyrics-driven strategies. This remains a significantly underreported area of research. Having safe spaces and a voice to express feelings, to understand one's strengths, to practice coping skills, to build life skills, and to engage in community improvements are transformational opportunities our newest generation of mental health professionals have taken a stand for.

CHAPTER 13

The Healing Power of Hip Hop:
The Next Forty Years

Hip Hop changes lives. The depth and complexity of its culture creates an explosion of ways the "body, brain, mind, conscious and unconscious systems" continuously work together.[1] Since the culture's birth, people of all races and ethnicities have turned to Hip Hop as a source of self and community improvement, while also recognizing its many earlier roots. This popularity has seen the culture become a global multibillion dollar industry, and some of its most visible creative artists become CEOs and approach billionaire status.

Hip Hop culture is able to capture aspects of the Black community's unique identities within distinct and evolving social environments that directly influence development, health, and well-being. This adds a powerful layer to its healing power. It is in this context that this book begins and ends. This final chapter will pull together major ideas and lessons learned in this exploration of Hip Hop's use across a range of scenarios and settings. Most importantly, it offers suggestions about how to use this evidence to plot a path forward so that individuals and communities can reach their potential.

WHAT WE NEED(ED)

After exploring Hip Hop's roots, Black racial identity, the ascendance of Hip into the mainstream, and early examples of its healing power, the subsequent chapters in this book contributed to the discussion in several important ways. Chapters 4 through 7 synthesized Hip Hop's cultural values of self and community improvement.

These values are consistently expressed in deejaying and production, b-boying/b-girling, graffiti, and emceeing. These values are the foundation of an evolving knowledge of self. Chapters 4 through 7 also explored Hip Hop's musical canon as a broad canvas to focus on developmental narratives often found in song hooks and lyrics. Narratives of esteem, resilience, growth, community, and change helped accentuate identity, illuminate context, and reinforce growth and skill-building for the purposes of solidarity and protest when necessary. These narratives are specific pathways of empowerment, offering direction and influencing learning and growth to improve individuals and communities. At the same time there is a recognition of potentially risky narratives, and research shows a steady increase over time in risky content, attitudes, and behaviors often glorified in more mainstream rap music.

Chapter 8 sought to unify some of the many research voices on music and well-being. It introduced several conceptual models, such as health-musicking to reinforce that music can trigger learning and growth through both formal and informal pathways. Further, much of music's impact comes from the evocation of emotions, and through a variety of very specific mechanisms such as imagination and memory. Finally, the chapter introduced a language and structure to help organize (i.e., ICE) and measure (i.e., EMPYD) Hip Hop–integrated pathways to learning and growth.

Chapters 9 through 12 described culturally meaningful strategies that use Hip Hop as a natural resource, using its artifacts and value driven narratives across professional settings and programs. Common across professional settings, whether classrooms, therapeutic relationships, health settings, or OST programs, was the desire to build communities of belonging for youth that promote positive relationships, confidence, mastery, reduced stress, and a community interest. These chapters also introduced committed and skilled leaders who are ushering in a new wave of innovation with research, development, and strategies to promote self and community improvement. Their embodiment of Hip Hop culture allows innovation in research and identification (of historic and contemporary artifacts for use), development (of derivative artifacts and products), and creating strategies that employ artifacts for promoting learning and growth among youth (creating pathways to potential and possibility).

VOICES OF HEALING

A big part of Hip Hop's ability to heal stems from its ability to mature and expand as a source of strength. Each new beat, hook, lyric, move, sample, and piece goes into the archives as another branch of the culture to be discovered, repurposed, and used as a source of learning and growth. The nature of the culture is to sample what is available and consider the most creative and helpful use for it so that it says something personal about the communities the artist values.

We heard from many of Hip Hop's cultural ambassadors who are on the front line, working directly to serve youth and communities. The culture's ambassadors understand this healing power not just intellectually but personally. They too are an embodiment of Hip Hop's branches of learning and growth.

Tupac's famous poem, *The Rose That Grew from Concrete*, as amazing as it is, did not allow a complete description of his vision. Roses are not singular. They grow as part of a bush. Every rose is connected to other strong stems and is anchored by a life-giving bush with grounded roots. Ambassadors of Hip Hop culture understand the culture and its narratives. They recognize the importance of confidence, motivation, mastery, and inspiration from a legacy of strength and solidarity, and how all of these things help individuals prevail despite life's roughest patches. They understand the range of Hip Hop's artifacts, from the most basic to the complexities of its aesthetics and how they can transform the mundane into something extraordinary. They realize Hip Hop's core values of self and community improvement as gifts that keep on giving. They also realize how much Black lives really do matter, and these beliefs permeate their words and the culture of their classrooms, offices, and workspaces.

WHO DOES HIP HOP HEAL?

Hip Hop's cultural ambassadors are leaders in advancing strategies that leverage Hip Hop culture to help all youth and communities. They recognize everyone's strengths and potential. They also embrace Hip Hop's core value of unity. At the same time, their voices also recognize the unique lived reality of the Black community in the United States, and that it *is* different for Black youth. They understand the research evidence that shows the pathways by which social determinants influence health development, psychological well-being, and education. As a result, many construct opportunities for youth that are context-specific, with opportunities to build awareness, critically analyze, and be a voice for social justice. At the end of the day, these ambassadors take a stand for the culture and its transformative potential and use it to construct opportunities for all youth to learn and grow in a wide range of settings.

HIP HOP IS MORE THAN A YOUTH CULTURE: GROWTH AND THE LIFE COURSE

While it is critical that we show youth they are valued and that investment in their growth and potential is important, we must extend that vision for the later stages of their health development as well. Alexis Maston's research on Hip Hop culture, empowerment, and adult development was evidence of Hip Hop's transformative power among adults.[2] We must recognize that Hip Hop is not a distinctly youth culture and move beyond the belief that only youth need to grow and improve. Timothy Jones spoke about his own personal growth from early life as a fan and artist, to later in life, still a fan and artist, but also as critic, role model, and father. His passion for the culture has not waned but he listens with a wiser, more experienced ear. He interacts with Hip Hop culture as an artist, educator, and role model in ways he thinks will best represent the culture and most benefit his teenage son and youth in general.[3] During his discussion he described why he is so passionate about the oft-forgotten importance of continued learning and growth and mentorship in the lives of young adults between the ages of 18 and 24:

> Society is telling you, you're grown. But where is there room for you to say "I'm grown but . . ." Any person aged 18 to 24, think about the changes in your life from when you graduate high school. Even if you graduated college when you are a couple of years out, on your own by yourself; your life has done a 180 during that six year span. In some ways there is a greater change than from birth to 18 years. But there is less purposeful, "Yo, let me hold your hand on that, let me holler at you with that, let me talk with you about that." A lot of times, there are so many holes in that socioemotional piece.[4]

HOW DOES HIP HOP HEAL? WHAT WE LEARN, HOW WE GROW

We have been able to identify specific things people learn and specific ways people grow via Hip Hop culture. Learning and growth are both identity-driven and context-specific. Through the appropriation of music and the culture, emotional connections are made and attitudes and behaviors are prompted that are pathways to well-being. People are able to learn lifelong skills and develop insights about their own growth and development. Equally important is the ability of young people to learn about the world and their place in it, since individual identities are embedded within social identities and social circumstances.

For Black youth, their identities are embedded in pressing conditions that warrant attention. Left unaddressed, there will be continued threats to nutrition, physical activity, psychological well-being, educational mastery, and health development. Looming large are issues of employment and poverty with education being a key cog in this pipeline. However, certain acute realities are especially prominent at the moment, including the relationship between the criminal justice system and the Black community. The more notable issues are suspension and expulsion in education, community surveillance and excessive force by law enforcement, and bias in legislation and adjudication resulting in significant disparities in incarceration rates. However, the most palpable aspect of these issues has been the perceived use of excessive force of law enforcement resulting in the deaths of Black U.S. residents, contributing greatly to the present Black Lives Matter social movement.

WHO CAN HELP WITH HEALING?

To continue, Hip Hop allows people to experience therapeutic growth that helps them thrive in challenging circumstances. In the best of circumstances is a level of personal transformation that inspires commitment to being a positive change agent in society. This book offers some conceptual background for a language and structure to describe this growth.

The individual and community empowerment (ICE) framework, which focuses on individual identity as much as social identity, is a growth-oriented model of well-being. However, it is specifically targeted at how people appropriate Hip Hop culture for self and community improvement. The framework also recognizes the potential for material to evoke something empowering and risky at the same time. This allows much greater flexibility in what and how Hip Hop materials are used to facilitate learning and growth. It is not wedded to problems, deficits, disorders, or disability.

The underlying conceptual model for ICE is the Empowerment-based Positive Youth Development (EMPYD) perspective. EMPYD is grounded in substantial research on the most promising pathways to positive development, confidence, connection, competence, caring, character, sense of community, and active and engaged citizenship. As important is that the model identifies unique and interrelated aspects of positive development specific to Black youth. Examples were given throughout this book about the importance of these concepts, especially from ambassadors like Natalie Davis, Elliot Gann, and Mazi Mutafa, representing out-of-school time strategies.

The core of the EMPYD model is connection, sense of community, and engaged citizenship. EMPYD as reflected through ICE and Hip Hop offers many points of leverage for how to approach learning and growth, and all are measurable within the context of other indicators of development. It is these opportunities for learning and growth that health professionals, educators, youth workers, and caregivers must continue to provide and capitalize on. It is these opportunities that funders can invest in.

HEALTH PROFESSIONALS (PHYSICAL AND MENTAL HEALTH)

The major challenges of physical and mental health for the Black community stem from the influence of social determinants on health development over the life-course. These pathways to health occur via nutrition, physical activity, stress, and trauma—all exacerbated by poverty and discrimination. At the same time, as with education, we have seen promise in working toward greater well-being through highly engaging, interactive experiences that use art and music as resources to build awareness about issues and to change attitudes and behaviors, but also policies. These strategies, with youth as creators or receivers of art, have shown to work with prevention and intervention efforts.

Violence and Mass Incarceration as Public Health Concerns

Progress in reducing violence and mass incarceration among Black communities should also be a major objective for physical health, but equally for mental health outcomes. Tremendous stress and trauma develops and accumulates from being in violent environments and from the residual effects of involvement in the criminal justice system. These realities are wildly disproportionate for the Black community. It is an excessive wear and tear that wreaks havoc on the body and mind that health professionals must focus on as they consider the varied possibilities for integrating Hip Hop culture.

Hip Hop narratives are most notable for capturing these realities, but sustained momentum toward changing the conditions that spawn them is no longer a reality among mainstream outlets. Professionals and settings that integrate Hip Hop must steer clear of focusing only on the problem. For example, in the area of violence, deficit-oriented approaches seek merely to cope, prevent further violence, and build awareness about the disparity.

Empowering approaches seek to build self-efficacy, orient toward long-term goals and thriving, achieve mastery and develop life skills, and embed youth in prosocial communities where they feel engaged and personally invested as active decision makers. Many artists do offer these narratives and many programs, like Words, Beats, and Life, Inc.; AAHH; and the Austin Healthy Adolescent program take the latter approach. These types of initiatives exemplify Hip Hop's healing power in the context of community well-being and deserve more collaborative opportunities and material investments. Artists who are serious about investing in the health and well-being of communities must be afforded pathways to meaningful employment within city, county, and state departments of education and departments of health.

EDUCATORS

Before anything else, educators have to prioritize their role in enhancing learning opportunities for Black youth. Positive relationships, equitable treatment, high expectations, and a highly engaged community of belonging drive academic outcomes. Educators must also think carefully about the role of identity and context in their curricula. Most importantly, they must be explicit in demonstrating how invested they are in creating learning environments that affirm identities, promote mastery, and value the ability of Black youth to be lifelong learners. It is in these contexts that innovative educational strategies must emerge.

Educators can embrace Hip Hop in class and in school from a range of perspectives to capture many of its cultural and engagement concerns. At the very least they can connect with artists to augment the classroom experience while deepening their own understanding of Hip Hop culture to better recognize its educational and therapeutic potentials. Educators can take the more straightforward approach of linking materials to educational activities, or they can use the culture's aesthetics to transform the learning environment—either of the class, or, as in projects like Science Genius, entire schools. Educators can look to conferences, research literature, social media sources, and actual practitioners for ideas and resources.

Critical Hip Hop pedagogies take on issues of culture and engagement too, but they also seek to shed more light on equity and justice issues. Goals are as much about increasing awareness of equity and justice issues in the material discussed as they are about inspiring youth involvement in working toward positive change in those discussed areas. For example, educational topics could be about trends and determinants of incarceration disparities, life expectancy disparities, or disparities in suspensions and expulsions. These topics could be prompts for research, tests, or community service projects to raise community awareness.

The nontraditional nature of some of the aforementioned topics, particularly prior to higher education, relates to one last major point and that is for educators to increase the interdisciplinary nature of how certain topics are explored. Cooper and Condon's discussion about the interdisciplinary application of music and teaching offers an excellent template for how subjects counted as electives can be part of mainstream educational content in a serious manner ready for critical analysis.[5] Topics like psychology, urban studies, women studies, political science, international relations, health care and wellness, criminal justice and law enforcement, and business and economics all intersect with core academic subjects and, as highlighted in earlier chapters, are consistent with Hip Hop's narratives of self and community improvement.

On a related note, educators can also work with mental health professionals to integrate learning and growth.[6] Teachers face an increasing burden to respond to student's contextual realities while maintaining rigorous standards and high expectations. School mental health workers are often under pressure to serve more students with less time. Hip Hop culture offers opportunities to create safe spaces where therapeutic and justice-oriented activities can occur alongside the ability to learn.

In today's climate of limited funding, and with trust issues and stigma around mental health in communities of color, we need to utilize any opportunities that can foster improved mental health and well-being. Other opportunities include providing supplemental resources to augment self-health and everyday listening. In other words, when people are not accessing formal services, it can help for them to have a range of Hip Hop–integrated therapeutic materials and resources to help cope and facilitate improvement.

YOUTH WORKERS (AND COMMUNITIES OF MASTERY)

Youth workers are the anchors of learning and growth for youth who often fall through the cracks of traditional learning environments. Youth workers are the leaders who cultivate the talents and strengths of youth that are overlooked, dismissed, and otherwise forgotten about in many school systems. Youth workers create safe community spaces where youth can be themselves, feel at home, and showcase their interests and abilities outside of the context of academic standards and standardized tests.

Less traditional arenas of work include social media settings. Technology must be leveraged, in these and in more traditional spaces, to maximize the information, capital, and collaborative opportunities available to both youth and youth workers. Initiatives like #HipHopEd and #CultureFix are international in scope and offer points of synergy for the most empowering uses of Hip Hop culture. They incorporate learning and growth for professionals, but also have room for youth and young adults. While it is an opportunity to learn, these cyphers are empowering places of knowledge sharing in the spirit of "each one teach one" and the biblical phrase from Proverbs "as iron sharpens iron, so one man sharpens another."

Theory

These are the spaces that have enjoyed the most freedom integrating Hip Hop strategies and are poised to continue being bastions of innovation. Several opportunities exist for youth workers and out-of-school time spaces within which they operate. First, it is important that they operate using a Hip Hop–oriented model and theory of change that helps capture the story of the amazing work that is being done.

For example, the ICE and EMPYD frameworks capture the importance of one-on-one relationships, but also the increases in confidence and self-efficacy, the importance of a sense of belonging created in settings (or arenas), and an increase in mastery and skills. Programs can compare what is being done and decide to show where and how they are aligned with a growth model that is empowerment based, culturally specific, and attentive to both youth and their social environments. This may inspire programs to renew their commitment to the excellent model and work they have in place, or they may be interested in making program refinements and updates to better correspond to new models of youth development.

Measurement

Youth workers and OST settings that they operate within must also increase the quality of evaluation and measurement of the great work that is being done. This includes the specific links between Hip Hop–integrated activities and well-being. In the same way that certain programs can be identified and compared to a conceptual model (above), they can also be measured to determine potential change over time. Significant positive influences on the lives of program participants must be documented to properly capture program efficacy.

CAREGIVERS

Even before looking to use Hip Hop culture or music, caregivers must recognize how positive of an influence their role is as the primary supportive relationship for young people.[7] This relationship and connection is the wellspring of all other aspects of young people's positive development.

Caregivers help shape the context within which identity develops. Caregivers are the anchor from which belonging emerges, and it is the quality of youth-caregiver relationships that often influences where else youth go to find belonging.

Caregivers must also think about how racial and cultural socialization messages influence how youth respond to social and environmental stressors connected to race. Are youth being armed more with fear and resentment, or caution and pride? Are caregivers building young people's academic confidence by staying actively involved with their home learning *and* their child's learning environment (i.e., school)? And, how well are caregivers modeling a lifestyle of healthy nutrition and physical activity that invests in their child's health development? This is not meant to be an accountability checklist per se, but to emphasize that the emotions evoked from interacting with music and other art are context-driven. Caregivers help provide that first layer of context. But youth have additional layers, stressors, and challenges related to identity. Youth have to cope with their own intersectionality of identity by race, gender, and class which has an impact on day-to-day life through experiences with teachers, friends, other significant adults, and even media.

When looking at caregivers and Hip Hop, caregivers must be cautious of how they mediate music and media involvement. Music is a doorway to a young person's life, a version of their voice they may not be able to fully access. Their music is a way to cope with their reality. At its most risky, the music/art may be an escape, or an attempt to portray the high-risk values of an identity that resonates with him or her. However, at its most empowering, music, art, dance, or deejaying/production can be a vehicle for learning and growth. While youth evoke emotions most strongly from their own self-selected music, it does not mean caregivers cannot co-listen, mediate, or suggest their own preferred music for opportunities to connect.

When opportunities for discussions surface, caregivers will benefit from a framework to help organize thoughts as opposed to fishing for answers or lecturing. For example, the ICE dimensions of esteem, resilience, growth, community, and change start with identity and move through to community interest. You have opportunities to create a safe place to reflect, share, and create empowering messages with them, while being realistic and educational about the risky ones. You can explore issues of identity, fatherhood, interactions with law enforcement, and simply coping with everyday stressors. More importantly, you may be able to find out about aspects of their context and environment you can help support. And while I concentrated on beats, hooks, and lyrics, the creation or interaction with *any aspect of Hip Hop culture* is an opportunity for sharing and discussion. Thus, providing opportunities to create music or for other expression, like dance and art, are equally meaningful.

WHAT CAN FUNDERS DO? BUILDING AN ALTERNATIVE SELF-SUSTAINING HIP HOP ECONOMY

The global Twitter chat for #CultureFix on April 7, 2015, spearheaded by Natalie Crue and Nora Rahimian was focused on "Building an Alternative Hip Hop Economy." The idea is that while acknowledging limitations presented by a global entertainment industry in how Hip Hop culture is developed, disseminated, and digested, there must be energy invested in creating an alternative system that leverages its empowering, prosocial, and healthy elements.

Investors can be at the forefront of investing in the healing power of Hip Hop, in both the basic research and the applied or practice work. Research scholars exist across disciplines on all coasts of the United States and in between. Artists and professionals who are doing the work on the ground also exist all across the United States. Asheru talked about the major financial dilemma for artists because the belief is that there are not sufficient paid opportunities to create art that promotes individual and community well-being. He quoted the often invoked "Moment of Clarity" line from Jay Z, "Truthfully I want to rhyme like Common Sense, but I did 5 mill'—I ain't been rhyming like Common since." Mazi Mutafa felt a little differently, and that his program's success has stemmed from youth seeing the financial self-sufficiency in the creative economy, and nurturing successful organizational relationships.

The importance of artists being in professional roles to promote health and well-being can also be seen in Tomas Alvarez's Beats, Rhymes, and Life, Inc. Their unique therapist-artist combination is integral for facilitating their therapeutic groups. Tim Eubanks and The Austin Healthy Adolescent Program's experimentation with Hip Hop artists and public health is another example of creating pathways for art driven empowerment and well-being. All of these ideas speak to the universal truth that financial investors have an incredible opportunity to use their resources to help unleash unprecedented talent and expertise, and usher in a new era of Hip Hop inspired health and well-being for youth and young adults.

THE REWIND FACTOR

To best capitalize on the healing power of Hip Hop, more deliberate interactions must be made with creative content. This will allow individuals increased opportunities to analyze and unpack the creativity of artists. Each track and album is a treasure of material to be explored and built upon. This is true for other aspects of Hip Hop culture too. Visual art is worthy of critique and discussion. Dance performances can be analyzed for themes and effect. Ultimately, when interacting with any aspect of Hip Hop culture, the questions should start with, "What can we learn? How can we grow?" If personalized more directly, "What can I learn? How can I grow?"

EXPANDING PRODUCT LINES AND TALIB KWELI'S COLOUR OF COALITIONS

We must expand the product line for ways to access the empowering aspects of the culture, to be used in everyday listening, strategically in self-musicking, and across professional settings. Talib Kweli's collective Colours of the Culture is a step in this direction uniting musicians, filmmakers, comedians, and emcees to develop projects. In our discussion of the future of these possibilities, Chris Emdin accentuates the idea of generating more products from the empowering aspects of the culture and our identities, saying,

> We haven't given people enough. [So they know where to go when their self-talk is . . .] "What can I wear that promotes positivity and this brand? I'm looking for something to chat about online. I want a book to read." Every domain should be infiltrated with multiple aspects of who we are, to create for young people this notion that there is more to us than that.[8]

Asheru similarly talked about the importance of diversifying products but also in developing coalitions so that Hip Hop culture and skill sets can be used in different ways, in different settings, and in different regions.

REGIONAL IMPORTANCE AND ARCHIVES

Cendrine Robinson also talked about regional importance in her work, with the tendency for youth to listen to and identify with local artists. But even mainstream Hip Hop hails from all over the United States and Canada (thanks Drake). Timothy Jones spoke similarly about how regional identity was an important part of youth development for youth in Washington, DC, because of its unique go go-integrated culture. These localized identities are important and must be unpacked, explored, and built upon through a Hip Hop and empowerment perspective, distinct from other regions. In effect, every area should have a localized, regional-specific pipeline of researchers, artists, educators, therapists, OST workers, and public health professionals working in partnership with caregivers and health and social service agencies, street level community organizers, and youth to promote the healing power of Hip Hop. This will allow the circulation of ideas, knowledge, and products through both formal institutions and settings, and more organic community settings (i.e., "the streets").[9] Further, regional efforts can be linked to Hip Hop's varied archives to help introduce and maintain a connection to these localized sources.

Hip Hop archives and collections, big and small, from Harvard's Hip Hop Archive, to the regional William & Mary Hip Hop Collection, to the Mixtape Collective co-signed by the web-based Mixtape Museum, are of the utmost priority for preserving materials and solidifying the connections between archiving, learning, and growth within the culture. We have to treat Hip Hop as an interactive library, in the same manner as deejays and producers dig for samples. We can learn and grow from artist catalogs—Lupe, Nas, Jay, or Pac—as much as collections of individual tracks. But more importantly, we have to determine new and engaging ways to explore and build upon their work. The website genius that allows annotaction of lyrics is but one starting point.

The Twitter-driven initiative #thelistening is a great example of step one, slowing down the process of enjoying and sharing thoughts, ideas, and inspiration from art in a prosocial community space. The next step must be the expansion of structured opportunities to dissect, analyze, critique, and exchange ideas for the purposes of building upon the art in a way that prompts learning and growth. #HipHopEd is an excellent example of this, where the rationale for critique and sharing is not the merit of the art as "good" or "bad" in quality. Rather, the emphasis is an analysis and critique of the possibilities of how best to use art or what it inspires as an educational tool. Building upon this must be a wide range of ideas to allow the ability to recreate or transform art and its inspirations (remix) to re-engage individuals and communities in opportunities to learn and grow.

FlowStory's Muzuze system includes a range of resources to promote this next level of critical interaction with Hip Hop music. For example, in 2013, it used the #HipHopEd Twitter chat-inspired Top 40 educational Hip Hop tracks of all time to create the #404040 Toolkit. It represented the forty years since the formation of UZN and (close to) the beginning of Hip Hop culture, the forty identified educational tracks, and forty unanswered questions that the songs inspired (questions that are still relatively unanswered in the collective conscience of our communities). In the toolkit, each of the forty tracks had its own feature, themes to articulate, questions to explore, and community resources that related to the exploration of those questions.

The purpose of these toolkit activities was to encourage a community-wide exploration of these ideas and prompt efforts toward self and community improvement. In Austin, Texas, a community event was held to examine the developed themes, celebrate the tracks, begin a community dialogue on the issues, and build awareness of available resources.

We must continue to share the most empowering aspects of Hip Hop culture. These are not assumed, and, in fact, many people come from a place of disbelief when discussing the empowering aspects of the culture. We most readily hear about its most controversial and high-risk elements, like "all that foul language." Its ability to transform must not be a secret.

TIME FOR SOME ACTION!

Finally, we must act. We cannot sit on the sidelines. Our experiences of personal growth can be shared through mentoring and being a role model for others. The strength of mentoring and modeling relationships can inspire involvement in other activities in working toward positive change. Ultimately, we must create the spaces and opportunities for what is already happening to manifest in the most health-enhancing manner possible.

If this is all new for you, how can you get started in this process? First, think about your own musical collection. Go listen to five of your favorite songs. Think about the feelings and emotions they inspire and how they helped you to learn and grow. Chances are they are not much different than those feelings and emotions experienced by the young people in your life when they listen to their favorite songs. For many of them, Hip Hop culture is their pathway to potential. Also think about your own individual and social identities, and what this means in relation to the Black American experience. Finally, ask yourself, "How can I help promote health and well-being for all?" and "What role(s) can Hip Hop play in these efforts?"

We cannot create a new youth culture, and frankly there is no need to, but we can celebrate and recognize the best in Hip Hop and its capacity to empower. We can explain why Hip Hop shows up in the various forms it does. We can explain and demonstrate how consistent Hip Hop is with Black history's long legacy of innovative and empowering art. We can educate ourselves more about the current grassroots and community-based efforts that are actively working at community change as much as they are youth development—balancing those over and inner views of Black social identity. And we can get involved.

Remember: Listen . . . Think . . . Act.

Notes

INTRODUCTION

1. Matthias Mauch, Robert MacCallum, Mark Levy, and Armand Leroi, "The Evolution of Popular Music: USA 1960–2010," *Royal Open Society* 2 (2015): 1–9.

CHAPTER 1

1. Reiland Rabaka, *Hip Hop Inheritance: From the Harlem Renaissance to the Hip Hop Feminist Movement* (Blue Ridge Summit, PA: Lexington Books, 2011); Joseph Schloss, *Foundation: B-Boys, B-Girls, and Hip-Hop Culture in New York* (Cary, NC: Oxford University Press, 2009).

2. Edgar H. Schein, "Organizational Culture," *American Psychologist* 45, no. 2 (February 1990): 109–19.

3. Kevin Avruch, *Culture & Conflict Resolution* (Washington, DC: United States Institute of Peace Press, 1998).

4. H. Samy Alim, *Roc the Mic Right: The Language of Hip Hop Culture* (Florence, KY: Routledge, 2006); Emery Petchauer, "Starting with Style: Toward a Second Wave of Hip-Hop Education Research and Practice," *Urban Education* 50, no. 1 (January 2015): 79.

5. Chris Emdin, "The Rap Cipher, the Battle, and Reality Pedagogy: Developing Communication and Argumentation in Urban Science Education," in *Schooling Hip-Hop: Expanding Hip-Hop Based Education Across the Curriculum*, ed. Marc L. Hill and Emery Petchauer (New York: Teachers College Press, 2013); Petchauer, "Starting with Style," 78–105.

6. Jeff Chang, *Can't Stop, Won't Stop: A History of the Hip-Hop Generation* (New York: St. Martin's Press, 2005); Tricia Rose, *Hip-Hop Wars: What We Talk About When We Talk About Hip-Hop—And Why It Matters* (New York: Basic Civitas, 2008).

7. Tricia Rose, *Black Noise: Rap Music and Black Culture in Contemporary America* (Hanover, NH: Wesleyan University Press, 1994); Emdin, "The Rap Cipher"; Petchauer, "Starting with Style."

8. Schloss, *Foundation*, 18.

9. Ibid.

10. Gregory Snyder, *Graffiti Lives: Beyond the Tag in New York's Urban Underground* (New York: New York University Press, 2009), 26.

11. *Scratch*, directed by Doug Pray (New York, NY: Palm Pictures, 2001), DVD.

12. Rose, *Black Noise*; Schloss, *Foundation*; Cheryl Keyes, *Rap Music and Street Consciousness* (Urbana, IL: University of Illinois Press, 2002).

13. Chang, *Can't Stop, Won't Stop*.

14. Ibid., 105.

15. Ibid., 101.

16. Ibid., 106.

17. Reiland Rabaka, *Hip Hop's Amnesia: From Blues and the Black Women's Club Movement to Rap and the Hip Hop Movement* (Lanham, MD: Lexington Books, 2012).

18. *Public Enemy: Prophets of Rage*, directed by James Hale (London: British Broadcasting Corporation, 2011), DVD.

19. Rose, *Black Noise*, 163.

20. *Something from Nothing: The Art of Rap*, directed by Ice-T and Andy Baybutt (London: Kaleidoscope Film Distribution, 2012), DVD; Rose, *Black Noise*.

21. Chris Emdin, *They Connect to the Listener*, #hiphoped, 2014.

22. Keyes, *Rap Music and Street Consciousness*; Reiland Rabaka, *Hip Hop Movement: From R and B and the Civil Rights Movement to Rap and the Hip Hop Generation* (Blue Ridge Summit, PA: Lexington Books, 2013), 236–37.

23. Imani Perry, *Prophets of the Hood: Politics and Poetics in Hip Hop* (Durham, NC: Duke University Press, 2004).

24. *Scratch*, DVD.

25. Perry, *Prophets of the Hood*, 93.

26. Bronwen Low, Eloise Tan, and Jacqueline Celemencki, "The Limits of 'Keepin' It Real': The Challenges for Critical Hip Hop Pedagogies of Discourses of Authenticity," in *Schooling Hip-Hop: Expanding Hip-Hop Based Education across the Curriculum*, ed. Marc L. Hill and Emery Petchauer (New York: Teachers College Press, 2013), 120.

27. Ibid.

28. Keyes, *Rap Music and Street Consciousness*; Rabaka. *Hip Hop Movement*, 236–37; Rose, *Black Noise*, 163.

29. *Scratch*, DVD; Ron Lawrence and Hassan Pore, eds., "Hip Hop Did Not Start in the Bronx," in *Founding Fathers: The Untold Story of Hip Hop*, accessed April 15, 2015, at http://hiphopandpolitics.com/2014/02/05/founding-fathers-documentary-hip-hop-start-bronx/.

30. *Founding Fathers*.

31. Jeffrey Ogbar, *Hip-Hop Revolution: The Culture and Politics of Rap* (Lawrence, KS: University Press of Kansas, 2007), 4.

32. Ibid.

33. Joseph Schloss, *Making Beats: The Art of Sample-Based Hip-Hop* (Middletown, CT: Wesleyan University Press, 2004), 92; Schloss, *Foundation*.

34. *Scratch*, DVD.

35. Ibid; Keyes, *Rap Music and Street Consciousness*, 57.

36. Ibid.

37. Lawrence and Pore, *Founding Fathers*.

38. Keyes, *Rap Music and Street Consciousness*, 54.

39. *Scratch*.

40. Schloss, *Making Beats*, 144.

41. Schloss, *Making Beats*; Schloss, *Foundation*.

42. Chuck D., "It takes a nation of millions to hold us back," interview by Pitchfork, April 5, 2012.

43. Jared Ball, *I Mix What I Like! A Mixtape Manifesto* (Baltimore, MD: AK Press, 2011); Kembrew McLeod and Benjamin Franzen, *Copyright Criminals* (United States: Changing Images, 2009).

44. *Scratch*, DVD.

45. DJ Shadow, "Renegades of Rhythm," accessed September 11, 2014 at http://acl-live.com/calendar/renegades-of-rhythm.

46. Rose, *Black Noise*.

47. Keyes, *Rap Music and Street Consciousness*, 140–41; Rose, *Black Noise*.

48. Rose, *Black Noise*.

49. Keyes, *Rap Music and Street Consciousness*, 145.

50. Ibid., 147.

51. Jorge Pabon, "Physical Graffiti: The History of Hip Hop Dance," in *Total Chaos: The Art and Aesthetics of Hip-Hop*, ed. Jeff Chang (New York: Basic Civitas Books, 2007), 19.

52. *Scratch*, DVD.

53. Pabon, "Physical Graffiti."

54. Ibid., 20–21.

55. Ibid.

56. Ibid.

57. Ibid., 21.

58. Chang, *Can't Stop, Won't Stop*.

59. Pabon, "Physical Graffiti."

60. Ibid., 23.

61. Ibid.

62. Ibid., 24–25.

63. *Style Wars*, Films On Demand, 2011, accessed April 15, 2015, from http://digital.films.com/PortalPlaylists.aspx?aid=1706&xtid=50730.

64. Craig Castleman, *Getting Up: Subway Graffiti in New York* (Cambridge, MA: MIT Press, 1982); Nicholas Ganz, *Graffiti World: Street Art from Five Continents*, ed. Tristan Manco (New York: Abrams, 2009).

65. Castleman, *Getting Up*.

66. Ibid.

67. Ganz, *Graffiti World*.

68. Ibid., 7.

69. Ibid., 10.

70. *Scratch*, DVD.

71. Castleman, *Getting Up*.

72. Tia DeNora, *Music in Everyday Life* (New York: Cambridge University Press, 2000), 5.

CHAPTER 2

1. Jeffrey Ogbar, *Hip-Hop Revolution: The Culture and Politics of Rap* (Lawrence, KS: University Press of Kansas, 2007).

2. Imani Perry, *Prophets of the Hood: Politics and Poetics in Hip Hop* (Durham, NC: Duke University Press, 2004).

3. Ibid., 20.

4. Mark Fenster, "Understanding and Incorporating Rap: The Articulation of Alternative Popular Musical Practices within Dominant Cultural Practices and Institutions," *Howard Journal of Communications* 5, no. 3 (Spring 1995): 223–44.

5. Jeff Chang, *Can't Stop, Won't Stop: A History of the Hip-Hop Generation* (New York: St. Martin's Press, 2005); Ogbar, *Hip-Hop Revolution*; Perry, *Prophets of the Hood*.

6. Henry Chalfant, *From Mambo to Hip Hop: A South Bronx Tale* (New York: City Lore, 2006).

7. Cheryl Keyes, *Rap Music and Street Consciousness* (Urbana, IL: University of Illinois Press, 2002), 54.

8. Ogbar, *Hip-Hop Revolution*, 41.

9. Ibid.

10. Jorge Pabon, "Physical Graffiti: The History of Hip Hop Dance," in *Total Chaos: The Art and Aesthetics of Hip-Hop*, ed. Jeff Chang (New York: Basic Civitas Books, 2006), 18–26; *Scratch*, directed by Doug Pray (New York, NY: Palm Pictures, 2001), DVD; Gregory Snyder, *Graffiti Lives: Beyond the Tag in New York's Urban Underground* (New York: New York University Press, 2009), 26.

11. Reiland Rabaka, *Hip Hop Inheritance: From the Harlem Renaissance to the Hip Hop Feminist Movement* (Blue Ridge Summit, PA: Lexington Books, 2011).

12. Brad Porfilio and Michael Viola, "Introduction," in *Hip-Hop(e): The Cultural Practice and Critical Pedagogy of International Hip-Hop*, ed. Brad Porfilio and Michael Viola (New York: Peter Lang, 2012), 1–19.

13. Perry, *Prophets of the Hood*, 21.

14. Eugene Robinson, *Disintegration: The Splintering of Black America* (New York: Doubleday, 2010); Christina Greer, *Black Ethnics: Race, Immigration, and the Pursuit of the American Dream* (New York: Oxford University Press, 2013).

15. Craig Watkins, *Hip Hop Matters: Politics, Pop Culture, and the Struggle for the Soul of a Movement* (Boston, MA: Beacon Press, 2005), 151.

16. Raphael Travis and Scott W. Bowman, "Ethnic Identity, Self-Esteem and Variability in Perceptions of Rap Music's Empowering and Risky Influences," *Journal of Youth Studies* 15, no. 4 (June 2012): 455–78.

17. Robinson, *Disintegration*; Greer, *Black Ethnics*.

18. MK Asante Jr., *It's Bigger than Hip Hop: The Rise of the Post-Hip-Hop Generation* (New York: St. Martin's Press, 2008), 238–39.

19. Nsenga Burton, "Foreclosure Crisis: Class Is Becoming a Growing Issue in Black Communities," *The Root*, February 28, 2011, accessed May 1, 2015 from http://www.theroot.com/articles/culture/2011/02/foreclosure_crisis_class_is _becoming_a_growing_issue_in_black_communities.html.

20. Asante, *It's Bigger than Hip Hop*; Robinson, *Disintegration,* 103.

21. Robinson, *Disintegration*, 106.

22. Greer, *Black Ethnics*, 8.

23. Thomas Hale, *Griots and Griottes: Masters of Words and Music* (Bloomington: Indiana University Press, 1998).

24. Jeff Chang, *Can't Stop, Won't Stop*, 96.

25. Ibid., 60.

26. *Scratch*, DVD.

27. Thomas Hale, "From the Griot of Roots to the Roots of Griot: A New Look at the Origins of a Controversial African Term for Bard," *Oral Tradition* 12 no. 2 (October 1997): 249–78.

28. *Adama Drame: A Griot's Story*, directed by Adam Rozanski, Ozumi Films (New York: Filmakers Library, 2007).

29. Ibid.

30. Hale, "From the Griot of Roots to the Roots of Griot."

31. Ibid.

32. *Merriam-Webster*, s.v. "prophet." http://www.merriam-webster.com/dictionary /prophet (accessed 20 May, 2015).

33. Reiland Rabaka, *Hip Hop Movement: From R&B and the Civil Rights Movement to Rap and the Hip Hop Generation* (Blue Ridge Summit, PA: Lexington Books, 2013), 291.

34. Ibid.

35. Davey D., "Black History Fact: Exploring the Historic Links of Early Hip-Hop and Gang Culture," in *Davey D's Hop Hop Corner*, February 22, 2010, accessed

April 16, 2015 from http://hiphopandpolitics.com/2010/02/22/black-history-fact
-exploring-historic-links-of-early-hip-hop-and-gang-culture/.

36. *80 Blocks from Tiffany's*, directed by Gary Weis (New York: Above Average Productions Inc., 1979).

37. Rabaka, *Hip Hop Inheritance*, 88–90.

38. Ibid., 99–100.

39. Rabaka, *Hip Hop Movement*, 161.

40. Ibid., 163.

41. Ibid., 161.

42. Rabaka, *Hip Hop Inheritance*, 103.

43. Shana Redmond, *Anthem: Social Movements and the Sound of Solidarity in the African Diaspora* (New York: New York University Press, 2014), 165.

44. Ibid., 265.

45. Ibid.

46. Dan Charnas, *The Big Payback: The History of the Business of Hip-Hop* (New York: New American Library, 2010), 148.

47. Ibid., 173.

48. Ibid., 236.

49. Jared Ball, *I Mix What I Like!: A Mixtape Manifesto* (Baltimore, MD: AK Press, 2011); Charnas, *The Big Payback*.

50. Tricia Rose, *Black Noise: Rap Music and Black Culture in Contemporary America* (Hanover, NH: Wesleyan University Press, 1994); Joseph Schloss, *Foundation: B-Boys, B-Girls, and Hip-Hop Culture in New York* (Cary, NC: Oxford University Press, 2009).

51. Carl Bialik, "Is the Conventional Wisdom Correct in Measuring Hip-Hop Audience?," *Wall Street Journal*, May 5, 2005.

52. GfK MRI, "Consumer Insights: Product Usage," accessed May 9, 2015, from http://www.gfkmri.com/consumerinsights/productusage.aspx.

53. Pitchfork Media, *Public Enemy: It Takes a Nation of Millions to Hold Us Back—Special Presentation*, produced by RJ Bentler (Chicago: Pitchfork Media, 2012).

54. Ogbar, *Hip-Hop Revolution*, 110.

55. Tricia Rose, *Hip-Hop Wars: What We Talk About When We Talk About Hip-Hop—And Why It Matters* (New York, NY, USA: Basic Civitas, 2008), 9.

56. Helen Spencer-Oatey, "What Is culture? A Compilation of Quotations," GlobalPAD Core Concepts, 2012.

57. Ball, *I Mix What I Like!*; Bettina Love, *Hip Hop's Li'l Sistas Speak: Negotiating Hip Hop Identities and Politics in the New South* (New York: Peter Lang, 2012); Rose, *Hip-Hop Wars*.

58. Love, *Hip Hop's Li'l Sistas Speak,* 106.

59. Charnas, *The Big Payback*.

60. Chang, *Can't Stop, Won't Stop*, 258.

61. James Peterson, "Rewriting the Remix: College Composition and the Educational Elements of Hip Hop," in *Schooling Hip Hop: Expanding Hip Hop Based*

Education across the Curriculum, ed. Marc L. Hill and Emery Petchauer (New York, NY: Teachers College Press, 2013), 47–65.

62. Love, *Hip Hop's Li'l Sistas Speak*; Rose, *Hip-Hop Wars*; Natasha Sharma, *Hip Hop Desis: South Asian Americans, Blackness, and a Global Race Consciousness.* (Durham, NC: Duke University Press, 2010), 161.

63. Love, *Hip Hop's Li'l Sistas Speak*.

64. Ball, *I Mix What I Like!*, 123; Bakari Kitwana, *The Hip Hop Generation: Young Blacks and the Crisis in African American Culture* (New York: Basic Books, 2012).

65. Ball, *I Mix What I Like!*, 26; Kitwana, *The Hip Hop Generation*; Love, *Hip Hop's Li'l Sistas Speak*; Rose, *Hip-Hop Wars*.

66. Joe Coscarelli, "Street Image Helps a Young Rapper, Until It Doesn't," *The New York Times*, February 22, 2015.

67. Charnas, *The Big Payback*.

68. Ibid.

69. Victoria Rideout, *Parents, Children & Media* (Menlo Park, CA: Kaiser Family Foundation, 2007).

70. Office of Disease and Health Promotion, "HP2020 Database," accessed May 10, 2015 from http://www.healthypeople.gov/2020/data-search/Search-the -Data.

71. The Associated Press, "TV Networks Make Unequal Progress Toward On-Screen Diversity," *The New York Times*, January 20, 2015.

72. Dominic Patten, "'Empire' Finale Ratings Rise Even More, Best New Series Result in 10 Years," *Deadline*, March 19 2015, accessed May 10, 2015 from http://deadline.com/2015/03/empire-finale-ratings-high-fox-danny-strong-1201395097/.

73. Jane Rhodes, *Framing the Black Panthers: The Spectacular Rise of a Black Power Icon* (New York: The New Press, 2007), 308.

74. Questlove, "MCA (What Does It Mean?)—Questlove and Respect To The End," *Okayplayer*, 2012, accessed May 9, 2015 from http://www.okayplayer.com /news/mca-what-does-it-mean-by-questlove.html.

75. Dan Hyman, "Chance the Rapper on Staying Independent: 'It's a Dead Industry,'" *Rolling Stone*, September 27, 2013, accessed May 9, 2015 from http://www .rollingstone.com/music/news/chance-the-rapper-on-staying-independent-its-a -dead-industry-20130927.

CHAPTER 3

1. Jeff Chang, *Can't Stop, Won't Stop: A History of the Hip-Hop Generation* (New York: St. Martin's Press, 2005), 104–5.

2. Jorge Pabon, "Physical Graffiti: The History of Hip Hop Dance," in *Total Chaos: The Art and Aesthetics of Hip-Hop*, ed. Jeff Chang (New York: Basic Civitas Books, 2006), 19.

3. Jane Rhodes, *Framing the Black Panthers: The Spectacular Rise of a Black Power Icon* (New York: The New Press, 2007), 117.

4. Ibid., 111.

5. Federal Bureau of Investigation, *The Vault: COINTELPRO, Black Extremist*, August 25, 1967, accessed May 9, 2015 from http://vault.fbi.gov/cointel-pro/cointel -pro-black-extremists/cointelpro-black-extremists-part-01-of/view; David Cunningham and Barb Browning, "The Emergence of Worthy Targets: Official Frames and Deviance Narratives Within the FBI," *Sociological Forum* 19, no. 3 (September 2004): 347–69.

6. Chang, *Can't Stop, Won't Stop.*

7. Ibid., 52.

8. *Flyin' Cut Sleeves*, directed by Henry Chalfant and Rita Fecher (Pottstown, PA: MVD Visual, 1993).

9. Chang, *Can't Stop, Won't Stop*, 63.

10. Ibid., 101.

11. Melbourne S. Cummings and Abhik Roy, "Manifestations of Afrocentricity in Rap Music," *Howard Journal of Communications* 13, no. 1 (January 1995): 59–76; Cheryl Keyes, *Rap Music and Street Consciousness* (Urbana, IL: University of Illinois Press, 2002), 54.

12. Andreana Clay, *The Hip-Hop Generation Fights Back: Youth, Activism and Post-Civil Rights Politics* (New York: New York University Press, 2012); Anthony B. Pinn, "'How Ya Livin'?': Notes on Rap Music and Social Transformation," *The Western Journal of Black Studies* 23, no. 1 (Spring 2012): 10–21.

13. Michele Collison, "'Fight the Power': Rap Music Pounds Out a New Anthem for Many Black Students," *Chronicle of Higher Education* 36, no. 22 (February 1990): A1–A30.

14. Erin Trapp, "The Push and Pull of Hip-Hop: A Social Movement Analysis," *American Behavioral Scientist* 48, no. 11 (July 2005): 1482–95.

15. Edward G.Armstrong, "The Rhetoric of Violence in Rap and Country Music," *Sociological Inquiry* 63, no.1 (January 1993): 64–83; Christine Hall Hansen, "Predicting Cognitive and Behavioral Effects of Gangsta Rap," in *Basic and Applied Social Psychology* 16, no. 1–2 (1995): 43–52; Dolf Zillmann, Charles F. Aust, Kathleen D. Hoffman, Curtis C. Love, Virginia Ordman, Janice Pope, Patrick Seigler, and Rhonda Gibson, "Radical Rap: Does It Further Ethnic Division?," in *Basic and Applied Social Psychology* 16, no. 1–2 (1995): 1–25.

16. Gregory Snyder, *Graffiti Lives: Beyond the Tag in New York's Urban Underground* (New York: New York University Press, 2009), 97; Joseph Schloss, *Foundation: B-Boys, B-Girls, and Hip-Hop Culture in New York,* (Cary, NC: Oxford University Press, 2009), 75–85.

17. Snyder, *Graffiti Lives*, 97.

18. Schloss, *Foundation,* 75–85.

19. H. Samy Alim, *Roc the Mic Right: The Language of Hip Hop Culture* (Florence, KY: Routledge, 2006), 98; Erik Pihel, "A Furified Freestyle: Homer and Hip Hop," *Oral Tradition* 11, no. 2 (1996): 249–69.

20. Alim, *Roc the Mic Right*, 98.

21. *Scratch*, directed by Doug Pray (New York, NY: Palm Pictures, 2001), DVD.

22. Snyder, *Graffiti Lives*, 26; Myra Frances Taylor, "Addicted to the Risk, Recognition and Respect that the Graffiti Lifestyle Provides: Towards an Understanding of the Reasons for Graffiti Engagement," *International Journal of Mental Health and Addiction* 10, no. 1 (February 2012): 54–68.

23. Schloss, *Foundation*; Snyder, *Graffiti Lives*, 26.

24. Snyder, *Graffiti Lives*, 97.

25. *Getting Up: A Graffiti Documentary*, directed by Caskey Ebeling (USA: Ebeling Group, 2010).

26. Schloss, *Foundation*; Snyder, *Graffiti Lives*, 26.

27. *Style Wars*, directed by Tony Silver (USA: Public Art Films: 1983).

28. William Grimes, "Michael Martin, Subway Graffiti Artist Iz the Wiz, Is Dead at 50," *The New York Times*, June 29, 2009.

29. Hansen, "Predicting."

30. Tia DeNora, *Music in Everyday Life* (New York: Cambridge University Press, 2000), 5; Patrik N. Juslin, Simon Liljeström, Petri Laukka, Daniel Västfjäll, and Lars-Olov Lundqvist, "Emotional Reactions to Music in a Nationally Representative Sample of Swedish Adults: Prevalence and Causal Influences," *Musicae Scientiae* 15, no. 2 (2011): 174–207; Viggo Krüger and Brynjulf Stige, "Between Rights and Realities—Music as a Structuring Resource in Child Welfare Everyday Life: A Qualitative Study," *Nordic Journal of Music Therapy* 24, no. 2 (2015): 99–122.

31. DeNora, *Music*; Katrina Skewes McFerran and Suvi Saarikallio, "Depending on Music to Feel Better: Being Conscious of Responsibility when Appropriating the Power of Music," *The Arts in Psychotherapy* 41, no. 1 (2014): 89–97.

32. Tia DeNora. *Music*, 153; Peter J. Rentfrow, Lewis R. Goldberg, and Daniel J. Levitin, "The Structure of Musical Preferences: A Five-Factor Model," *Journal of Personality and Social Psychology* 100, no. 6 (2011): 1139–57.

33. Thomas Schäfer, Peter Sedlmeier, Christine Städtler, and David Huron, "The Psychological Functions of Music Listening," *Frontiers in Psychology* 4 (2013).

34. McFerran and Saarikallio, "Depending on Music"; Brad H. Reddick and Eugene V. Beresin, "Rebellious Rhapsody: Metal, Rap, Community, and Individuation," *Academic Psychiatry: The Journal of the American Association of Directors of Psychiatric Residency Training and the Association for Academic Psychiatry* 26, no. 1 (2002): 51–59; Suvi Saarikallio and Jaakko Erkkilä, "The Role of Music in Adolescents' Mood Regulation," *Psychology of Music* 35, no. 1 (2007): 88–109.

35. Raphael Travis and Anne Deepak, "Empowerment in Context: Lessons from Hip-Hop Culture for Social Work Practice," *Journal of Ethnic & Cultural Diversity in Social Work: Innovation in Theory, Research & Practice* 20, no. 3 (2011): 203–22.

36. Raphael Travis, "Rap Music and the Empowerment of Today's Youth: Evidence in Everyday Music Listening, Music Therapy, and Commercial Rap Music," *Child and Adolescent Social Work Journal* 30, no. 2 (2013): 139–67.

37. Tia DeNora, "Resounding the Great Divide: Theorising Music in Everyday Life at the End of Life," *Mortality* 17, no. 2 (2012): 92–105; Julian Koenig, Marco

Warth, Rieke Oelkers-Ax, Alexander Wormit, Hubert J. Bardenheuer, Franz Resch, Julian F. Thayer, and Thomas K. Hillecke, "I Need to Hear Some Sounds That Recognize the Pain in Me: An Integrative Review of a Decade of Research in the Development of Active Music Therapy Outpatient Treatment in Patients with Recurrent or Chronic Pain," *Music and Medicine* 5, no. 3 (2013): 150–61; Suvi Saarikallio, "Music as Emotional Self-Regulation Throughout Adulthood," *Psychology of Music* 39, no. 3 (July 2011): 307–27; Schäfer, et al., "Psychological Functions of Music Listening."

38. DeNora, *Music*, 153.

39. Neal Halfon, Kandyce Larson, Michael Lu, Ericka Tullis, and Shirley Russ, "Lifecourse Health Development: Past, Present and Future," *Maternal and Child Health Journal* 18, no. 2 (2014): 344–65; D. Kuh, Y. Ben-Shlomo, J. Lynch, J. Hallqvist, and C. Power, "Life Course Epidemiology," *Journal of Epidemiology and Community Health* 57, no. 10) (2013): 778–83; Travis, "Rap Music and the Empowerment of Today's Youth"; Raphael Travis Jr. and Tamara G. J. Leech, "Empowerment-Based Positive Youth Development: A New Understanding of Healthy Development for African American Youth," *Journal of Research on Adolescence* 24, no. 1 (2014): 93–116.

40. DeNora. "Resounding the Great Divide"; Saarikallio, "Music as Emotional Self-Regulation."

41. Mona Lisa Chanda and Daniel J. Levitin, "The Neurochemistry of Music," *Trends in Cognitive Sciences* 17, no. 4 (April 2013): 179–93.

42. Edgar H. Tyson, Paul Duongtran, and Gregory Acevedo, "Hip Hop Perceptions and Exposure as Predictors of School Outcomes for Black and Latino Adolescents," *Journal of Human Behavior in the Social Environment* 22, no. 3 (March 2012): 235–54.

43. Chanda and Levitin, "The Neurochemistry of Music"; Galina Mindlin, Don Durousseau, and Joseph Cardillo, *Your Playlist Can Change Your Life* (Naperville, IL: Sourcebooks, 2012).

44. Tia DeNora, *Music in Everyday Life* (New York: Cambridge University Press, 2000).

45. Reiland Rabaka, *Hip Hop Movement: From R&B and the Civil Rights Movement to Rap and the Hip Hop Generation* (Blue Ridge Summit, PA: Lexington Books, 2013).

46. Schloss, *Foundation*, 48.

47. Chris Emdin, *Urban Science Education for the Hip Hop Generation: Essential Tools for the Urban Science Educator and Researcher* (Boston, MA: Sense Publishers, 2010); Emery Petchauer, "Starting with Style: Toward a Second Wave of Hip-Hop Education Research and Practice," *Urban Education* 50, no. 1 (2015): 78–105.

48. Schloss, *Foundation*, 74.

49. Rabaka, *Hip Hop Movement*.

50. Adrian C. North and David J. Hargreaves, "Pop Music Subcultures and Well-being," in *Health and Wellbeing*, ed. Raymond A. R. MacDonald, Gunter Kreutz, and Laura Mitchell (New York: Oxford University Press, 2012), 502–12.

51. Schloss, *Foundation*, 75–85.

52. Stefan Koelsch, "Music-Evoked Emotions: Principles, Brain Correlates, and Implications for Therapy," *Annals of the New York Academy of Sciences* 1337 (March 2015): 193–201.

53. Imani Perry, *Prophets of the Hood: Politics and Poetics in Hip Hop* (Durham, NC: Duke University Press, 2004), 21.

54. Brynjulf Stige, "Health Musicking: A Perspective on Music and Health as Action and Performance," in *Health and Wellbeing*, ed. Raymond A. R. MacDonald, Gunter Kreutz, and Laura Mitchell (New York: Oxford University Press, 2012), 183–95.

CHAPTER 4

1. Mazi Mutafa, interview with author, Washington, DC, September 2014.

2. Timothy Jones, interview with author, Washington, DC, September 2014.

3. James Peterson, "It's Yours: Hip Hop Worldviews in the Lyrics of Nas," in *Born to use Mics*, ed. Michael Eric Dyson and Sohail Daulatzai (New York: Basic Civitas Books, 2010), 82.

4. Michael Hughes et al., "Racial Identity and Well-Being Among African Americans," *Social Psychology Quarterly* 78, no. 1 (March 2015): 25–48; Elizabeth M. Lusk et al., "Biracial Identity and Its Relation to Self-Esteem and Depression in Mixed Black/White Biracial Individuals," *Journal of Ethnic & Cultural Diversity in Social Work: Innovation in Theory, Research & Practice* 19, no. 2 (April 2010): 109–26.

5. Valerie Adams-Bass, Howard C. Stevenson, and Diana Slaughter Kotzin, "Measuring the Meaning of Black Media Stereotypes and Their Relationship to the Racial Identity, Black History Knowledge, and Racial Socialization of African American Youth," *Journal of Black Studies* 45, no. 5 (July 2014): 367–95.

6. *Something from Nothing: The Art of Rap*, directed by Tracy Marrow and Andy Baybutt (United States: Indomina Releasing, 2012), DVD.

7. Tricia Rose, *Hip-Hop Wars: What We Talk About When We Talk About Hip-Hop—And Why It Matters* (New York: Basic Civitas, 2008), 9.

8. Reiland Rabaka, *Hip Hop Inheritance: From the Harlem Renaissance to the Hip Hop Feminist Movement* (Blue Ridge Summit, PA: Lexington Books, 2011).

9. Imani Perry, *Prophets of the Hood: Politics and Poetics in Hip Hop* (Durham, NC: Duke University Press, 2004), 23.

10. Tia DeNora, *Music in Everyday Life* (New York: Cambridge University Press, 2000), 32–34.

11. Kim Hong Nguyen, "Hearing What We See: Censoring 'Nigga,' Vernaculars, and African American Agentic Subjects," *Howard Journal of Communications*, 24, no. 3 (July 2013): 293–308.

12. Tupac Shakur, *The Rose That Grew from Concrete* (New York: MTV Books, 2009).

13. *Merriam-Webster*, s.v. "negus." http://www.merriam-webster.com/dictionary /negus (accessed 20 May, 2015).

14. Nguyen, "Hearing What We See."

15. Roy R. Baumeister, Jennifer D. Campbell, Joachim J. Krueger, and Kathleen D. Vohs, "Exploding the Self-Esteem Myth," in *Navigating the Mindfield: A User's Guide to Distinguishing Science from Pseudoscience in Mental Health*, ed. Scott O. Lilienfeld, John Ruscio, Steven Jay Lynn (Amherst, NY: Prometheus Books, 2008), 575–87.

16. Elizabeth Sweet, "'If Your Shoes Are Raggedy You Get Talked About': Symbolic and Material Dimensions of Adolescent Social Status and Health," *Social Science & Medicine* 70, no. 12 (June 2010): 2029–35.

17. Dian A. Vries et al., "Adolescents' Social Network Site Use, Peer Appearance-Related Feedback, and Body Dissatisfaction: Testing a Mediation Model," *Journal of Youth and Adolescence* (forthcoming).

18. Jean M. Twenge, "The Evidence for Generation Me and Against Generation We," *Emerging Adulthood* 1, no. 1 (March 2013): 11–16.

19. Robin Roberts, "Ladies First: Queen Latifah's Afrocentric Feminist Music Video," *African American Review* 28, no. 2 (1994): 245–57.

20. Billyjam, "Women in Hip Hop Part III: 1990 & 1991," *Amoeba Music* (blog), March 24, 2009, http://www.amoeba.com/blog/2009/03/jamoeblog/women-in -hip-hop-part-iii-1990-1991.html.

21. Danice L. Brown, Rhonda White-Johnson, and Felicia Griffin-Fennell, "Breaking the Chains: Examining the Endorsement of Modern Jezebel Images and Racial-Ethnic Esteem among African American Women," *Culture, Health & Sexuality* 15, no. 5 (May 2013): 525–39.

22. Christina Oney, Elizabeth Cole, and Robert Sellers, "Racial Identity and Gender as Moderators of the Relationship between Body Image and Self-Esteem for African Americans," *Sex Roles* 65, no. 7 (October 2011): 619–31.

23. Reiland Rabaka, *Hip Hop Movement: From R&B and the Civil Rights Movement to Rap and the Hip Hop Generation* (Blue Ridge Summit, PA: Lexington Books, 2013), 195.

24. Bettina Love, *Hip Hop's Li'l Sistas Speak: Negotiating Hip Hop Identities and Politics in the New South* (New York: Peter Lang, 2012), 76.

25. Ibid., 109.

26. Cheryl Keyes, *Rap Music and Street Consciousness* (Urbana, IL: University of Illinois Press, 2002); Tricia Rose, *Black Noise: Rap Music and Black Culture in Contemporary America* (Hanover, NH: Wesleyan University Press, 1994), 59.

27. Robin D. G. Kelley, *Race Rebels* (New York: The Free Press, 1994).

28. Ibid., 194.

29. Rabaka, *Hip Hop Movement*, 167.

30. Michelle Alexander, *The New Jim Crow: Mass Incarceration in the Age of Colorblindness* (New York: The New Press, 2010), 185–87.

31. Elliot McLaughlin, "We're Not Seeing More Police Shootings, Just More News Coverage," CNN, April 21, 2015, http://www.cnn.com/2015/04/20/us /police-brutality-video-social-media-attitudes/.

32. Claudio G. Vera Sanchez and Ericka B. Adams, "Sacrificed on the Altar of Public Safety: The Policing of Latino and African American Youth," *Journal of Contemporary Criminal Justice* 27, no. 3 (August 2011): 322–41.

33. Complex TV. *Special Ed—"I Got It Made" | Magnum Opus*, http://www .complex.com/tv/shows/magnum-opus/new-series-magnum-opus-featuring -special-ed-i-got-it-made.

34. Timothy Jones, interview with author, Washington, DC, September 2014.

35. Gabriel "Asheru" Benn, interview with author, Washington, DC, September 2014.

36. Ndidi Okeke-Adeyanju et al., "Celebrating the Strengths of Black Youth: Increasing Self-Esteem and Implications for Prevention," *Journal of Primary Prevention* 35, no. 5 (October 2014): 357–69.

37. L.J. Shrum et al., "Reconceptualizing Materialism as Identity Goal Pursuits: Functions, Processes, and Consequences," *Journal of Business Research* 66, no. 8 (August 2013): 1179–85.

CHAPTER 5

1. L. J. Shrum, *The Psychology of Entertainment Media: Blurring the Lines Between Entertainment and Persuasion* (2nd ed.), ed. L. J. Shrum (New York: Routledge/Taylor & Francis Group, 2012); Robert S. Wyer Jr. and L. J. Shrum, "The Role of Comprehension Processes in Communication and Persuasion," *Media Psychology* 18, no. 2 (April 2015): 163–95.

2. Mickey Hess, "From Bricks to Billboards: Hip-Hop Autobiography," *Mosaic: A Journal for the Interdisciplinary Study of Literature* 39, no. 1 (March 2006): 61–77; Stefan Koelsch, "Music-Evoked Emotions: Principles, Brain Correlates, and Implications for Therapy," *Annals of the New York Academy of Sciences* 1337 (March 2015): 193–201.

3. Natalie Davis, interview with author, Florida, December 2014.

4. Madelijn Strick et al., "Striking the Right Chord: Moving Music Increases Psychological Transportation and Behavioral Intentions," *Journal of Experimental Psychology: Applied* 21, no. 1 (March 2015): 57–72.

5. Raphael Travis, "Rap Music and the Empowerment of Today's Youth: Evidence in Everyday Music Listening, Music Therapy, and Commercial Rap Music," *Child and Adolescent Social Work Journal* 30, no. 2 (April 2013): 139–67.

6. Ian Levy, interview with author, New York, NY, April 2015.

7. Melanie C. Green, Timothy C. Brock, and Geoff F. Kaufman, "Understanding Media Enjoyment: The Role of Transportation into Narrative Worlds," *Communication Theory* 14, no. 4 (November 2004): 311–27.

8. Melanie C. Green and Timothy C. Brock, "The Role of Transportation in the Persuasiveness of Public Narratives," *Journal of Personality and Social Psychology* 79, no. 5 (November 2000): 701–21.

9. Robert Marriott, "Allah's on Me," in *And It Don't Stop! The Best American Hip Hop Journalism of the Last 25 Years*, ed. Raquel Cepeda (New York: Faber and Faber, 2004), 187–201.

10. Bettina Love, *Hip Hop's Li'l Sistas Speak: Negotiating Hip Hop Identities and Politics in the New South* (New York: Peter Lang, 2012), 5.

11. James Peterson, "It's Yours: Hip Hop Worldviews in the Lyrics of Nas," *Born to Use Mics*, ed. Michael Eric Dyson and Sohail Daulatzai (New York: Basic Civitas Books, 2010), 76.

12. Anita Chandra and Ameena Batada, "Exploring Stress and Coping among Urban African American Adolescents: The Shifting the Lens Study," *Preventing Chronic Disease: Public Health Research and Policy* 32, no. 2 (2006): 1–10.

13. Nieson Himmel, "LAPD's Battering Ram Roars Back into Action," *Los Angeles Times*, Feb. 19, 1986. http://articles.latimes.com/1986-02-19/news/mn-9506_1_ram-battering-action.

14. Paula S. Nurius, Dana M. Prince, and Anita Rocha, "Cumulative Disadvantage and Youth Well-Being: A Multi-Domain Examination with Life Course Implications," *Child and Adolescent Social Work Journal* (forthcoming).

15. Eli Somer and Yochai Ataria, "Adverse Outcome of Continuous Traumatic Stress: A Qualitative Inquiry," *International Journal of Stress Management* (forthcoming); Garth Stevens et al., "Continuous Traumatic Stress: Conceptual Conversations in Contexts of Global Conflict, Violence and Trauma," *Peace and Conflict: Journal of Peace Psychology* 19, no. 2 (May 2013): 75–84.

16. Cendrine Robinson, interview with author, Chicago, IL, December 2014.

17. Chris Emdin, interview with author, New York, NY, March 2015.

18. Stephen Peck et al., "Racial/Ethnic Socialization and Identity Development in Black Families: The Role of Parent and Youth Reports," in *Developmental Psychology* 50, no. 7 (July 2014): 1897–1909.

19. Gregory Snyder, *Graffiti Lives: Beyond the Tag in New York's Urban Underground* (New York: New York University Press, 2009), 100–101.

20. Troy Harden, "Street Life-Oriented African American Males and Violence as a Public Health Concern," *Journal of Human Behavior in the Social Environment* 24, no. 6 (August 2014): 678–93.

21. Michelle Alexander, *The New Jim Crow: Mass Incarceration in the Age of Colorblindness* (New York: The New Press, 2010).

22. Eloise Dunlap et al., "Macro-Level Social Forces and Micro-Level Consequences: Poverty, Alternate Occupations, and Drug Dealing," *Journal of Ethnicity in Substance Abuse* 9, no. 2 (April 2010): 115–27.

23. Beau Kilmer et al., *How Big Is the U.S. Market for Illegal Drugs?* (Santa Monica, CA: RAND Corporation, 2014), accessed May 9, 2015 from http://www.rand.org/pubs/research_briefs/RB9770.

24. Alexander, *The New Jim Crow*, 51–52.

25. Ibid.; Roland G. Fryer et al., "Measuring Crack Cocaine and Its Impact," *Economic Inquiry* 51, no. 3 (July 2013): 1651–81; Alan Lizotte, Marvin D. Krohn, and James C. Howell, "Factors Influencing Gun Carrying among Young Urban Males over the Adolescent–Young Adult Life Course," *Criminology* 38, no. 3 (August 2000): 811–34.

26. MK Asante Jr., *It's Bigger Than Hip Hop: The Rise of the Post-Hip-Hop Generation* (New York: St. Martin's Press, 2008).

27. Marriott, "Allah's on Me," 195.

28. Ibid., 193.

CHAPTER 6

1. Alexis C. Maston, *Spiritualizing Hip Hop with I.C.E.: The Poetic Spiritual Narratives of Four Black Educational Leaders from Hip Hop Communities,* PhD dissertation, Texas State University, May 2014.

2. Reiland Rabaka, *Hip Hop's Amnesia: From Blues and the Black Women's Club Movement to Rap and the Hip Hop Movement* (Lanham, MD: Lexington Books, 2012), 81.

3. Ali S. Muhammad and Frannie Kelley, "Nas: I'm Still Charged 20 Years After 'Illmatic,'" *NPR,* April 23, 2014, http://www.npr.org/sections/microphonecheck /2014/04/23/305629896/nas-im-still-charged-20-years-after-illmatic.

4. Alicia Maule, "Rapsody Raps to Inspire the Next Generation of Black Girls," *MSNBC,* Feb. 6, 2015, http://www.msnbc.om/msnbc/rapsody-raps-inspire-the -next-generation-black-girls.

5. Shana Redmond, "*Anthem: Social Movements and the Sound of Solidarity in the African Diaspora* (New York: New York University Press, 2014), 191.

6. Ibid., 184.

7. Muhammad and Kelley, *Nas.*

8. Redmond, *Anthem.*

9. Ibid., 181.

10. Muhammad and Kelley, *Nas.*

11. Reiland Rabaka, *Hip Hop Movement: From R&B and the Civil Rights Movement to Rap and the Hip Hop Generation* (Blue Ridge Summit, PA, USA: Lexington Books, 2013), 332–34.

12. Cheryl Keyes, *Rap Music and Street Consciousness* (Urbana, IL: University of Illinois Press, 2002), 228.

13. Bronwen Low, Eloise Tan, and Jacqueline Celemencki, "The Limits of 'Keepin' it Real': The Challenges for Critical Hip Hop Pedagogies of Discourses of Authenticity," in *Schooling Hip-Hop: Expanding Hip-Hop Based Education across the Curriculum,* ed. Marc L. Hill and Emery Petchauer (New York: Teachers College Press, 2013), 118–36.

14. Dan Charnas, *The Big Payback: The History of the Business of Hip-Hop* (New York: New American Library, 2011), 177.

15. Reiland Rabaka, *Hip Hop Inheritance: From the Harlem Renaissance to the Hip Hop Feminist Movement* (Blue Ridge Summit, PA: Lexington Books, 2011), 50; Yuval Taylor and Jake Austen, *Darkest America: Black Minstrelsy from Slavery to Hip Hop* (New York: W. W. Norton & Company, 2012), 73.

16. Rabaka, *Hip Hop Inheritance,* 51.

17. Yuval Taylor and Jake Austen, *Darkest America,* 72–73.

18. William E. Cross Jr., "The Historical Relationship between Black Identity and Black Achievement Motivation," in *African American Children and Mental Health, Volume 1: Development and Context*, ed. N. Hill, T. Mann, and H. Fitzgerald (Santa Barbara, CA: Praeger, 2011), 16.

19. Azmat Khan, "Derrion Albert: The Death That Riled the Nation," in *PBS*, Feb. 14, 2012, http://www.pbs.org/wgbh/pages/frontline/social-issues/interrupters /derrion-albert-the-death-that-riled-the-nation.

20. Cross, "The Historical Relationship," 17; "Chicago Police Seek 3 More in Teen's Death," *CNN*, Sep. 30, 2009, http://edition.cnn.com/2009/CRIME/09/29 /chicago.teen.beating/.

21. Jeffrey Fagan and Bernard Harcourt, *Fact Sheet in Richmond County (Staten Island) Grand Jury in Eric Garner Homicide* (New York: Columbia Law School, 2015).

22. Adam Waytz, Kelly Marie Hoffman, and Sophie Trawalter, "A Superhumanization Bias in Whites' Perceptions of Blacks," *Social Psychological and Personality Science* 6, no. 3 (April 2015): 352–59.

23. Kimberly Kindy, "Fatal Police Shootings in 2015 Approaching 400 Nationwide," *The Washington Post*, May 30, 2015, http://www.washingtonpost.com /national/fatal-police-shootings-in-2015-approaching-400-nationwide/2015/05 /30/d322256a-058e-11e5-a428-c984eb077d4e_story.html; "The Counted: People Killed by Police in the United States," *The Guardian*, accessed June 6, 2015, from http://www.theguardian.com/us-news/ng-interactive/2015/jun/01/the-counted -police-killings-us-database.

24. Lizette Alvarez and Cara Buckley, "Zimmerman Is Acquitted of Killing Trayvon Martin," *The New York Times*, July 14, 2013, http://www.nytimes.com/2013 /07/15/us/george-zimmerman-verdict-trayvon-martin.html?_r=0.

25. Joycelyn Pollock, Steven Glassner, and Angela Krajewski, "Examining the Conservative Shift from Harsh Justice," *Laws* 4, no. 1 (2015): 107–24.

26. James Peterson, "It's Yours: Hip Hop Worldviews in the Lyrics of Nas," in *Born to Use Mics*, ed. Michael Eric Dyson and Sohail Daulatzai (New York: Basic Civitas Books, 2010), 76.

27. Maria Piacentini and Kathy Hamilton, "Consumption Lives at the Bottom of the Pyramid," *Marketing Theory* 13, no. 3 (September 2013): 397–400.

28. Michael Rutter, "Annual Research Review: Resilience–Clinical implications," *Journal of Child Psychology and Psychiatry* 54, no. 4 (April 2013): 474–87.

29. Madelijn Strick et al., "Striking the Right Chord: Moving Music Increases Psychological Transportation and Behavioral Intentions," *Journal of Experimental Psychology: Applied* 21, no. 1 (March 2015): 57–72.

CHAPTER 7

1. Adam Bradley and Andrew Dubois, *The Anthology of Rap* (New Haven, CT: Yale University Press, 2011), 32–33.

2. Peter Spirer, *Beef*, ed. Denis Hennelly, Casey Suchan, and Peter Spirer (Chatsworth, CA: Image Entertainment, 2003).

3. "Here's Why I Won't Support the Coonery of 'Empire,'" Dr. Boyce Watkins, All Hip Hop, January 20, 2015, http://allhiphop.com/2015/01/20/dr-boyce-watkins -heres-why-i-wont-support-the-coonery-of-empire/.

4. Jay Z and Dream Hampton, *Decoded* (New York: Spiegel & Grau, 2011), 203.

5. "Tef Poe is More than a Rapper—He's Becoming the Voice of Ferguson," Tom Barnes, Music.Mic, January 8, 2015. http://mic.com/articles/108042/tef-poe -isn-t-just-a-rapper-he-s-becoming-the-voice-of-ferguson.

6. Cheryl Corley, "With Ferguson Protests, 20-Somethings Become First-Time Activists," in *NPR*, October 24, 2014,. http://www.npr.org/2014/10/24/358054785 /with-ferguson-protests-20-somethings-become-first-time-activists.

7. Jamal Watson, "Sharpton Responds to Criticism That His Movement Excludes Younger Activists," in *The Root*, December 15, 2014, http://www.theroot .com/articles/culture/2014/12/rev_sharpton_responds_to_his_critics.html.

8. Kirsten W. Savali, "The Fierce Urgency of Now: Why Young Protesters Bum-Rushed the Mic," *The Root*, December 14, 2014, http://www.theroot.com/articles /culture/2014/12/the_fierce_urgency_of_now_why_young_protesters_bum _rushed_the_mic.html?wpisrc=topstories.

9. Mike Miller, "Fifty Years Later, a Time for Evaluation," *Social Policy* 44, no. 1 (Spring 2014): 15–21.

10. Reiland Rabaka, *Hip Hop Inheritance: From the Harlem Renaissance to the Hip Hop Feminist Movement* (Blue Ridge Summit, PA: Lexington Books, 2011).

11. Imani Perry, *Prophets of the Hood: Politics and Poetics in Hip Hop* (Durham, NC: Duke University Press, 2004), 128.

12. Reiland Rabaka, *Hip Hop's Amnesia: From Blues and the Black Women's Club Movement to Rap and the Hip Hop Movement* (Lanham, MD: Lexington Books, 2012), 92.

13. Joan Morgan, *When Chickenheads Come Home to Roost: A Hip-Hop Feminist Breaks It Down* (Chicago, IL: Simon & Schuster, 2000), 70.

14. Brenda Stevenson, *The Contested Murder of Latasha Harlins: Justice, Gender, and the Origins of the LA Riots* (New York: Oxford University Press, 2013).

15. Zurbriggen et al., *Report of the APA Task Force on the Sexualization of Girls* (Washington, DC: American Psychological Association, 2010).

16. Tobias Greitemeyer, "Effects of Songs With Prosocial Lyrics on Prosocial Behavior: Further Evidence and a Mediating Mechanism," *Personality and Social Psychology Bulletin* 35, no. 11 (November 2009): 1500–1511.

17. Lance Hannon, Robert DeFina, and Sarah Bruch, "The Relationship between Skin Tone and School Suspension for African Americans," *Race and Social Problems* 5, no. 4 (June 2013): 281–95; Carla Monroe, "Colorizing Educational Research: African American Life and Schooling as an Exemplar," *Educational Researcher* 42, no. 1 (2013): 9–19.

18. Amy L. Ai et al., "Racial/Ethnic Identity and Subjective Physical and Mental Health of Latino Americans: An Asset Within?," *American Journal of Community Psychology* 53, nos. 1–2 (March 2014): 173–84; Michael Hughes, K. J. Kiecolt, Verna M. Keith, and David H. Demo, "Racial Identity and Well-Being among African Americans, *Social Psychology Quarterly* 78, no. 1 (2015): 25–48; Monnica T. Williams et al., "The Role of Ethnic Identity in Symptoms of Anxiety and Depression in African Americans," *Psychiatry Research* 199, no. 1 (August 2012): 31–36.

CHAPTER 8

1. Brynjulf Stige, "Health Musicking: A Perspective on Music and Health as Action and Performance," *Music, Health, and Wellbeing*, ed. Raymond A. R. MacDonald, Gunter Kreutz, and Laura Mitchell (New York: Oxford University Press, 2012), 183–95.

2. Stefan Koelsch, "Music-Evoked Emotions: Principles, Brain Correlates, and Implications for Therapy," *Annals of the New York Academy of Sciences* 1337 (March 2015): 193–201.

3. Raphael Travis Jr. and Anne Deepak, "Empowerment in Context: Lessons from Hip-Hop Culture for Social Work Practice," *Journal of Ethnic & Cultural Diversity in Social Work: Innovation in Theory, Research & Practice* 20, no. 3 (July 2011): 203–22.

4. Raphael Travis Jr., and Tamara G. J. Leech, "Empowerment-Based Positive Youth Development: A New Understanding of Healthy Development for African American Youth," *Journal of Research on Adolescence* 24, no. 1 (March 2014): 93–116.

5. Stige, "Health Musicking."

6. Ibid., 189.

7. Ibid., 188–89.

8. Koelsch, *Music-Evoked Emotions.*

9. Patrik N. Juslin, László Harmat, and Tuomas Eerola, "What Makes Music Emotionally Significant? Exploring the Underlying Mechanisms," *Psychology of Music* 42, no. 4 (July 2014): 599–623.

10. Koelsch, *Music-Evoked Emotions.*

11. Ibid., 197.

12. Ibid., 193.

13. Ibid., 194.

14. Ibid., 195.

15. Ibid., 196.

16. Ibid., 197.

17. Ibid., 197–98.

18. Ibid., 198.

19. Travis and Deepak, "Empowerment in Context"; Raphael Travis Jr., "Rap Music and the Empowerment of Today's Youth: Evidence in Everyday Music Lis-

tening, Music Therapy, and Commercial Rap Music," *Child and Adolescent Social Work Journal* 30, no. 2 (April 2013): 139–67.

20. Travis and Leech, *Empowerment-Based Positive Youth Development.*

21. Travis, *Rap Music.*

22. Stige, "Health Musicking," 188.

23. Ibid.

24. Ibid., 186.

25. Daniel Västfjäll, Patrik N. Juslin, and Terry Hartig, "Music, Subjective Well-being, and Health: The Role of Everyday Emotions" in *Music, Health, and Wellbeing,* ed. Raymond A. R. MacDonald, Gunter Kreutz, and Laura Mitchell (New York: Oxford University Press, 2012), 405–23.

26. Stige, "Health Musicking," 188.

27. Ibid., 187.

28. Ibid.

CHAPTER 9

1. J. O. Connelly, T. Berryman, and E. A. Tolley, "Rap Video vs. Traditional Video for Teaching Nutrition," *The Journal of Biocommunication* 23, no.4 (1996): 17–21; Steve Sussman et al., "Empirical Development of Brief Smoking Prevention Videotapes Which Target African-American Adolescents," *The International Journal of the Addictions* 30, no. 9 (1995): 1141–64; J. B. Tucker et al., "Violence Prevention: Reaching Adolescents with the Message," *Pediatric Emergency Care* 15, no. 6 (1999): 436–39.

2. Mona Lisa Chanda and Daniel J. Levitin, "The Neurochemistry of Music," *Trends in Cognitive Sciences* 17, no. 4 (2013): 179–93.

3. Maria Pothoulaki, Raymond MacDonald, and Paul Flowers, "The Use of Music in Chronic Illness: Evidence and Arguments," in *Music, Health, and Wellbeing,* ed. Raymond A. R. MacDonald, Gunter Kreutz, and Laura Mitchell (New York: Oxford University Press, 2012), 239–56.

4. Gunther Bernatzky et al., "Music as Non-Pharmacological Pain Management in Clinics," in *Music, Health, and Wellbeing,* ed. Raymond A. R. MacDonald, Gunter Kreutz, and Laura Mitchell (New York: Oxford University Press, 2012), 257–75.

5. Pothoulaki, MacDonald, and Flowers, "The Use of Music in Chronic Illness," 249.

6. Bernatzky et al., "Music as Non-Pharmacological Pain Management," 257–75.

7. Neal Halfon et al., "Lifecourse Health Development: Past, Present and Future," *Maternal and Child Health Journal* 18, no. 2 (2014): 344–65.

8. Michael Byrd and Linda Clayton, *An American Health Dilemma: A Medical History of African Americans and the Problem of Race: Beginnings to 1900* (New York: Routledge, 2000).

9. Ibid., 292.

10. Gallup, *Healthways Well-being Index*, 2015, accessed June 8, 2015, from http://www.gallup.com/poll/182348/uninsured-rate-dips-first-quarter.aspx.

11. Halfon et al., "Lifecourse Health Development;" U.S. Department of Health and Human Services, *HHS Action Plan to Reduce Racial and Ethnic Health Disparities* (Washington, DC: Department of Health and Human Services, 2014), http://minorityhealth.hhs.gov/assets/pdf/hhs/HHS_Plan_complete.pdf.

12. Centers for Disease Control and Prevention, *MMWR, CDC Health Disparities and Inequalities Report—United States, 2013* 62 (Supplement 3).

13. Stephen P. Gulley, Elizabeth K. Rasch, and Leighton Chan, "Difference, Disparity, and Disability: A Comparison of Health, Insurance Coverage, and Health Service Use on the Basis of Race/Ethnicity among U.S. Adults with Disabilities, 2006–2008," *Medical Care* 52, no. 10 (2014): S9–S16; Benjamin Lê Cook, Colleen L. Barry, and Susan H. Busch, "Racial/Ethnic Disparity Trends in Children's Mental Health Care Access and Expenditures from 2002 to 2007," *Health Services Research* 48, no. 1 (2013): 129–49.

14. U.S. Department of Health and Human Services, *HHS Action Plan to Reduce Racial and Ethnic Health Disparities*.

15. Byrd and Clayton, *An American Health Dilemma*, 520.

16. Centers for Disease Control and Prevention, *MMWR, CDC Health Disparities and Inequalities*.

17. Yingru Li et al., "Childhood Obesity and Community Food Environments in Alabama's Black Belt Region," *Child: Care, Health and Development* (October 2014): 1–9; Lorraine Reitzel et al., "Density and Proximity of Fast Food Restaurants and Body Mass Index among African Americans," *American Journal of Public Health* 104, no. 1 (2014): 110–16.

18. Ibid.

19. Sean C. Lucan, Frances K. Barg, and Judith A. Long, "Promoters and Barriers to Fruit, Vegetable, and Fast-Food Consumption among Urban, Low-Income African Americans—A Qualitative Approach," *American Journal of Public Health* 100, no. 4 (2010): 631–35.

20. Phillip S. Gardiner, "The African Americanization of Menthol Cigarette Use in the United States," *Nicotine & Tobacco Research* 6, no. 2 (2004): S55–65.

21. Jennifer B. Unger et al., "Menthol and Non-Menthol Cigarette Use among Black Smokers in Southern California," *Nicotine & Tobacco Research* 12, no. 3 (February 2010): 398–407.

22. Neal L. Benowitz, Brenda Herrera, and Peyton Jacob II, "Mentholated Cigarette Smoking Inhibits Nicotine Metabolism," *The Journal of Pharmacology and Experimental Therapeutics* 310, no. 3 (2004): 1208–15.

23. Navid Hafez and Pamela M. Ling, "Finding the Kool Mixx: How Brown & Williamson Used Music Marketing to Sell Cigarettes," *Tobacco Control* 15, no. 5 (2006): 359–66.

24. Brown and Williamson Tobacco Corporation, "Kool Music Property," 1981, accessed June 8, 2015, http://legacy.library.ucsf.edu/tid/tyu63f00/pdf;jsessionid=C A6AA4B6F90069E674B0596063FA815C.tobacco03.

25. Ibid.

26. Ibid.

27. Unger et al., "Menthol and Non-Menthol Cigarette Use," 404.

28. Robert H. DuRant et al., "Violence and Weapon Carrying in Music Videos: A Content Analysis," *Archives of Pediatrics & Adolescent Medicine* 151, no. 5 (1997): 443–48; Clarke S. Harris, Richard J. Bradley, and Sharon K. Titus, "A Comparison of the Effects of Hard Rock and Easy Listening on the Frequency of Observed Inappropriate Behaviors: Control of Environmental Antecedents in a Large Public Area," *Journal of Music Therapy* 29, no. 1 (1992): 6–17; Kevin J. Took and David S. Weiss, "The Relationship between Heavy Metal and Rap Music and Adolescent Turmoil: Real or Artifact?" *Adolescence* 29, no. 115 (1994): 613.

29. Denise Herd, "Changing Images of Violence in Rap Music Lyrics: 1979–1997," *Journal of Public Health Policy* 30, no. 4 (2009): 395–406; Denise Herd, "Changes in the Prevalence of Alcohol Use in Rap Song Lyrics, 1979–97," *Addiction* 100, no. 9 (2005): 1258–69; Denise Herd, "Changes in Drug Use Prevalence in Rap Music Songs, 1979–1997," *Addiction Research & Theory* 16, no. 2 (2008): 167–80; Brian A. Primack et al., "Content Analysis of Tobacco, Alcohol, and Other Drugs in Popular Music," *Archives of Pediatrics & Adolescent Medicine* 162, no. 2 (2008): 169–75.

30. Mark A. Bellis et al., "Elvis to Eminem: Quantifying the Price of Fame through Early Mortality of European and North American Rock and Pop Stars," *Journal of Epidemiology and Community Health* 61, no. 10 (2007): 896–901.

31. Ibid., 899.

32. Megan S. C. Lim et al., "A Cross-Sectional Survey of Young People Attending a Music Festival: Associations between Drug Use and Musical Preference," *Drug and Alcohol Review* 27, no. 4 (2008): 439–41.

33. Herd, "Changes in the Prevalence of Alcohol Use."

34. Ibid.

35. Lynette Holloway, "Hip-Hop Sales Pop: Pass the Courvoisier and Count the Cash," *The New York Times*, September 2, 2002, accessed June 8, 2015, http://www.nytimes.com/2002/09/02/business/media-hip-hop-sales-pop-pass-the-courvoisier-and-count-the-cash.html.

36. Ibid.

37. Brian A. Primack et al., "Alcohol Brand Appearances in US Popular Music," *Addiction* 107, no. 3 (2012): 557–66.

38. Christian Schemer et al., "Does "Passing the Courvoisier" Always Pay Off? Positive and Negative Evaluative Conditioning Effects of Brand Placements in Music Videos," *Psychology & Marketing* 25, no. 10 (2008): 923–43.

39. Carla E. Stokes, "Representin' in Cyberspace: Sexual Scripts, Self-Definition, and Hip Hop Culture in Black American Adolescent Girls' Home Pages," *Culture, Health & Sexuality* 9, no. 2 (2007): 169–84.

40. Meng-Jinn Chen et al., "Music, Substance Use, and Aggression," *Journal of Studies on Alcohol* 67, no. 3 (2006): 373–81.

41. Shani H. Peterson et al., "Images of Sexual Stereotypes in Rap Videos and the Health of African American Female Adolescents," *Journal of Women's Health* 16, no. 8 (2007): 1157–64.

42. Adrian C. North and David J. Hargreaves, "Pop Music Subcultures and Wellbeing," in *Music, Health & Wellbeing*, ed. Raymond A. R. MacDonald, Gunter Kreutz, and Laura Mitchell (New York: Oxford University Press, 2012), 502–12.

43. Ibid., 588.

44. Derek K. Iwamoto, John Creswell, and Leon Caldwell, "Feeling the Beat: The Meaning of Rap Music for Ethnically Diverse Midwestern College Students—A Phenomenological Study," *Adolescence* 42, no. 166 (2007): 337.

45. Miguel Muñoz-Laboy et al., "Condom Use and Hip Hop Culture: The Case of Urban Young Men in New York City," *American Journal of Public Health* 98, no. 6 (2008): 1081–85.

46. Partnership for a Healthier America, "Songs for a Healthier America," 2014, accessed April 19, 2015, http://ahealthieramerica.org/songs/.

47. Hip Hop Public Health Education Center, *Hip Hop Stroke Center*, accessed June 8, 2015, http://home2.nyc.gov/html/hhc/harlem/html/services/hip-hop.shtml.

48. Olajide Williams et al., "Child-Mediated Stroke Communication Findings from Hip Hop Stroke," *Stroke* 43, no. 1 (2012): 163–69.

49. Hip Hop Public Health Education Center, *Hip Hop Stroke Center*.

50. Ibid.

51. Renetia Martin and Florence Stroud, "Delivering Difficult Messages: AIDS Prevention and Black Youth," in *AIDS Challenge: Prevention Education for Young People*, ed. Marcia Quackenbush and M. Nelson (Santa Cruz, CA: Network Publications, 1988), 345–59.

52. Steve Sussman et al., "Empirical Development of Brief Smoking Prevention Videotapes Which Target African-American Adolescents," *International Journal of the Addictions* 30, no. 9 (1995): 1141–64.

53. J. O. Connelly, T. Berryman and E. A. Tolley, "Rap Video vs. Traditional Video for Teaching Nutrition," *The Journal of Biocommunication* 23, no. 4 (1995): 17–21.

54. James B. Tucker et al., "Violence Prevention: Reaching Adolescents with the Message," *Pediatric Emergency Care* 15, no. 6 (1999): 436–39.

55. Centers for Disease Control and Prevention, *HIV among African Americans* (Atlanta, GA: Centers for Disease Control and Prevention, 2015), accessed April 29, 2015, http://www.cdc.gov/hiv/risk/racialethnic/aa/facts/index.html#ref1.

56. Anna Johnson et al., "HIV Infection—United States, 2008 and 2010," *MMWR, CDC Health Disparities and Inequalities Report—United States, 2013* 62, no. 3 (November 2013): 112–19.

57. Martin and Stroud, "Delivering Difficult Messages."

58. S. Keller, "Media Can Contribute to Better Health," *Network* 17 (3): 29–31.

59. Torrance Stephens, Ronald L. Braithwaite, and Sandra E. Taylor, "Model for Using Hip-Hop Music for Small Group HIV/AIDS Prevention Counseling with African American Adolescents and Young Adults," *Patient Education and Counseling* 35, no. 2 (1998): 127–37.

60. Don Elligan, "Rap Therapy: A Culturally Sensitive Approach to Psychotherapy With Young African American Men," *Journal of African American Studies* 5, no. 3 (2000): 27–36.

61. Camily Alves Peres et al., "Developing an AIDS Prevention Intervention for Incarcerated Male Adolescents in Brazil," *AIDS Education and Prevention* 14, no. 5 Supplement (2002): 36–44.

62. Ibid., 42.

63. Carla Boutin-Foster et al., "Reducing HIV and AIDS through Prevention (RHAP): A Theoretically Based Approach for Teaching HIV Prevention to Adolescents through an Exploration of Popular Music," *Journal of Urban Health* 87, no. 3 (2010): 440–51; Jocelyn Turner-Musa et al., "Hip-Hop to Prevent Substance Use and HIV among African-American Youth: A Preliminary Investigation," *Journal of Drug Education* 38, no. 4 (2009): 351–65.

64. SAMSHA, *Hip-Hop 2 Prevent Substance Abuse and HIV (H2P)* (The National Registry of Evidence-based Programs and Practices [NREPP], 2015), http://www.nrepp.samhsa.gov/ViewIntervention.aspx?id=84.

65. Marian L. Fitzgibbon et al., "Hip-Hop to Health Jr. for Latino Preschool Children," *Obesity* 14, no. 9 (September 2006): 1616–25.

66. Ibid.

67. Ibid.

68. Ibid.

69. *Hip Hop to Health Jr. Hip Hop to Health*, 2015, accessed June 8, 2015, http://www.hiphoptohealth.com/.

70. Sungwoon Kim and Jingu Kim, "Mood after Various Brief Exercise and Sport Modes: Aerobics, Hip-Hop Dancing, Ice Skating, and Body Conditioning," *Perceptual and Motor Skills* 104, no. 3c (2007): 1265–70.

71. Young Ran Tak et al., "[The Effects of a Physical Activity-Behavior Modification Combined Intervention (PABM-Intervention) on Metabolic Risk Factors in Overweight and Obese Elementary School Children]," *Taehan Kanho Hakhoe Chi* 37, no. 6 (2007): 902–13.

72. Sophie Lindner, "Urban Dance Health," 2015, accessed June 8, 2015, http://sophielindner.com/blog/.

73. Project Breakalign, *Project Breakalign: Reducing Injuries for Dancers*, 2015, accessed June 8, 2015, http://projectbreakalign.wix.com/projectbreakalign.

74. Rani Whitfield, *About H2D*, 2015, http://h2doc.com/main/#home.

75. Michael "Ice-Blue" Harris, "Hip Hop Doc Rani G. Whitfield Drops New CD and Talks Health and the Black Community," *Hip Hop Enquirer*, 2013, accessed June 8, 2015, http://hiphopenquirer.com/hip-hop-doc-rani-g-whitfield/.

76. Khnum "Stic" Ibomu, "7 Ways to Eat Good on a Hood Budget," *Plant Based on a Budget*, 2015, accessed June 8, 2015, http://plantbasedonabudget.com/7-ways -to-eat-good-while-on-a-hood-budget-by-stic-of-dead-prez/.

77. Khnum "Stic" Ibomu, *Eat Plants Lift Iron* (Atlanta, GA: Yojo Culture LLC, 2015).

78. RBG Fit Club, "Raising the Bar: Well Rounded Well Being," *RBG Fit Club*, 2015, accessed June 8, 2015, http://www.rbgfitclub.com/.

79. Daniel Västfjäll, Patrik N. Juslin, and Terry Hartig, "Music, Subjective Wellbeing, and Health: The Role of Everyday Emotions," in *Music, Health, and Wellbeing*, ed. Raymond A. R. MacDonald, Gunter Kreutz, and Laura Mitchell (New York: Oxford University Press. 2012).

80. Pothoulaki, MacDonald, and Flowers, "The Use of Music in Chronic Illness," 241.

81. David J. Elliott and Marissa Silverman, "Why Music Matters: Philosophical and Cultural Foundations," in *Music, Health, and Wellbeing*, eds. Raymond A. R. MacDonald, Gunter Kreutz, and Laura Mitchell (New York: Oxford University Press. 2012).

82. Lauri Nummenmaa et al., "Bodily Maps of Emotions," *Proceedings of the National Academy of Sciences* 111, no. 2 (January 2014): 646–51.

83. Stefan Koelsch, "Brain Correlates of Music-Evoked Emotions," *Nature Reviews Neuroscience* 15, no. 3 (2014): 170–80.

84. Hector F. Myers et al., "Cumulative Burden of Lifetime Adversities: Trauma and Mental Health in Low-SES African Americans and Latino/as," *Psychological Trauma: Theory, Research, Practice, and Policy* 7, no. 3 (2015): 243.

85. Tom Booth et al., "Association of Allostatic Load with Brain Structure and Cognitive Ability in Later Life," *Neurobiology of Aging* 36, no. 3 (2015): 1390–99; Lauren A. Doamekpor and Gniesha Y. Dinwiddie, "Allostatic Load in Foreign-Born and US-Born Blacks: Evidence from the 2001–2010 National Health and Nutrition Examination Survey," *American Journal of Public Health* 105, no. 3 (2015): 591–97.

86. Ibid.

87. Centers for Disease Control and Prevention, *MMWR, CDC Health Disparities and Inequalities Report*.

88. Kendell L. Coker et al., "The Effect of Social Problem Solving Skills in the Relationship between Traumatic Stress and Moral Disengagement among Inner-City African American High School Students," *Journal of Child & Adolescent Trauma* 7, no. 2 (2014): 87–95.

89. Kenneth D. Kochanek, Elizabeth Arias, and Robert N. Anderson, "How Did Cause of Death Contribute to Racial Differences in Life Expectancy in the United States in 2010," *NCHS Data Brief* 125 (2013): 1–8.

90. Joseph E. Logan et al., "Homicides—United States, 2007 and 2009," *CDC Health Disparities and Inequalities Report—United States, 2013* 62, no. 3 (2013): 164.

91. Raymond E. Barranco and Edward S. Shihadeh, "Business Structure, Ethnic Shifts in Labor Markets, and Violence: The Link Between Company Size, Local

Labor Markets, and Non-Latino Homicide," *Social Science Research* 49 (January 2015): 156–66.

92. Michelle Billies, "Surveillance Threat as Embodied Psychological Dilemma," *Peace and Conflict: Journal of Peace Psychology* 21, no. 2 (2015): 168–86; Hannah L. F. Cooper, "War on Drugs, Policing and Police Brutality," *Substance Use & Misuse* 50, no. 8–9 (2015): 1–7.

93. Halfon et al., *Lifecourse Health Development*, 351.

CHAPTER 10

1. Broderick Johnson and Jim Shelton, "My Brother's Keeper Taskforce Report to the President," *My Brother's Keeper Taskforce*, 2014, accessed June 8, 2015, http://www.whitehouse.gov/sites/default/files/docs/053014_mbk_report.pdf.

2. William E. Cross Jr., "The Historical Relationship between Black Identity and Black Achievement Motivation," *African American Children and Mental Health, Vol. 1: Development and Context*, ed. N. Hill, T. Mann, and H. Fitzgerald (Santa Barbara, CA: Praeger, 2011), 1–28.

3. Grey Gundaker, "Hidden Education among African Americans during Slavery," *Teachers College Record* 109, no. 7 (July 2007): 1591–1612.

4. Graziella Bertocchi and Dimico Arcangelo, "Slavery, Education, and Inequality," *European Economic Review* 70 (August 2014): 197–209.

5. Cross, "The Historical Relationship"; J. Diamond and J. Huguley, "Black/White Disparities in Educational Outcomes: Rethinking Issues of Race, Culture and Context," in *African American Children and Mental Health, Volume 1: Development and Context*, ed. N. Hill, T. Mann, and H. Fitzgerald (Santa Barbara, CA: Praeger, 2011), 63–94.

6. Ibid.

7. Ivory Toldson, *Breaking Barriers 2: Plotting the Path Away from Juvenile Detention and Toward Academic Success for School-Age African American Males* (Washington, DC: Congressional Black Caucus Foundation, Inc., 2011).

8. Chris Emdin, *Urban Science Education for the Hip Hop Generation: Essential Tools for the Urban Science Educator and Researcher* (Boston, MA: Sense Publishers, 2010), 30–32.

9. Yasser Arafat Payne and Tara M. Brown, "The Educational Experiences of Street-Life-Oriented Black Boys: How Black Boys Use Street Life as a Site of Resilience in High School," *Journal of Contemporary Criminal Justice* 26, no. 3 (August 2010): 316–38.

10. Russell W. Rumberger and Susan Rotermund, "The Relationship Between Engagement and High School Dropout," in *Handbook of Research on Student Engagement*, ed. Sandra L. Christenson, Amy L. Reschly, and Cathy Wylie (New York: Springer Science + Business Media, 2012), 491–513; Toldson, *Breaking Barriers 2*.

11. Journal of Blacks in Higher Education, *"Major Progress in Black Student Graduation Rates at Top-ranked Colleges and Universities,"* 2014, accessed June 8, 2015, http://www.jbhe.com/2014/11/major-progress-in-black-student-graduation-rates-at-top-ranked-colleges-and-universities/.

12. Raise DC, *District of Columbia Graduation Pathways Project Summary,* 2014, https://static1.squarespace.com/static/543dae78e4b09e17b7b6c5fe/t/547e3 06ce4b07096b3bd3f67/1417556076915/DME_GradPathways_FinalReport _20140924_vF.pdf.

13. Kathryn Monahan et al., "From the School Yard to the Squad Car: School Discipline, Truancy, and Arrest," *Journal of Youth and Adolescence* 43, no. 7 (July 2014): 1110–22.

14. U.S. Department of Education Office for Civil Rights, *Civil Rights Data Collection Data Snapshot: School Discipline Issue Brief No. 1,* 2014, https://www2 .ed.gov/about/offices/list/ocr/docs/crdc-discipline-snapshot.pdf.

15. Ibid.

16. Deborah Fowler et al., *Texas' School-to-Prison Pipeline: School Expulsion: The Path From Lockout to Dropout* (Austin, TX: Texas Appleseed, 2010); Daniel Losen et al., *Are We Closing the School Discipline Gap?* (Los Angeles, CA: The Center for Civil Rights Remedies, 2015).

17. Daniel Losen et al., "Disturbing Inequities: Exploring the Relationship between Racial Disparities in Special Education Identification and Discipline," *Journal of Applied Research on Children* 5, no. 2 (2014).

18. Lance Hannon, Robert DeFina, and Sarah Bruch, "The Relationship Between Skin Tone and School Suspension for African Americans," *Race and Social Problems* 5, no. 4 (June 2013): 281–95; Carla Monroe, "Colorizing Educational Research: African American Life and Schooling as an Exemplar," *Educational Researcher* 42, no. 1 (2013): 9–19.

19. Tiffany A. Ito et al., "Toward a Comprehensive Understanding of Executive Cognitive Function in Implicit Racial Bias," *Journal of Personality and Social Psychology* 108, no. 2 (February 2015): 187–218.

20. Patricia Clark and Eva Zygmunt, "A Close Encounter with Personal Bias: Pedagogical Implications for Teacher Education," *Journal of Negro Education* 83, no. 2 (Spring 2014): 147–61.

21. Carmen DeNavas-Walt, and Bernadette Proctor, *Income and Poverty in the United States: 2013,* 2014, accessed June 8, 2015, http://www.census.gov/content /dam/Census/library/publications/2014/demo/p60-249.pdf; Tony Fabelo, *Breaking Schools' Rules: A Statewide Study of how School Discipline Relates to Students' Success and Juvenile Justice Involvement,* 2011, http://csgjusticecenter.org/wp -content/uploads/2012/08/Breaking_Schools_Rules_Report_Final.pdf.

22. Emdin, *Urban Science Education,* 39.

23. Joe Brewster, Michele Stephenson, and Hilary Beard, *Promises Kept: Raising Black Boys to Succeed in School and in Life* (New York: Spiegel & Grau, 2014), 225.

24. Emdin, *Urban Science Education,* 36–37; Sam Seidel, *Hip Hop Genius: Remixing High School Education* (New York: Rowman & Littlefield Publishers, Inc., 2011), 28–29.

25. Marc L. Hill, *Beats, Rhymes, and Classroom Life: Hip Hop Pedagogy and the Politics of Identity* (New York: Teachers College Press, 2009), 130–31.

26. Emdin, *Urban Science Education,* 39; Seidel, *Hip Hop Genius.*

27. Hill, *Beats, Rhymes, and Classroom Life*, 130–31.

28. Seidel, *Hip Hop Genius,* 124.

29. Hill, *Beats, Rhymes, and Classroom Life*, 121.

30. Ibid., 56.

31. Emdin, *Urban Science Education.*

32. Michael Hughes et al., "Racial Identity and Well-Being among African Americans," *Social Psychology Quarterly* 78, no. 1 (2015): 25–48.

33. Tom McFadden, *Rosalind Franklin vs. Watson & Crick*, 2015, accessed June 8, 2015, http://genius.com/Tom-mcfadden-rosalind-franklin-vs-watson-and-crick-lyrics.

34. Chris Emdin, *Science Genius*, 2015, accessed June 8, 2015, http://chrisemdin.com/science-genius/.

35. Chris Emdin, interview with author, New York, NY, September 2014.

36. Merrill Schwerin, *School House Rapping with Wu-Tang Clan's GZA*, 2013, http://www.pbs.org/newshour/rundown/just-ask-wu-tang-clan-1/.

37. Marc L. Hill and Emery Petchauer, eds., *Schooling Hip-Hop: Expanding Hip-Hop Based Education across the Curriculum* (New York: Teachers College Press, 2013), 51–52.

38. Seidel, *Hip Hop Genius.*

39. Bronwen Low, Eloise Tan, and Jacqueline Celemencki, "The Limits of 'Keepin' It Real': The Challenges for Critical Hip Hop Pedagogies of Discourses of Authenticity," in *Schooling Hip-Hop: Expanding Hip-Hop Based Education across the Curriculum,* ed. Marc L. Hill and Emery Petchauer (New York: Teachers College Press, 2013), 120–21.

40. Amy Donnenwerth, "Song Communication Using Rap Music in a Group Setting with At-Risk Youth," in *Therapeutic Uses of Rap and Hip Hop,* ed. Susan Hadley and G. Yancey (New York: Routledge, 2012), 286–87; Hill, *Beats, Rhymes, and Classroom Life.*

41. Hill, *Beats, Rhymes, and Classroom Life*, 123.

42. Ibid., 119.

43. B. Lee Cooper and Rebecca Condon, eds., *The Popular Music Teaching Handbook: An Educator's Guide to Music-Related Print Resources* (Santa Barbara, CA: Libraries Unlimited, 2004).

44. Ibid., v.

45. Seidel, *Hip Hop Genius,* 124–25; Hill and Petchauer, *Schooling Hip-Hop*, 2–4.

46. Marcella Runell and Martha Diaz, *The Hip-Hop Education Guidebook: Volume 1* (New York: Hip-Hop Association, 2007).

47. Decoteau J. Irby and H. B. Hall, "Fresh Faces, New Places: Moving Beyond Teacher-Researcher Perspectives in Hip-Hop-Based Education Research," *Urban Education* 46, no. 2 (March 2011): 226–27.

48. Hill and Petchauer, *Schooling Hip-Hop*, 2–4.

49. Ksenija Simic-Muller, "Mathematizing Perceptions: Preservice Teachers' Use of Mathematics to Investigate Their Relationship with the Community," *Journal of Research in Mathematics Education* 4, no. 1 (February 2015): 30–51.

50. Edna Tan et al., *Empowering Science and Mathematics Education in Urban Schools* (Chicago, IL: University of Chicago Press, 2012).

51. Jonathan Osler, *A Guide for Integrating Issues of Social and Economic Justice into Mathematics Curriculum*, 2007, accessed April 30, 2015, http://www.radicalmath.org/docs/SJMathGuide.pdf.

52. Sage Salvo, "Understanding Literature through Hip Hop: Sage Salvo at TEDxMidAtlantic," *Youtube.com*, 2012, accessed June 8, 2015, https://www.youtube.com/watch?v=2kBc6M5XJw0.

53. Hip Hop Education Literacy Program, *Hip Hop Educational Literacy Program (H.E.L.P.)*, 2015, http://www.edlyrics.com/.

54. Gabriel "Asheru" Benn, interview with author, Washington, DC, September 2014.

55. Hill, *Beats, Rhymes, and Classroom Life*.

56. Runell and Diaz, *The Hip-Hop Education Guidebook*, 60.

57. David Yeager and Gregory Walton, "Social-Psychological Interventions in Education: They're Not Magic," *Review of Educational Research* 81, no. 2 (June 2011): 267–301.

58. Seidel, *Hip Hop Genius*.

59. Raphael Travis and Joshua Childs, "Why the Ed in #HipHopEd Is Not Enough: How Social Workers & Educators Can Change the Game," in #HipHopEd, ed. Chris Emdin (New York: Peter Lang, 2016).

60. Debangshu Roychoudhury and Lauren Gardner, "Taking Back Our Minds: Hip Hop Psychology's (HHP) Call for a Renaissance, Action, and Liberatory Use of Psychology in Education," in *Hip Hop(e): The Cultural Practice and Critical Pedagogy of International Hip Hop*, ed. Brad Porfilio and Michael Viola. (New York: Peter Lang, 2012), 245.

61. Hill, *Beats, Rhymes, and Classroom Life*, 37.

62. Ibid., 120.

63. Darius D. Prier, "Where Do Biases Start? A Challenge to Educators," *Education Week* 34, no. 8 (October 2015): 25–28.

64. Travis and Childs, "Why the Ed in #HipHopEd Is Not Enough;" Raphael Travis Jr. and Alexis Maston, "Hip-Hop and Pedagogy, More Than Meets the Eye," in *See You at the Crossroads: Hip Hop Scholarship at the Intersections*, ed. Brad Porfilio, Debangshu Roychoudhury, and Lauren M. Gardner (Boston, MA: Sense Publishers, 2014), 3–28.

65. Emdin, *Urban Science Education*.

66. MK Asante Jr., *It's Bigger than Hip Hop: The Rise of the Post-Hip-Hop Generation* (New York: St. Martin's Press, 2008).

CHAPTER 11

1. Karen Pittman and Wanda Fleming, *Testimony of Karen J. Pittman Before the House Select Committee on Children, Youth and Families* (Washington, DC: Academy for Educational Development, 1991).

2. Ibid.

3. Ibid.

4. Karen J. Pittman et al., *Preventing Problems, Promoting Development, Encouraging Engagement: Competing Priorities or Inseperable Goals?* (Takoma Park: The Forum for Youth Investment, 2001).

5. Ready by 21, *Ready by 21: Helping You to Improve the Odds That All Children and Youth Will Be Ready for College, Work and Life*, http://www.readyby21.org/.

6. Andreana Clay, *The Hip-Hop Generation Fights Back: Youth, Activism and Post-Civil Rights Politics* (New York: New York University Press, 2012), 102–3.

7. Melvin Delgado, *New Frontiers for Youth Development in the Twenty-First Century: Revitalizing and Broadening Youth Development* (New York: Columbia University Press, 2002).

8. Mazi Mutafa, interview with author, Washington, DC, September 2014.

9. Natalie Davis, interview with author, Miami, FL, November 2014.

10. Ibid.

11. Ibid.

12. Elliot Gann, interview with author, Oakland, CA, April 2015.

13. Ibid.

14. #HipHopEd. *#HipHopEd: The Intersections of Hip Hop and Education*, www.hiphoped.com.

15. Timothy D. Jones, interview with author, Washington, DC, September 2014.

16. Chris Emdin, interview with author, New York, NY, September 2014.

17. Melvin Delgado and Lee Staples, *Youth-Led Community Organizing: Theory and Action* (New York: Oxford University Press, 2007); Robert Wood Johnson Foundation, *How Does Where We Live, Work, Learn and Play Affect Our Health?* 2011, http://www.rwjf.org/content/dam/farm/reports/issue_briefs/2011/rwjf71339.

18. Raphael Travis Jr., "What They Think: Attributions Made by Youth Workers About Youth Circumstances and the Implications for Service-Delivery in Out-Of-School Time Programs" *Child & Youth Care Forum* 39, no. 6 (December 2010): 443–64.

19. Delgado and Staples, *Youth-Led Community Organizing*; Shawn Ginwright and Julio Cammarota, "New Terrain in Youth Development: The Promise of a Social Justice Approach," *Social Justice* 29, no. 4 (2002): 82–95; Katie Richards-Schuster et al., "What Constitutes Youth Organizing? Exploring the Role of Conservative Contexts in Understanding Practice," *Children and Youth Services Review* 35, no. 8 (August 2013): 1291–96.

20. Delgado and Staples, *Youth-Led Community Organizing*; Shawn Ginwright and Taj James, "From Assets to Agents of Change: Social Justice, Organizing, and Youth Development," in *Youth Participation: Improving Institutions and Communities*, ed. Benjamin Kirshner and Jennifer L. O'Donoghue (San Francisco, CA: Jossey-Bass, 2002), 27–46; P. Thandi Hicks Harper, *Hip-Hop Development: Exploring Hip-Hop Culture as a Youth Engagement Tool for Successful Community Building* (Clinton, MD: Billo Communications, Inc. and Youth Popular Culture Institute, 2008); Richard M. Lerner, *Liberty: Thriving and Civic Engagement Among America's*

Youth (Thousand Oaks, CA: SAGE Publications, 2004); Roderick J. Watts and Omar Guessous, "Sociopolitical Development: The Missing Link in Research and Policy on Adolescents," in *Beyond Resistance: Youth Activism and Community Change*, ed. Shawn Ginwright, Pedro Noguera, and Julio Cammarota (New York: Routledge, Taylor & Francis Group, 2006).

21. Delgado, *New Frontiers for Youth Development*; Delgado and Staples, *Youth-Led Community Organizing*.

22. Ginwright and Cammarota, "New Terrain in Youth Development," 82–95; Louise Jennings et al., "Toward a Critical Social Theory of Youth Empowerment," *Journal of Community Practice* 14, nos. 1–2 (2006): 31–55.

23. Ginwright and Cammarota, "New Terrain in Youth Development," 82–95.

24. Alberto Retana, "Why Latinos Should Speak Up for Black Lives," *Huffington Post*, 2015, http://www.huffingtonpost.com/alberto-retana/why-latinos-should-speak-up-for-black-lives_b_7218114.html.

25. Michelle A. Gambone et al., "Youth Organizing, Identity-Support, and Youth Development Agencies as Avenues for Involvement," *Journal of Community Practice* 14, nos. 1–2 (2006): 235–53.

26. Gambone et al., "Youth Organizing," 40.

27. A. Torres-Fleming, P. Valdes, and S. Pillai, *2010 Youth Organizing Field Scan* (New York: Funders Collaborative on Youth Organizing, 2010), 11.

28. Ibid., 11.

29. Constance Flanagan, Wim Beyers, and Rita Žukauskiene, "Political and Civic Engagement Development in Adolescence," *Journal of Adolescence* 35, no. 3 (June 2012): 471–73; Roderick Watts and Constance Flanagan, "Pushing the Envelope on Youth Civic Engagement: A Developmental and Liberation Psychology Perspective," *Journal of Community Psychology* 35, no. 6 (August 2007): 779–92.

30. Pedro D. Ferreira, Cristina N. Azevedo, and Isabel Menezes, "The Developmental Quality of Participation Experiences: Beyond the Rhetoric That 'Participation Is Always Good!'" *Journal of Adolescence* 35, no. 3 (June 2012): 599–610; Travis, "What They Think"; Adam Voight and Judith Torney-Purta, "A Typology of Youth Civic Engagement in Urban Middle Schools," *Applied Developmental Science* 17, no. 4 (October 2013): 198–212.

31. Ginwright and Cammarota, "New Terrain in Youth Development"; Ginwright and James, "From Assets to Agents of Change."

32. Tim Eubanks, interview with author, Austin, TX, April 2015.

33. Watts and Flanagan, "Pushing the Envelope."

34. Derrion "Chi" Borders, interview with author, Austin, TX, April 2015.

35. Ibid.

36. Wing Yi Chan, Suh-Ruu Ou, and Arthur J. Reynolds, "Adolescent Civic Engagement and Adult Outcomes: An Examination Among Urban Racial Minorities," *Journal of Youth and Adolescence* 43, no. 11 (November 2014).

37. Alison Rhodes and Rachel Schecter, "Fostering Resilience Among Youth in Inner City Community Arts Centers: The Case of the Artists Collective," *Education and Urban Society* 46, no. 7 (2014): 826–48.

38. Alan Crouch, Heather Robertson, and Patricia Fagan, "Hip Hopping the Gap—Performing Arts Approaches to Sexual Health Disadvantage in Young People in Remote Settings," *Australasian Psychiatry* 19, supp. 1 (2011): S34–37.

39. Borders, interview with author.

40. Eubanks, interview with author.

41. Jeffrey Ogbar, *Hip-Hop Revolution: The Culture and Politics of Rap* (Lawrence, KS: University Press of Kansas, 2007).

42. MK Asante Jr., *It's Bigger Than Hip Hop: The Rise of the Post-Hip-Hop Generation* (New York: St. Martin's Press, 2008), 4.

43. Ibid., 5.

44. Clay, *The Hip-Hop Generation*, 187.

45. Ibid., 186–88.

46. Asante, *It's Bigger Than Hip Hop*.

47. Delgado and Staples, *Youth-Led Community Organizing*, 169.

48. Ibid.

CHAPTER 12

1. Tia DeNora, "Health and Music in Everyday Life—a Theory of Practice," *Psyke & Logos* 28, no. 1 (2007): 271–87; Suvi Saarikallio, "Music as Emotional Self-Regulation Throughout Adulthood," *Psychology of Music* 39, no. 3 (July 2011): 307–27; Raphael Travis Jr., "Rap Music and the Empowerment of Today's Youth: Evidence in Everyday Music Listening, Music Therapy, and Commercial Rap Music," *Child and Adolescent Social Work Journal* 30, no. 2 (April 2013): 139–67.

2. D. Grocke et al., "Group Music Therapy for Severe Mental Illness: A Randomized Embedded-Experimental Mixed Methods Study," *Acta Psychiatrica. Scandinavica* 130, no. 2 (August 2014): 144–53; Sheri L. Robb et al., "Randomized Clinical Trial of Therapeutic Music Video Intervention for Resilience Outcomes in Adolescents/Young Adults Undergoing Hematopoietic Stem Cell Transplant: A Report from the Children's Oncology Group," *Cancer* 120, no. 6 (2014), 909–17.

3. Susan Hadley and George Yancey, eds., *Therapeutic Uses of Rap and Hip-Hop* (New York: Routledge, 2012).

4. Timothy Jones, interviewed by author, Washington, DC, September, 2014.

5. Cendrine Robinson, interviewed by author, Chicago, IL, April, 2015.

6. Beats, Rhymes, and Life, Inc., "Hip Hop Therapy," June 2015, http://brl-inc .org/programs/hiphoptherapy/.

7. Terry L. Mills and Susan Cody-Rydzewski, "Psychology of Older Adults: Exploring the Effects of Class and Culture on the Mental Health of African Americans," in *Handbook of Race and the Development of Mental Health*, ed. Edward C. Chang and Christina A. Downey (New York: Springer Science + Business Media, 2012), 67–85.

8. Centers for Disease Control and Prevention, "MMWR, CDC Health Disparities and Inequalities Report—United States, 2013" *MMWR* 62 (Supplement 3).

9. Lucas J. Schiller, B. Ward, and J. Peregoy, "Summary Health Statistics for U.S. Adults: National Health Interview Survey, 2010." *National Health Interview Survey* 10, no. 52 (2012).

10. Centers for Disease Control and Prevention, "MMWR, CDC Health Disparities and Inequalities Report."

11. Ivory Toldson, *Breaking Barriers 2: Plotting the Path Away from Juvenile Detention and Toward Academic Success for School-Age Black Males* (Washington, DC: Congressional Black Caucus Foundation, Inc., 2011).

12. Steven M. Kogan et al., "Racial Microstressors, Racial Self-Concept, and Depressive Symptoms Among Male African Americans During the Transition to Adulthood," *Journal of Youth and Adolescence* 44, no. 4 (April 2015): 898–909.

13. Centers for Disease Control and Prevention, "Unintentional Injuries and Violence," in *High School Youth Risk Behavior Survey* (Atlanta, GA: Centers for Disease Control and Prevention, 2013); National Center for Health Statistics, *Health, United States, 2011: With Special Feature on Socioeconomic Status and Health* (Hyattsville, MD: National Center for Health Statistics, 2012), http://www.cdc.gov/healthyyouth/data/yrbs/index.htm.

14. Tom Booth et al., "Association of Allostatic Load with Brain Structure and Cognitive Ability in Later Life," in *Neurobiology of Aging* 36, no. 3 (March 2015): 1390–99; Lauren Doamekpor and Gniesha Y. Dinwiddie, "Allostatic Load in Foreign-Born and US-Born Blacks: Evidence from the 2001–2010 National Health and Nutrition Examination Survey," *American Journal of Public Health* 105, no. 3 (2015): 591–97.

15. Doamekpor and Dinwiddie, "Allostatic Load."

16. Youth Risk Behavior Surveillance System, *Youth Online: High School YRBS, U.S. 2013* (Atlanta, GA: Centers for Disease Control and Prevention, 2015), http://nccd.cdc.gov/youthonline/App/Results.aspx?.

17. Ranbir Mangat Bains, "Black Adolescents and Mental Health Care: A Metasynthesis," *Journal of Child and Adolescent Psychiatric Nursing* 27, no. 2 (May 2014): 83–92; U.S. Department of Health and Human Services. *HHS action plan to reduce racial and ethnic health disparities*, United States Department of Health and Human Services, 2014. Available from http://minorityhealth.hhs.gov/assets/pdf/hhs/HHS_Plan_complete.pdf.

18. Agency for Healthcare Research and Quality. "Adults Who Received Mental Health Treatment or Counseling in the Last 12 Months, Table 17_3_1–2b" in *2010 National Healthcare Quality and Disparities Reports* (Rockville, MD, October 2014). Available at http://www.ahrq.gov/research/findings/nhqrdr/nhqrdr10/17_utilization/T17_3_1–2b.html.

19. Agency for Healthcare Research and Quality, "Adults With a Major Depressive Episode in the Last 12 Months Who Received Mental Health Treatment or Counseling, Table 17_1_1–2b" in 2010 National Healthcare Quality and Disparities Reports (Rockville, MD, October 2014). Available at http://www.ahrq.gov/research/findings/nhqrdr/nhqrdr11/7_mentalhealthsubstanceabuse/T7_1_1_2b.html.

20. Bains, "Black Adolescents and Mental Health"; Mills and Cody-Rydzewski, "Psychology of Older Adults"; Richard Thompson, Ernestine Briggs-King, and Sylvette LaTouche-Howard, "Psychology of Black Children: Strengths and Challenges," in *Handbook of Race and the Development of Mental Health*, ed. Edward C. Chang and Christina A. Downey (New York: Springer Science + Business Media, 2012), 27–43.

21. Thompson, Briggs-King, and LaTouche-Howard, "Psychology of Black Children."

22. Mills and Cody-Rydzewski, "Psychology of Older Adults."

23. Bains, "Black Adolescents and Mental Health."

24. Angela Duckworth and James J. Gross, "Self-Control and Grit: Related but Separable Determinants of Success," *Current Directions in Psychological Science* 23, no. 5 (October 2014): 319–25.

25. Michael Rutter, "Annual Research Review: Resilience—Clinical Implications," *Journal of Child Psychology and Psychiatry* 54, no. 4 (April 2013): 474–87.

26. Robert F. Valois, Keith J. Zullig, and Amy A. Hunter, "Association between Adolescent Suicide Ideation, Suicide Attempts and Emotional Self-Efficacy," *Journal of Child and Family Studies* 24, no. 2 (February 2015): 237–48.

27. Daniel Västfjäll, Patrik N. Juslin, and Terry Hartig, "Music, Subjective Well-being, and Health: The Role of Everyday Emotions," in *Music, Health, and Wellbeing*, ed. Raymond A. R. MacDonald, Gunter Kreutz, Laura Mitchell. (New York: Oxford University Press, 2012).

28. DeNora, "Health and Music in Everyday Life"; Don Elligan. "Rap Therapy: A Culturally Sensitive Approach to Psychotherapy With Young African American Men." *Journal of African American Men* 5, no. 3 (Winter 2000): 27; Ian Levy and Brian TaeHyuk Keum, "Hip-Hop Emotional Exploration in Men," *Journal of Poetry Therapy* 27, no. 4 (October 2014): 217–23; Edgar Tyson, "Rap Music in Social Work Practice With African-American and Latino Youth: A Conceptual Model With Practical Applications," *Journal of Human Behavior in the Social Environment* 8, no. 4 (2003): 1–21.

29. Grocke et al., "Group Music Therapy."

30. Ian Levy, interviewed by author, New York, NY, April, 2015.

31. Cheryl Keyes, *Rap Music and Street Consciousness* (Urbana, IL: University of Illinois Press, 2002); Tricia Rose, *Hip-Hop Wars: What We Talk about When We Talk about Hip-Hop—And Why It Matters* (New York: Basic Civitas, 2008).

32. Keyes. *Rap Music.*

33. Jeff Chang, *Can't Stop, Won't Stop: A History of the Hip-Hop Generation* (New York: St. Martin's Press, 2005), 104–5; S. Craig Watkins, *Hip hop Matters: Politics, Pop Culture, and the Struggle for the Soul of a Movement* (Boston, MA: Beacon Press, 2005).

34. Tony Mitchell, *Global Noise: Rap and Hip Hop outside the USA* (Middletown, CT: Wesleyan University Press, 2002); Brad Porfilio and Michael Viola, eds. *Hip-Hop(e): The Cultural Practice and Critical Pedagogy of International Hip-Hop* (New York: Peter Lang Publishing Inc., 2012).

35. Mona Lisa Chanda and Daniel J. Levitin, "The Neurochemistry of Music," *Trends in Cognitive Sciences* 17, no. 4 (April 2013): 192.

36. Ibid.

37. Ibid.

38. Stefan Koelsch, "Music-Evoked Emotions: Principles, Brain Correlates, and Implications for Therapy," *Annals of the New York Academy of Sciences* no. 1337 (March 2015): 193–201.

39. Alonzo DeCarlo and Elaine Hockman, "RAP Therapy: A Group Work Intervention Method for Urban Adolescents," *Social Work with Groups: A Journal of Community and Clinical Practice* 26, no. 3 (2003): 45–59; Edgar Tyson, "Rap Music in Social Work Practice."

40. Ibid.

41. Alonzo DeCarlo and Elaine Hockman, "RAP Therapy," 47; Don Elligan, "Rap Therapy: A Culturally Sensitive Approach," 61.

42. Alonzo DeCarlo and Elaine Hockman, "RAP Therapy"; Alonzo DeCarlo, "The Rise and Call of Group Rap Therapy: A Critical Analysis from Its Creator," *Group Analysis* 46, no. 2 (June 2013): 225–38.

43. Don Elligan, "Rap Therapy: A Culturally Sensitive Approach."

44. Travis, "Rap Music and the Empowerment"; Edgar Tyson, "Rap Music in Social Work Practice"; Adia Winfrey, *H.Y.P.E. Healing Young People Thru Empowerment: A Hip Hop Therapy Program for Black Teenage Boys* (createspace.com: Createspace, 2009).

45. Cendrine Robinson, interview.

46. Aaron J. Lightstone, "Yo! Can Ya Flow? Research Findings on Hip-Hop Aesthetics and Rap Therapy in an Urban Youth Shelter," in *Therapeutic Uses of Rap and Hip Hop*, ed. Susan Hadley and George Yancey (New York: Routledge, 2012), 46.

47. Aaron J. Lightstone, "The Importance of Hip-Hop for Music Therapists," in *Therapeutic Uses of Rap and Hip Hop*, ed. Susan Hadley and George Yancey (New York: Routledge, 2012), 39–56.

48. Ian Levy, interviewed by author, New York, NY, April, 2015.

49. Torrance Stephens, Ronald L. Braithwaite, and Sandra E. Taylor, "Model for Using Hip-Hop Music for Small Group HIV/AIDS Prevention Counseling With African American Adolescents and Young Adults," *Patient Education and Counseling* 35, no. 2 (October 1998): 127–37.

50. Jaleel Abdul-Adil, "Rap Music and Urban Rhapsody: Violence Prevention for Inner-City African American Male Adolescents," *The Journal of Urban Youth Culture* 4, no. 1 (2006); Alonzo DeCarlo and Elaine Hockman, "RAP Therapy"; Don Elligan, "Rap Therapy: A Culturally Sensitive Approach"; Tillie-Allen, "Exploring Hip-Hop Therapy With High-Risk Youth," *Praxis* 5 (Fall 2005): 30–36; Tyson, "Rap Music in Social Work Practice"; Adia Winfrey, *H.Y.P.E.*

51. Tyson, "Rap Music in Social Work Practice"; Tillie-Allen, "Exploring Hip-Hop."

52. DeCarlo, "The Rise and Call," 234.

53. Ian Levy, interviewed by author, New York, NY, April, 2015.

54. Winfrey, *H.Y.P.E.*, 16.

55. Ibid., 35.

56. Hadley and Yancey, *Therapeutic Uses.*

57. Tomas T. Alvarez III, "Beats, Rhymes, and Life: Rap Therapy in an Urban Setting," in *Therapeutic Uses of Rap and Hip Hop*, ed. Susan Hadley and George Yancey (New York: Routledge, 2012), 117–28.

58. Tomas T. Alvarez III, "Hip Hop Therapy for At-Risk Youth," in Ashoka, 2014. Available from https://www.youtube.com/watch?v=pNavHWM3fBY.

59. Ibid.

60. Felicity A. Baker, Genevieve A. Dingle, and Libby M. Gleadhill, "'Must Be the Ganja': Using Rap Music in Music Therapy for Substance Use Disorders," in *Therapeutic Uses of Rap and Hip Hop*, ed. Susan Hadley and George Yancey (New York: Routledge, 2012), 321–26.

61. Ibid., 331–32.

62. Edgar H. Tyson et al., "Therapeutically and Socially Relevant Themes in Hip-Hop Music: A Comprehensive Analysis of a Selected Sample of Songs," in *Therapeutic Uses of Rap and Hip Hop*, ed. Susan Hadley and George Yancey (New York: Routledge, 2012), 102.

63. Lightstone, "Yo! Can Ya Flow?"

64. Travis, "Rap Music and the Empowerment," 156–57.

65. Ibid.

66. Suvi Saarikallio, Christian Gold, and Katrina McFerran, "Development and Validation of the Healthy-Unhealthy Music Scale," *Child and Adolescent Mental Health* (Online first, May 2015).

67. Debangshu Roychoudhury and Lauren Gardner, "Taking Back Our Minds: Hip Hop Psychology's (HHP) Call for a Renaissance, Action, and Liberatory Use of Psychology in Education," in *Hip hop(e): The Cultural Practice and Critical Pedagogy of International Hip Hop*, ed. Brad Porfilio, Michael Viola (New York: Peter Lang, 2012), 237.

68. Jameca Falconer, "Close to Home: A Psychologist Reflects on Providing Crisis Counseling in Ferguson," *American Psychological Association*, October 14, 2014. http://psychologybenefits.org/2014/10/17/close-to-home-a-psychologist-reflects-on-providing-crisis-counseling-in-ferguson/ (accessed June 9, 2015).

69. Roychoudhury and Gardner, "Taking Back Our Minds," 245.

70. Andrew Belasco and Michael Trivette, "Aiming Low: Estimating the Scope and Predictors of Secondary Undermatch," *Journal of Higher Education* 86, no. 2 (March/April 2015): 233–63.

71. Sandra Black, Kalena Cortes, and Jane Lincove, "Academic Undermatching of High-Achieving Minority Students: Evidence from Race-Neutral and Holistic Admissions Policies," *American Economic Review: Papers & Proceedings* 105, no. 5 (May 2015): 604–10.

72. Michael Bastedo and Allyson Flaster, "Conceptual and Methodological Problems in Research on College Undermatch., *Educational Researcher* 43, no. 2 (March 2014): 93–99; Belasco and Trivette, "Aiming Low."

73. Raphael Travis Jr. and Scott W. Bowman, "Validation of the Individual and Community Empowerment Inventory: A Measure of Rap Music Engagement Among First-Year College Students," *Journal of Human Behavior in the Social Environment* 25, no. 2 (January 2015): 90–108.

74. Simon Liljeström, Patrik N. Juslin, and Daniel Västfjäll, "Experimental Evidence of the Roles of Music Choice, Social Context, and Listener Personality in Emotional Reactions to Music," *Psychology of Music* 41, no. 5 (September 2013): 579–99; Tyson, et al., "Therapeutically and Socially Relevant Themes."

CHAPTER 13

1. David Elliott and Marissa Silverman, "Why Music Matters: Philosophical and Cultural Foundations," in *Music, Health, and Well-being*, ed. Raymond A. R. MacDonald, Gunter Kreutz, and Laura Mitchell (New York: Oxford University Press, 2012), 38.

2. Alexis C. Maston, *Spiritualizing Hip Hop With I.C.E.: The Poetic Spiritual Narratives of Four Black Educational Leaders from Hip Hop Communities* (Ann Arbor, MI: ProQuest Information & Learning, 2015).

3. Tim Eubanks, interview with author, Austin, TX, April 2015.

4. Ibid.

5. B. Cooper and Rebecca Condon, eds., *The Popular Music Teaching Handbook: An Educator's Guide to Music-Related Print Resources* (Santa Barbara, CA: Libraries Unlimited, 2004).

6. Ian Levy, interview with author, New York, NY, April 2015; Debangshu Roychoudhury and Lauren Gardner, "Taking Back Our Minds: Hip Hop Psychology's (HHP) Call for a Renaissance, Action, and Liberatory Use of Psychology in Education," in *Hip Hop(e): The Cultural Practice and Critical Pedagogy of International Hip Hop*, ed. Brad Porfilio and Michael Viola (New York: Peter Lang, 2012), 237.

7. Meyran Boniel-Nissim et al. "Supportive Communication with Parents Moderates the Negative Effects of Electronic Media Use on Life Satisfaction During Adolescence," *International Journal of Public Health* 60, no. 2 (February 2015): 189–98.

8. Chris Emdin, interview with author, New York, NY, September 2014.

9. Decoteau Irby and Emery Petchauer, "Hustlin' Consciousness: Critical Education Using Hip Hop Modes of Distribution," in *Hip Hop(e): The Cultural Practice and Critical Pedagogy of International Hip Hop*, ed. Brad Porfilio and Michael Viola (New York: Peter Lang, 2012), 302–22; Yasser Arafat Payne and Tara M. Brown, "The Educational Experiences of Street-Life-Oriented Black Boys: How Black Boys Use Street Life as a Site of Resilience in High School," *Journal of Contemporary Criminal Justice* 26, no. 3 (August 2010): 316–38.

Index

About the Author

Raphael Travis Jr. is associate professor of social work at Texas State University in San Marcos, Texas. His published works include *Rap Music and the Empowerment of Today's Youth: Evidence in Everyday Music Listening, Music Therapy, and Commercial Rap Music*; *Empowerment-Based Positive Youth Development: A New Understanding of Healthy Development for African American Youth*; and *Ethnic Identity, Self-Esteem and Variability in Perceptions of Rap Music's Empowering and Risky Influences*. Travis holds a doctorate in public health from the University of California, Los Angeles, and a master of social work degree from the University of Michigan.

CPSIA information can be obtained
at www.ICGtesting.com
Printed in the USA
BVHW04*1459120918
527223BV00015B/205/P